IMAGES
of America

CITY OF WEST BEND

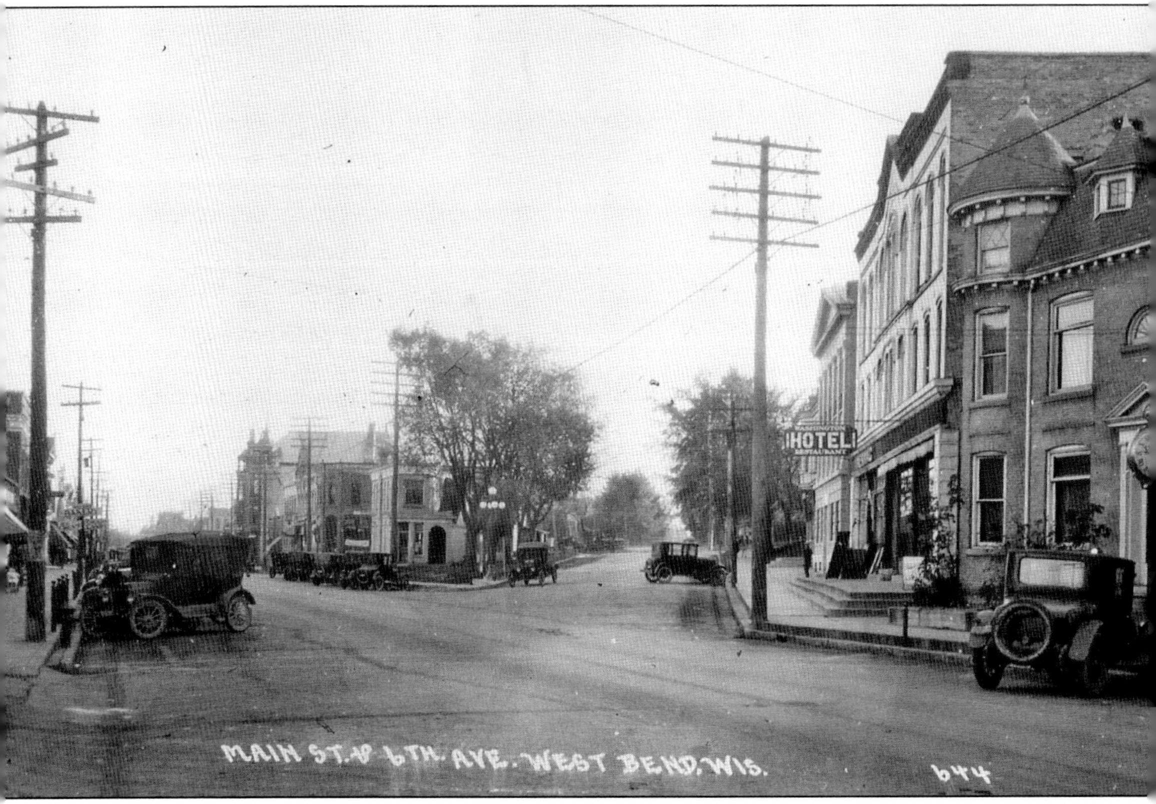

A view from Main Street at the intersection of Sixth Avenue, which veers off to the south, is seen here around 1920. On the right, with the pocket watch sign, is the shop and residence of Thomas Bruhy, who owned a jewelry store and the Washington House Hotel. At the intersection is the O'Meara Law Office, now the Old Settlers' Park. (Courtesy of the Washington County Historical Society.)

On the Cover: This photograph looks across the swimming lagoon at City Park. Construction on the park began in 1933 and used funds from the federal government New Deal programs. Most of the main construction projects were completed by 1935. The name was later changed to Regner Park in honor of the mayor who was instrumental in purchasing the original land. (Courtesy of the Washington County Historical Society, Inc.).

IMAGES
of America

CITY OF WEST BEND

Janean Mollet-Van Beckum
and the Washington County Historical Society

ARCADIA
PUBLISHING

ISBN 978-1-4671-1386-1

Published by Arcadia Publishing
Charleston, South Carolina

Printed in the United States of America

Library of Congress Control Number: 2014952694

For all general information, please contact Arcadia Publishing:
Telephone 843-853-2070
Fax 843-853-0044
E-mail sales@arcadiapublishing.com
For customer service and orders:
Toll-Free 1-888-313-2665

Visit us on the Internet at www.arcadiapublishing.com

Contents

Acknowledgments

This book would not have been possible without the dedication of the men and women of the Washington County Historical Society who, over the years, have collected a stunning array of photographs and documentation about West Bend and the county. Thank you to the volunteers who have worked countless hours cataloging, filing, identifying, researching, and caring for this collection. We also extend our sincere gratitude to the people of West Bend and Washington County who have helped in preserving the historical record. Unless otherwise noted, all photographs in this book are from the Washington County Historical Society Collection.

Introduction

Halfway between Milwaukee and Fond du Lac, the Milwaukee River makes a dramatic turn to the west. The area is marked by the Kettle Moraine landscape, a terrain of rolling hills and kettle lakes created when the most recent glaciers retreated around 20,000 years ago. It is here, at the river bend, that early settlers discovered a fast-paced current perfect for supplying waterpower and rich farmland beneath the dense forest. Europeans were not the first people in the area. When they arrived, the Potawatomi and Menomonee had already been here for generations. The interactions between these two cultures were peaceful, and trade was common between them.

In 1845, the state authorized a road between Fond du Lac and Milwaukee, and commissioners Byron Kilbourn, James Kneeland, and Dr. E.B. Wolcott purchased much of the area that would become West Bend in anticipation of the new road. Soon, a small village grew up along the river, with early industries and general stores. The first settlers to the area were eastern Yankees moving west to seek their fortunes. Soon after came the European immigrants, most of them from the Germanic region. Through word of mouth and letters sent to friends and family left in the Old Country, settlement increased quickly. Immigrants brought their trades with them and opened the first stores and factories in West Bend. Blacksmiths, harness makers, furniture builders, button makers, and general merchants were a few of these early entrepreneurs. Being on the road between the bustling city of Fond du Lac and the Port of Milwaukee also meant a constant stream of visitors and hotels quickly sprung up.

The railroad's arrival in 1872 resulted in a boost to manufacturing, as goods could be imported and shipped quickly and inexpensively. This caused a demand for skilled and unskilled workers, so much so that companies had to advertise for help outside of West Bend because of a worker shortage.

Education was a priority to West Bend, and classes held in private homes were started shortly after the first settlers arrived. The earliest record of a public school being formed is from 1846, with a total of 22 students. Public education was well established by the 1860s, and in 1861 the countywide curriculum-supervision system began, and a county superintendent of schools was elected. As the population of West Bend increased, more schools were built, and by the mid-20th century there was a heavy focus on the trades in higher grades. This meant a future workforce for the manufacturers of the city.

In addition to their families and trades, the settlers brought their faith. Places of worship were a priority to new settlers, granting a sense of community and the comfort of familiar rituals. Most congregations started by meeting in members' homes until enough funds were raised to construct a dedicated church building. Several of these congregations also felt a faith-based school was necessary for their children, and parochial schools soon followed.

Services to account for public safety were also in demand. Manufacturers were especially eager to protect their wooden buildings and perishable stock and equipment from fire. Several fire companies, each specializing in a different task of firefighting from pumping water to tearing down a burning building, were formed starting around 1860. These early companies were mainly funded by the businesses they were to protect. By 1885, the city council deemed a permanent fire department was needed, and the independent companies were merged into the West Bend Fire Department. In 1853, West Bend became the county seat, and the county sheriff's department and courts were also located here.

The story leading up to West Bend being the county seat is unique. Until 1853, the current counties of Washington and Ozaukee were one large county called Washington County. At the time, Port Washington was serving as the temporary county seat. In 1846, a public election was held to determine which city would permanently house the county offices. There was no clear winner. Over the next seven years, there were several ballots, but no decisive frontrunner. There were accusations of ballot-box stuffing and much public outcry. It was also becoming more difficult to complete government business because there was no permanent home of the government. In 1853, the state legislature decided to divide the county into two separate counties, making the old rivals West Bend and Port Washington each a county seat. Now there was the question of what to do with the original records of the old Washington County. They were housed in the former temporary county seat at Port Washington, and even with a court order Port Washington refused to surrender the documents. A midnight raid was planned by officials from West Bend to retrieve the records. Unfortunately, they were caught, and the records were quickly hidden by the Port Washington officials. Shortly after the foiled raid, a letter from a Port Washington newspaper editor gave the West Bend officials the hiding place of the records. A second midnight raid by West Benders to this secret location was successful, and all but one volume was recovered except "M," which was discovered in Port Washington and returned to West Bend in 1878.

While West Benders worked hard, they played hard too. The annual county fair, picnics, outings to the local lakes, trips to cities like Milwaukee, and local sporting games were common pastimes. An abundance of taverns, dance halls, and movie theaters came and went in West Bend, giving the locals refreshment and relaxation. Special occasions like presidential visits, anniversary celebrations, and cultural events were times to break the monotony of everyday life.

Through all of the changes, West Bend has had an eye toward its future. Preservation of its history, culture, and green space has always been a priority. With the first meeting of the Old Settlers' Club in 1874 and the creation of a city museum as part of the high school library in 1938, the foundations for preservation of the past were set. The museum collection was combined with the Old Settlers' Collection in 1962 when space became available in the Old Jailhouse. This was the beginning of the Washington County Historical Society as it exists today.

Along with cultural and material preservation, West Bend has a tradition of land preservation. Private, members-only parks were common in the 1800s. In 1935, the first public park, City Park, was dedicated. Today, West Bend boasts 39 open areas for play, preservation, and natural beauty, and it houses the headquarters of the Ozaukee/Washington County Land Trust. Public open areas are graced with 34 public art installations courtesy of the West Bend Friends of Sculpture.

Today, many of the big manufactures are gone from West Bend, but the city continues to thrive. Smaller manufactures and service industries continue to make West Bend their home. A thriving, historic downtown persists as the heart of the city, and various cultural offerings, from local theater to art and historical museums, ensure entertainment for locals and visitors alike.

One

Settlement

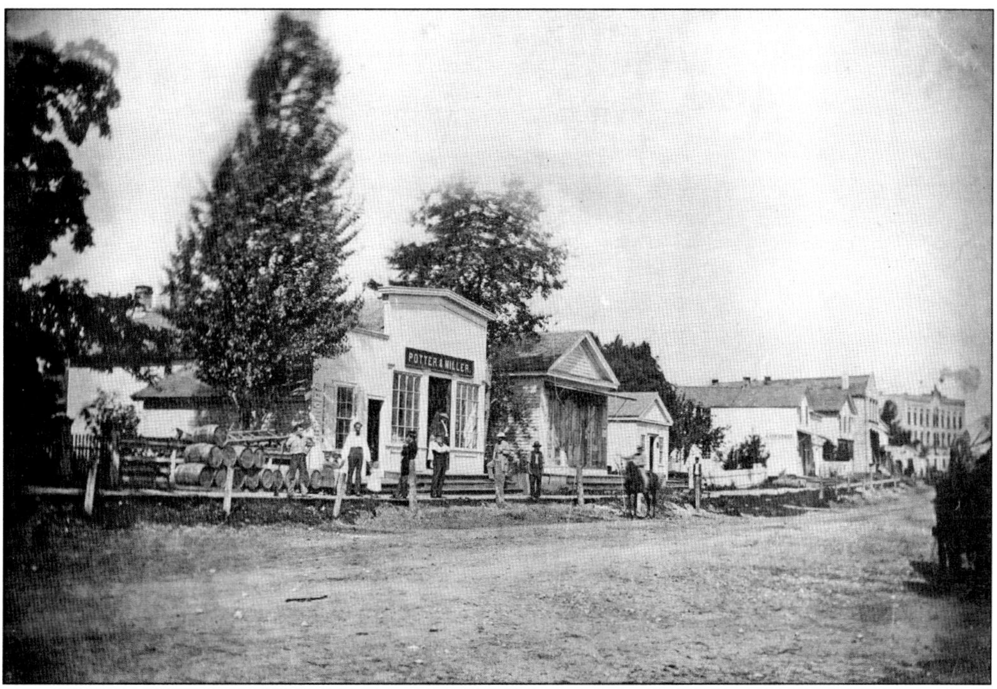

This is thought to be the earliest photograph of downtown West Bend, taken around 1870. Identified in the image are William Wightman and Hattie Miller, both members of West Bend pioneer families. The only building that survives today is the brick Washington House Hotel at the far end of the street; it is now a bar.

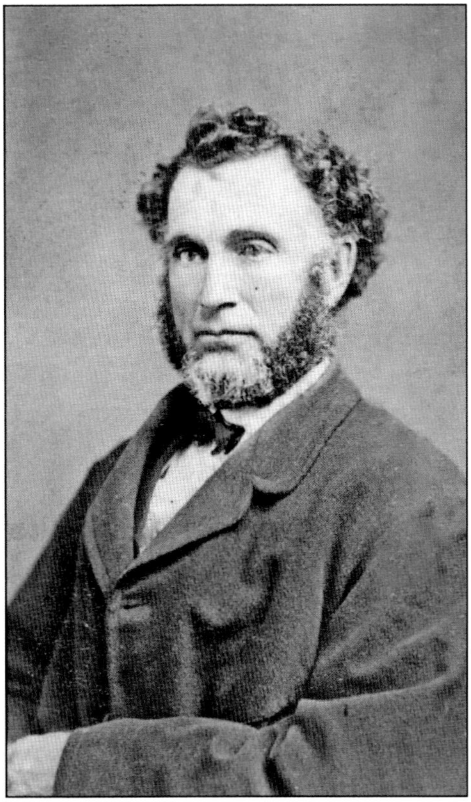

Anson Verbeck was a member of one of West Bend's pioneer families. The Verbecks moved to West Bend from Pennsylvania with M.A.T. Farmer and his family and owned a blacksmith shop. Anson was also the first bridegroom in West Bend. He served in the Civil War as part of the 36th Wisconsin Infantry Regiment. He was discharged because of wounds and later moved to and died in Kansas.

The McDonalds were one of the early pioneer families in West Bend. Hannah McDonald, pictured here, is listed as the first bride in West Bend. She married Anson Verbeck, a member of one of the earliest families living in West Bend. The marriage took place in 1846 and was performed by Jacob E. Young, the first justice of the peace.

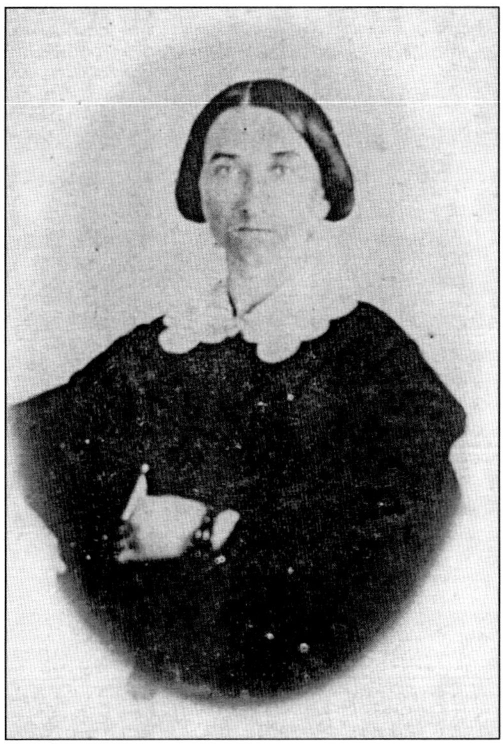

Elizabeth Wightman was born in New York and came to West Bend in 1846 with her husband, William. They, along with Byron Kilbourn, James Kneeland, and E.B. Wolcott, donated the land for what was then known as "the Park." It was meant to be used for the benefit of the county forever. Today, it is home to the Washington County Historical Society museums and the Veterans' Memorial Plaza.

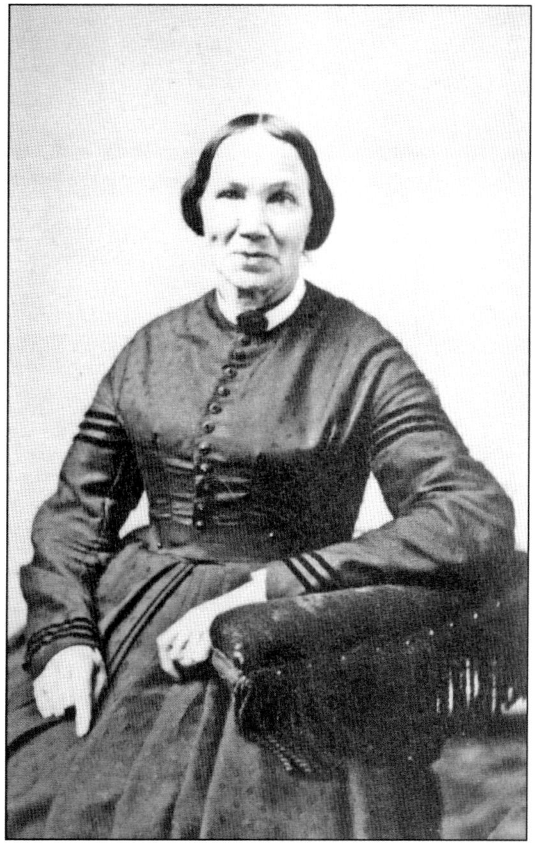

This house located on Carl and Minnie Eckert's farm was a typical log building from the late 1800s. Early settlers usually built a simple one- or two-room structure and added on as needed with the growth of their families and wealth. This house was located at what is now Park and Eighteenth Avenues. It was torn down in the 1990s when the city extended Eighteenth Avenue north.

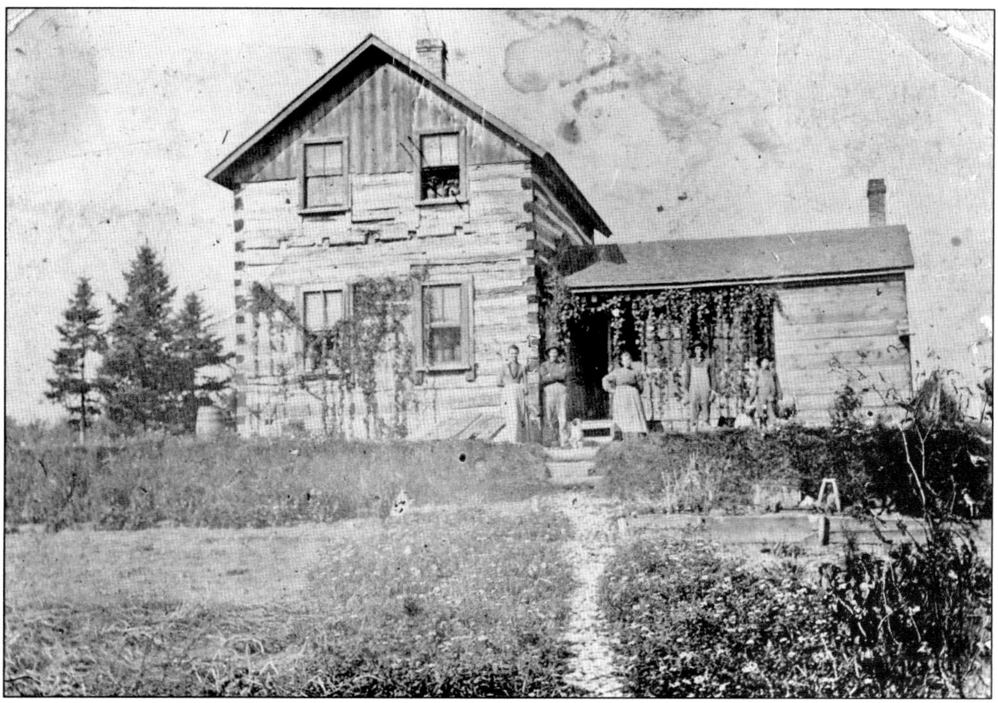

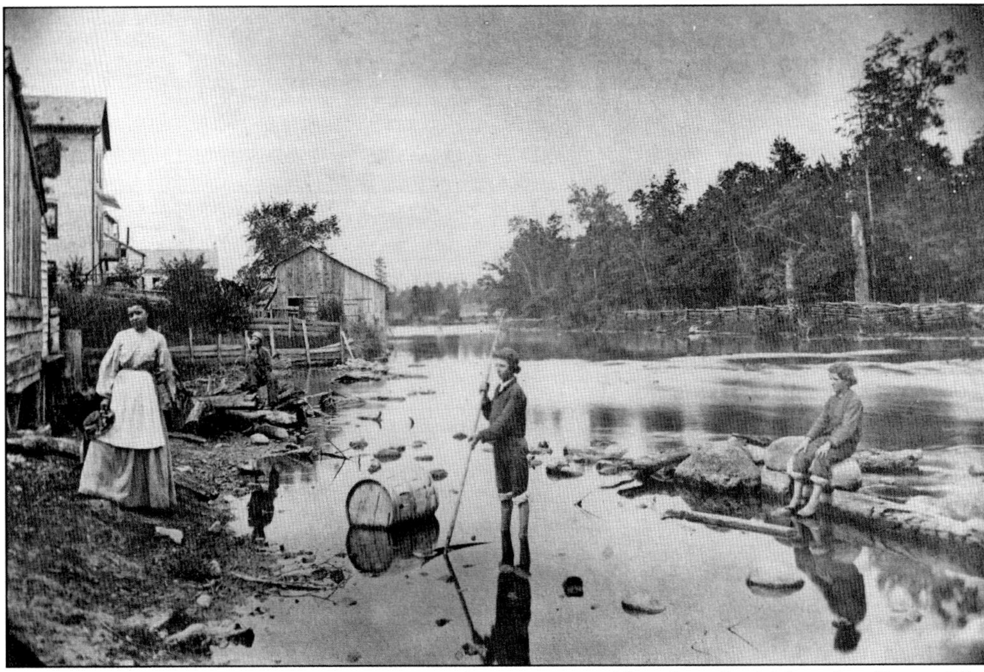

West Bend was named for its location on a large westward bend in the Milwaukee River. This early photograph of unidentified settlers shows the Milwaukee River and a few of the very early buildings constructed along it. The floating barrel likely contains food, which is kept cool by the river water. (Photograph by D.W. Wheeler.)

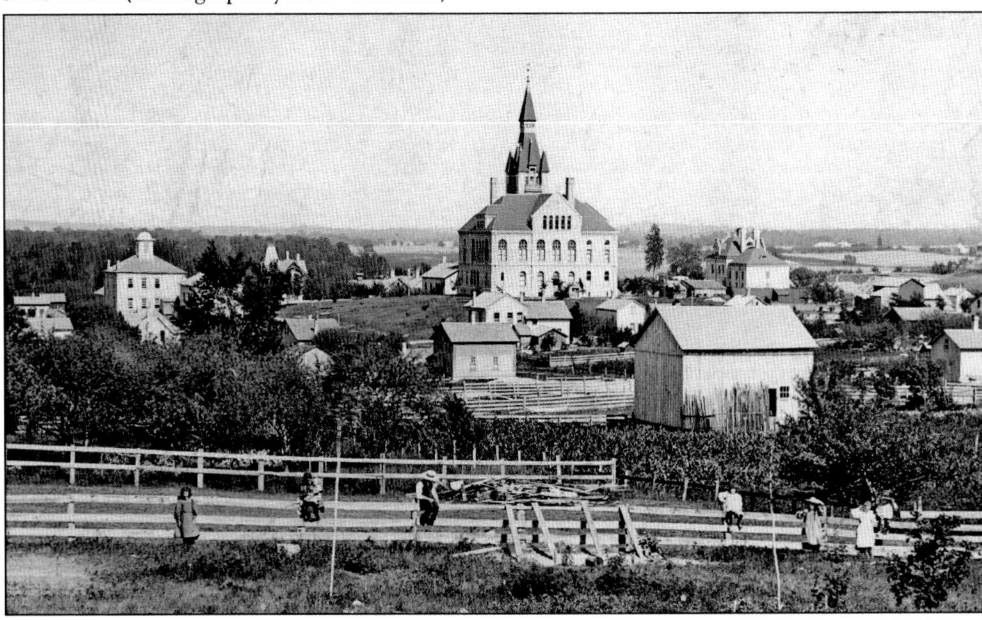

Taken around 1895, this view shows the Washington County Courthouse and its nearby buildings. The fence where the boys are sitting lines today's Eighth Avenue. The large building to the left of the courthouse is South School, which was used as a school until 1892. In 1893, Enger-Kress Pocketbook Company moved into the building and stayed until 1902. Old South School was torn down in 1907.

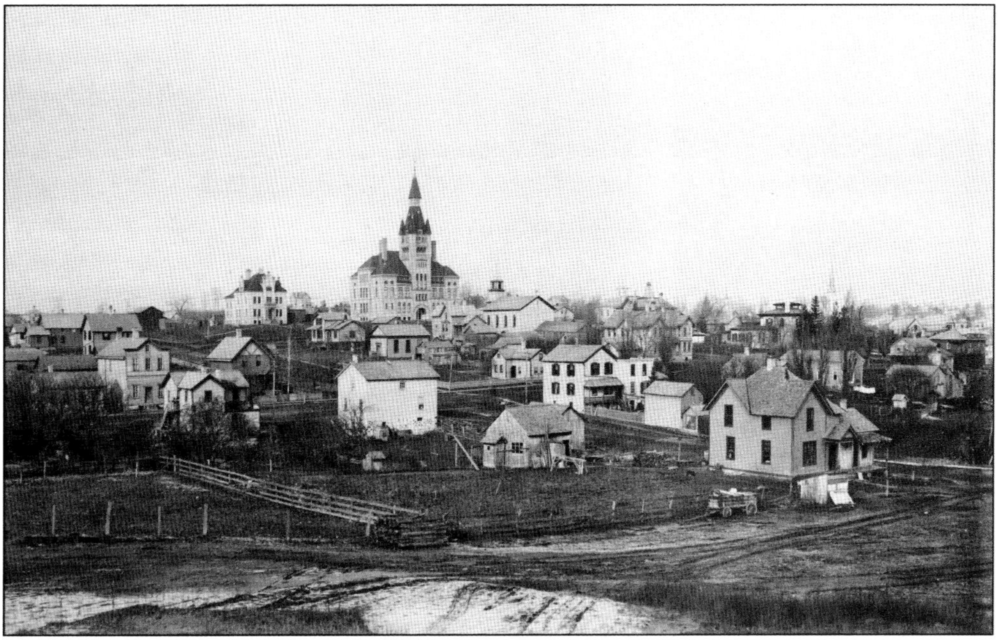

This photograph was taken from Sand Hill, which was near the intersection of modern-day Indiana Avenue and Decorah Road. The tallest building in the image, and the second-tallest building in the county, is the Washington County Courthouse, now the Old Courthouse Museum and Research Center, home of the Washington County Historical Society. This photograph was taken around 1897.

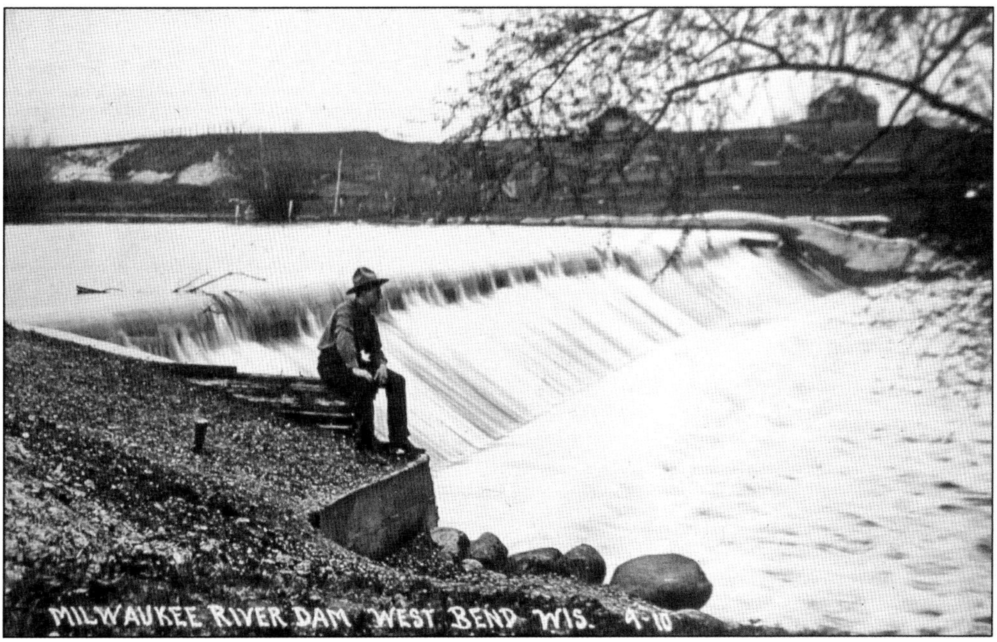

The Milwaukee River Dam in West Bend was one of the first things founders built. The first dam was constructed in 1846. The dam in this photograph from around 1900 was built in 1881. Several industries were constructed nearby to harness the dam's power, including a sawmill, gristmill, tannery, woolen mill, and electric company.

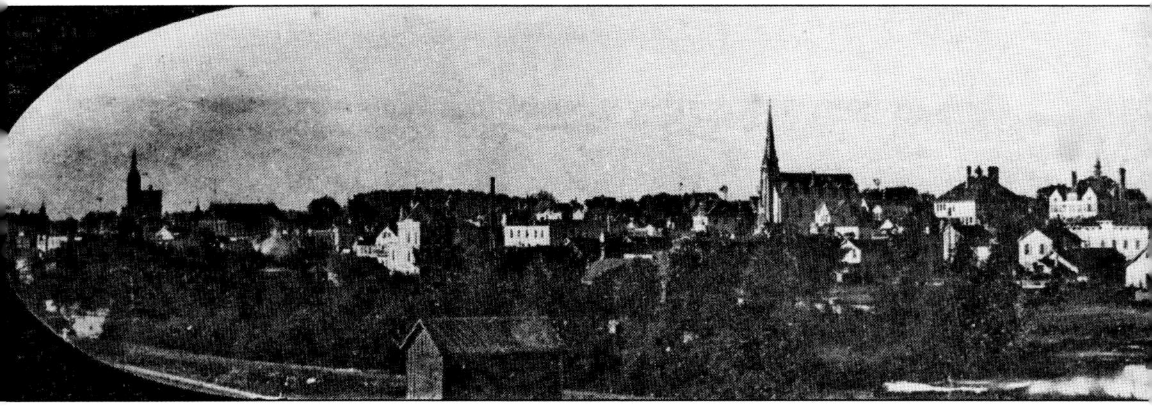

This photograph of West Bend dates to around 1900 and was taken from Pleasant Hill, northeast of the city. Pleasant Hill would later be the location of the county fairgrounds and today is the site of Fair Park Elementary School and the current Washington County Courthouse. Holy Angels

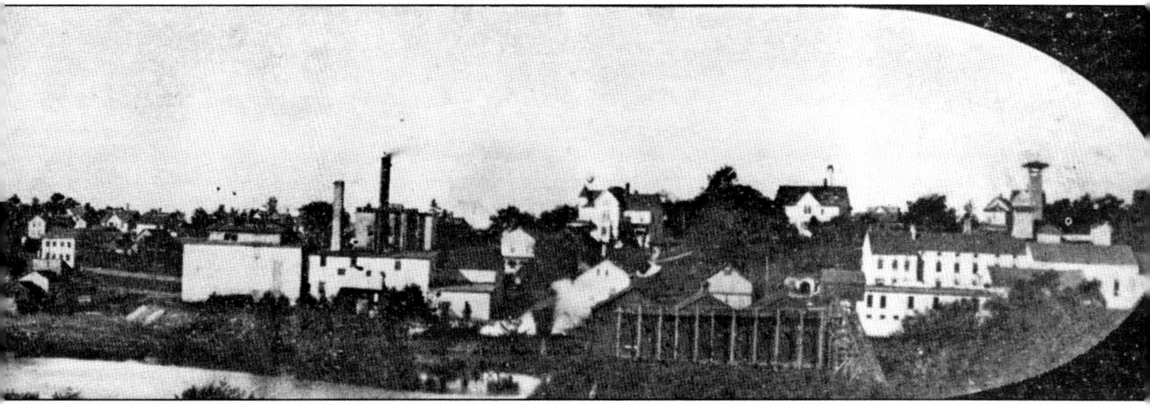

Catholic Church's Gothic construction can be seen prominently in the center left. (Photograph by Louis Schreiber).

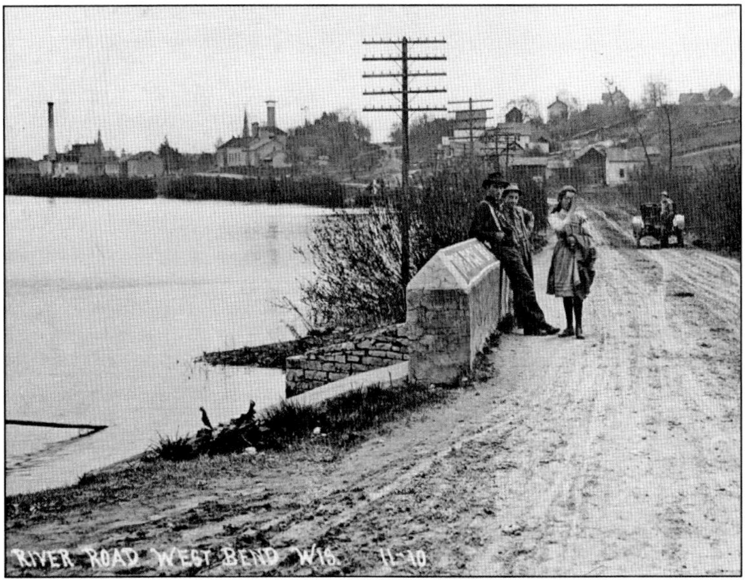

Taken around 1900, this photograph shows the bridge on River Road, today known as North Main Street, that crossed Silver Creek next to the millpond, just south of Kuester Island. On the left is the current entrance to Regner Park. Unfortunately, the people in the photograph are unidentified.

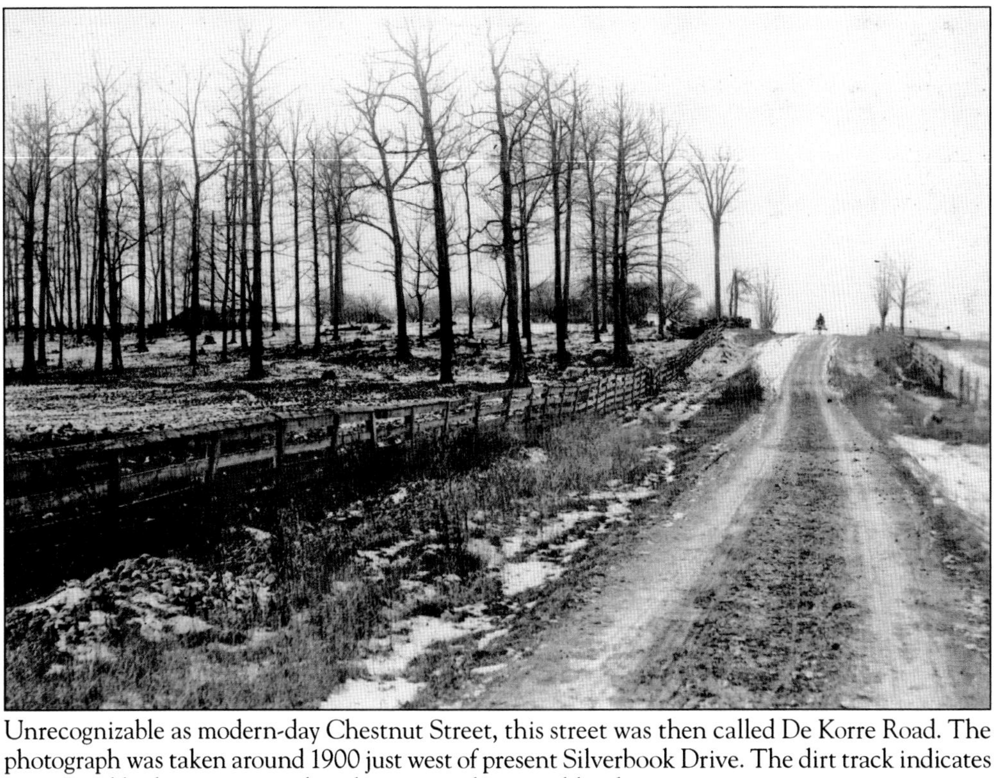

Unrecognizable as modern-day Chestnut Street, this street was then called De Korre Road. The photograph was taken around 1900 just west of present Silverbook Drive. The dirt track indicates West Bend had not yet spread to the surrounding rural landscape.

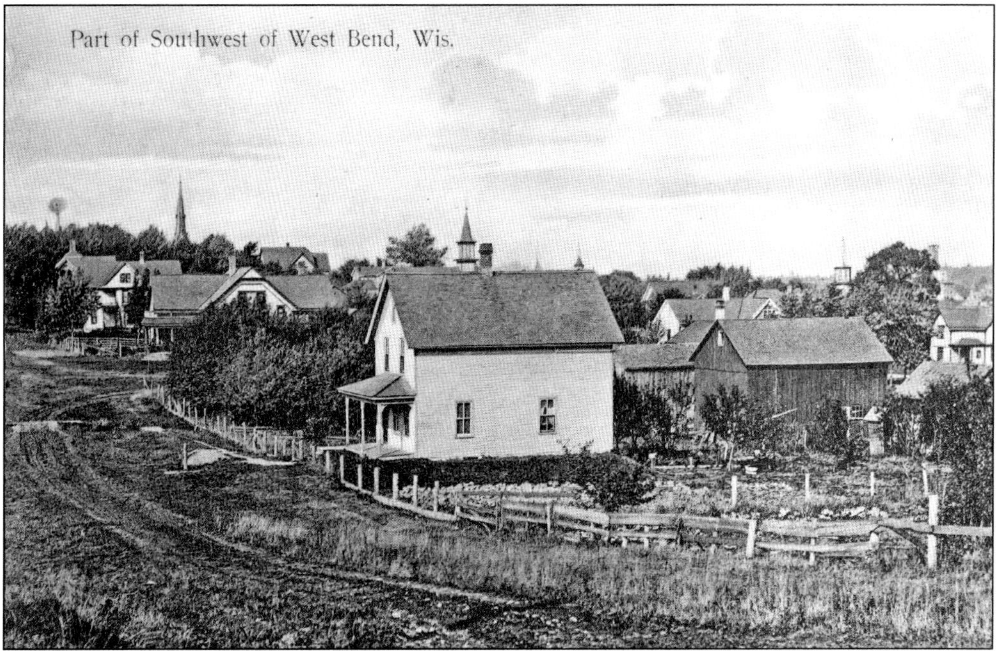

This photograph was taken of the southwest portion of West Bend around 1890, near the edge of the developed part of the city. The house in the center is located halfway between modern-day Chestnut and Poplar Streets on Eighth Avenue. The spire of Holy Angels Catholic Church can be seen in the background on the left.

The families of Dr. Daniel W. Lynch and James Finnegan are pictured around 1880 outside of a house located at what is now the 400 block of North Eighth Avenue. James Finnegan was the Washington County superintendant of schools. The house was built by Baruch Schleisinger Weil, the founder of Slinger, Wisconsin.

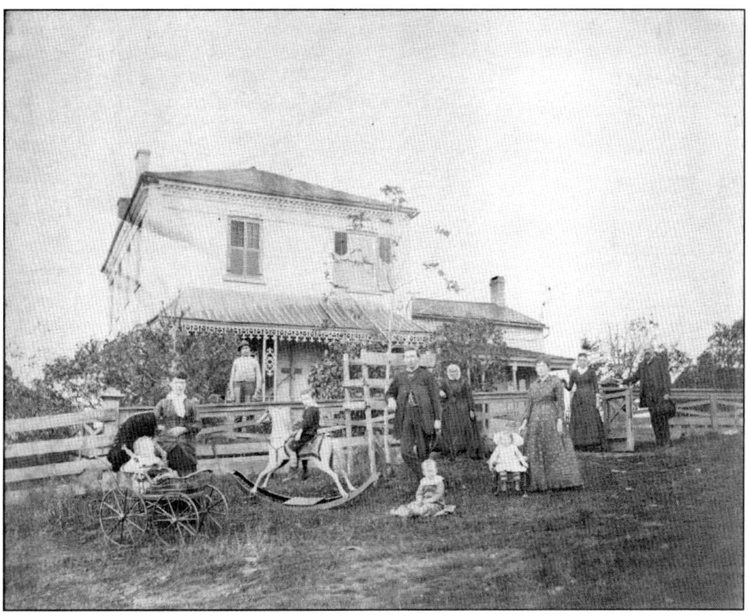

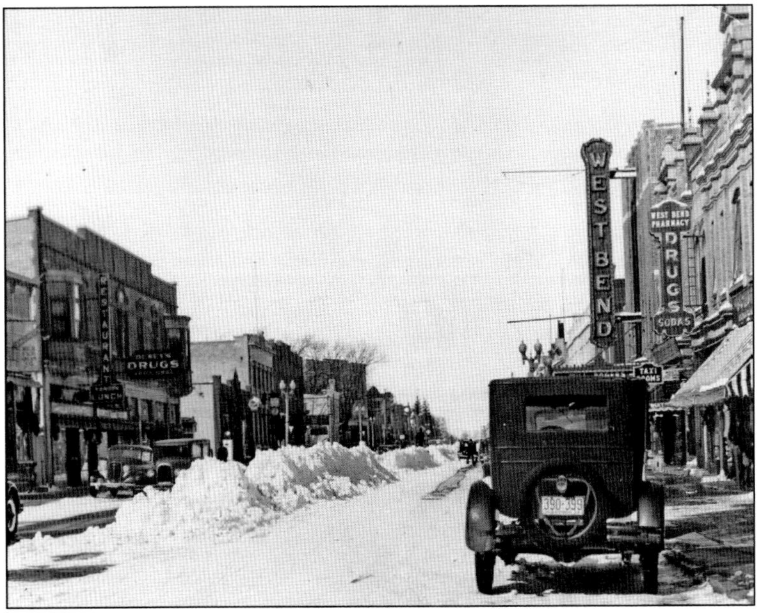

This view of West Bend's downtown Main Street looks north during the winter of 1928. On the right is the distinctive West Bend Theater sign, still in existence today and often used as a downtown landmark. Also on the left is the sign for the West Bend Pharmacy. Signs for the Beacon Restaurant and Dewy Drug Co. can be seen on the right.

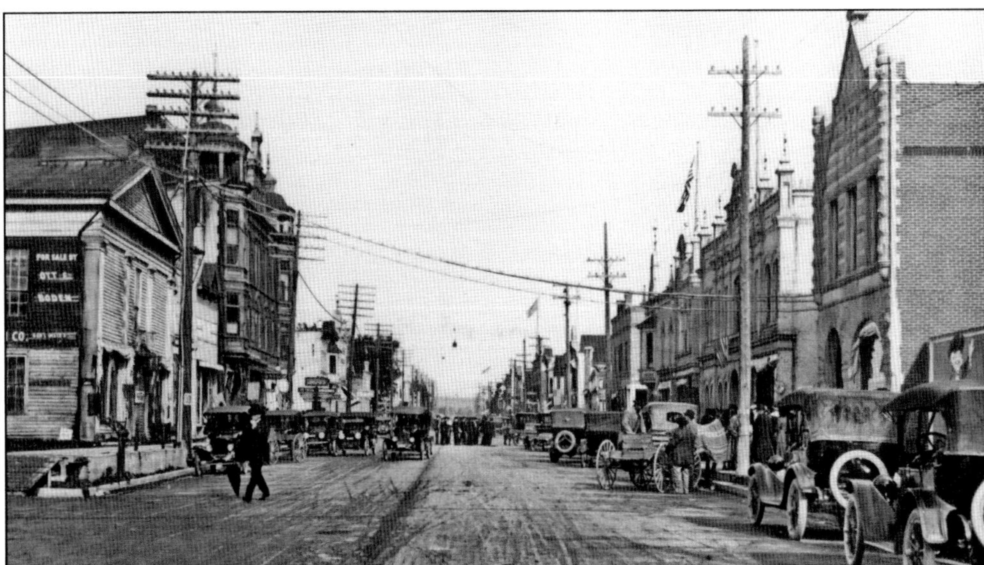

This photograph of Main Street was taken near the intersection of Hickory Street around 1915. The first building on the left is the original county courthouse, which was moved in 1889 when a new brick building was constructed. The edifice was remodeled and housed Ott and Boden Hardware Store before being torn down.

Two

Infrastructure, Business, and Industry

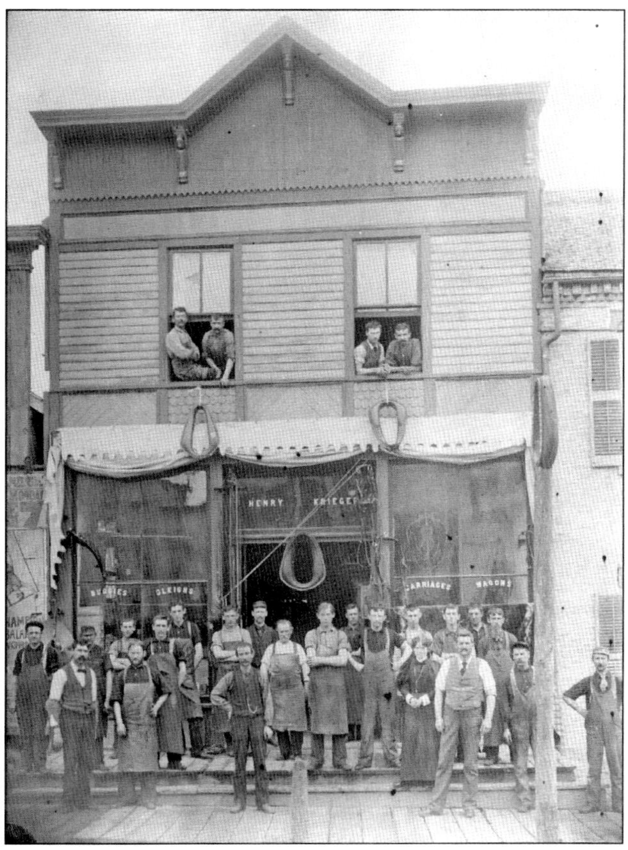

Henry Krieger Manufacturing Company made horse harnesses and saddle products. Founded in 1891, the company was in business for 11 years. At one point, Krieger combined his business with that of Adolf G. Schnepf, a wagon dealer, and located himself on Main Street. Adolf Schnepf is front and center in this photograph, wearing a vest and watch chain.

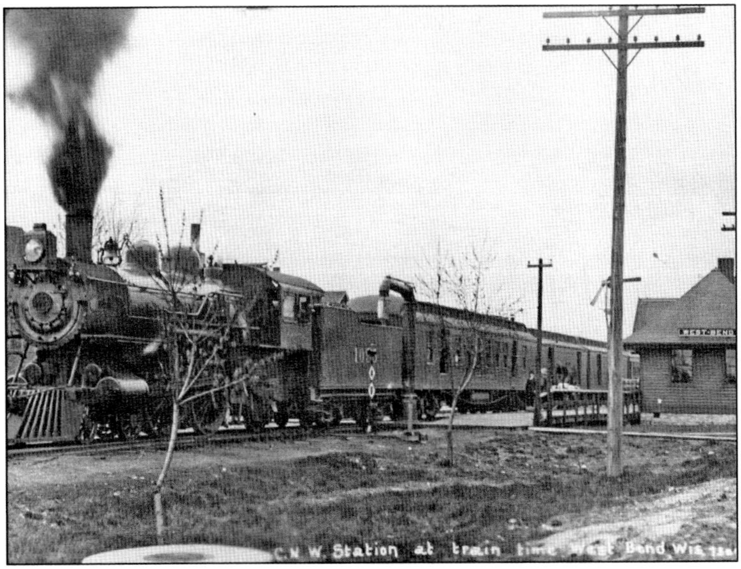

The Chicago & North Western Railway arrived in West Bend in 1872. The rail caused an increase in business and industry as manufactures were able to get raw materials and ship finished products easily and cheaply. It also allowed locals to travel easily to Milwaukee, Fond du Lac, and beyond. This photograph of a train at the depot was taken around 1910.

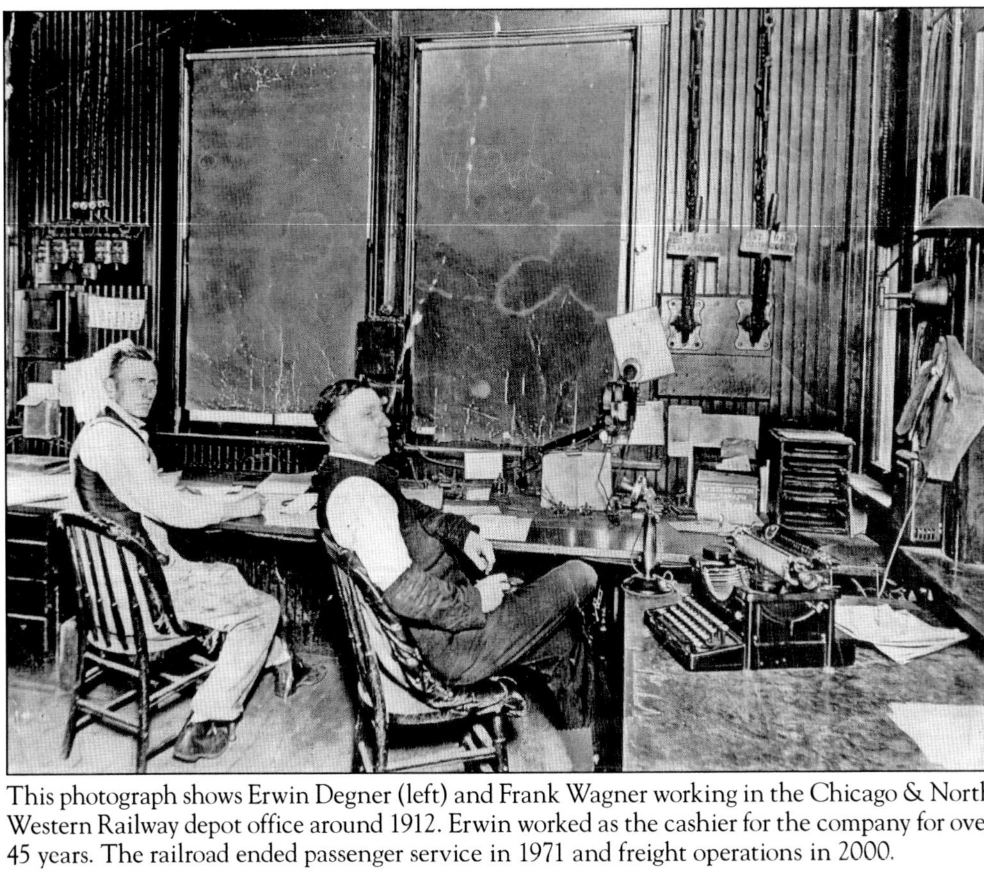

This photograph shows Erwin Degner (left) and Frank Wagner working in the Chicago & North Western Railway depot office around 1912. Erwin worked as the cashier for the company for over 45 years. The railroad ended passenger service in 1971 and freight operations in 2000.

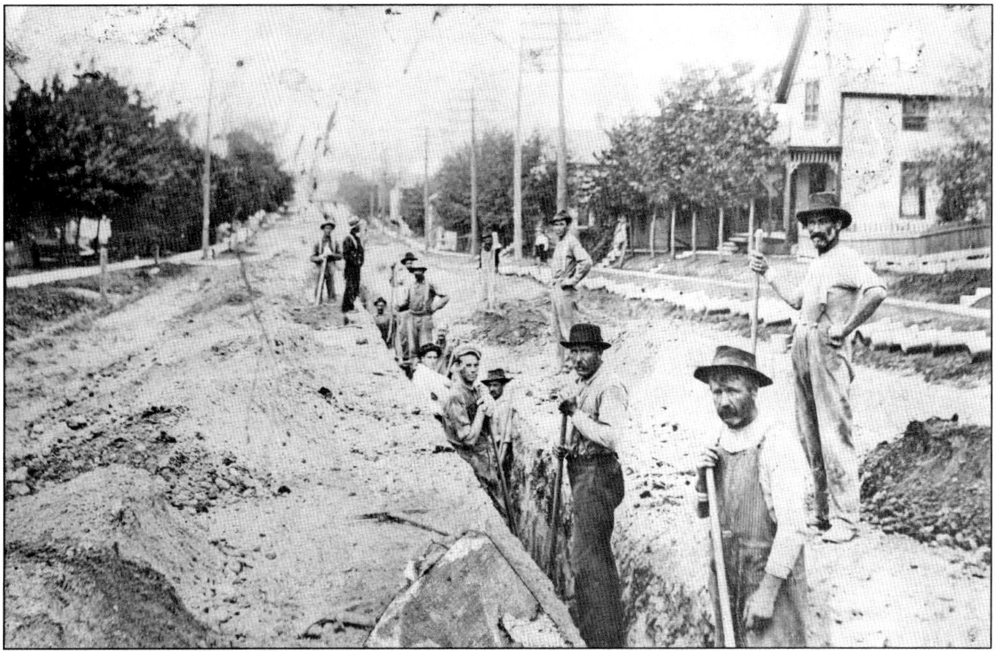

By 1908, West Bend had grown to the point that it was in dire need of a public water and sewer system. The men in this photograph are digging trenches to lay the pipes. The first public water service was heavily regulated to prevent waste. It cost a homeowner $10 to sign up for service. By 1913, only 65 houses had signed up; most still used private wells and outhouses.

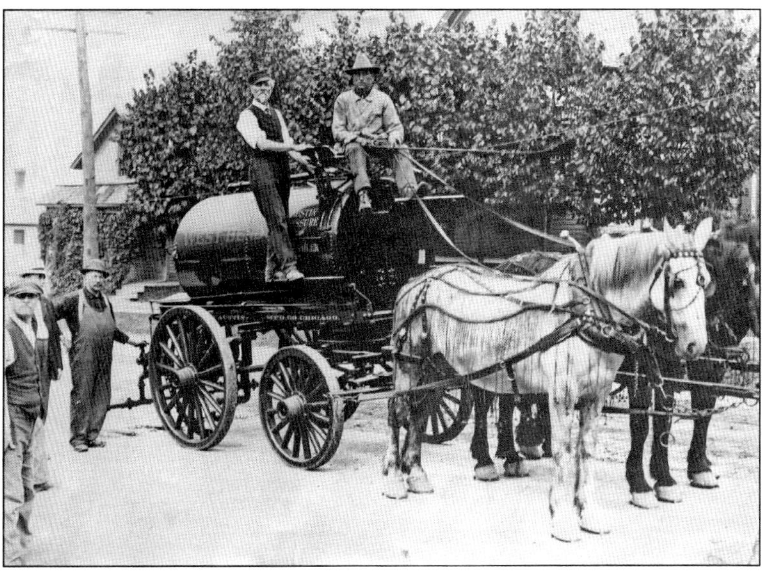

Street oiling and watering was common on dirt roads. It helped keep the dust down and also preserved the road surface by hardening it and preventing ruts. Here, a Mr. Lohr is standing on the Austin Pressure Street Oiler. It is being driven by a Mr. Schachelmeier and Fred Heipp (on the left) of Heipp's General Store.

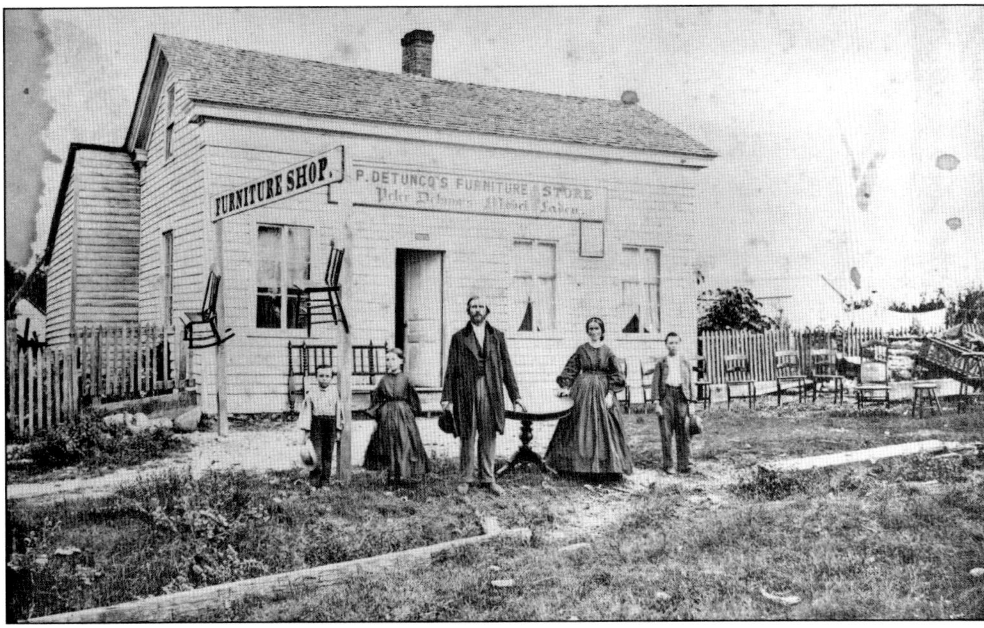

Around 1856, craftsman Pierre DeTuncq settled in West Bend and opened a furniture store. Originally from France, DeTuncq, like many immigrants, spent several years in New York before moving west. Along with furniture and detailed woodwork in local homes, the DeTuncq family expanded into coffins and hearses and added a funeral parlor to their Main Street store.

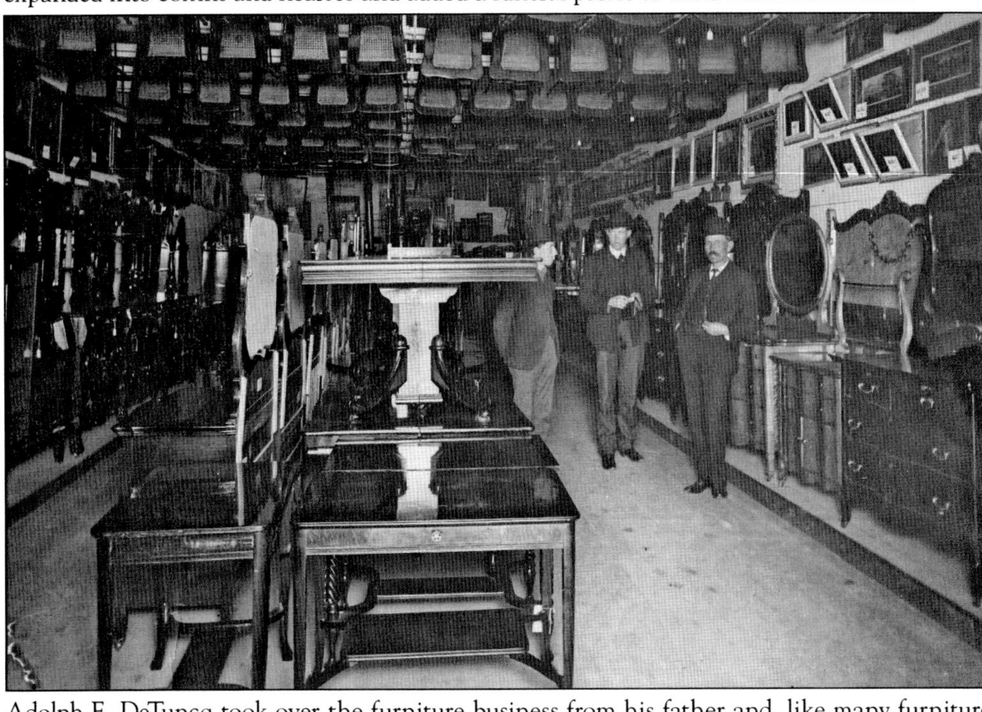

Adolph E. DeTuncq took over the furniture business from his father and, like many furniture makers of the time, expanded into undertaking and coffins. This photograph is of the interior of his shop and funeral parlor on Main Street near Hickory Street around 1910. From left to right are Arthur DeTuncq, Louis Richter, and Adolph DeTuncq.

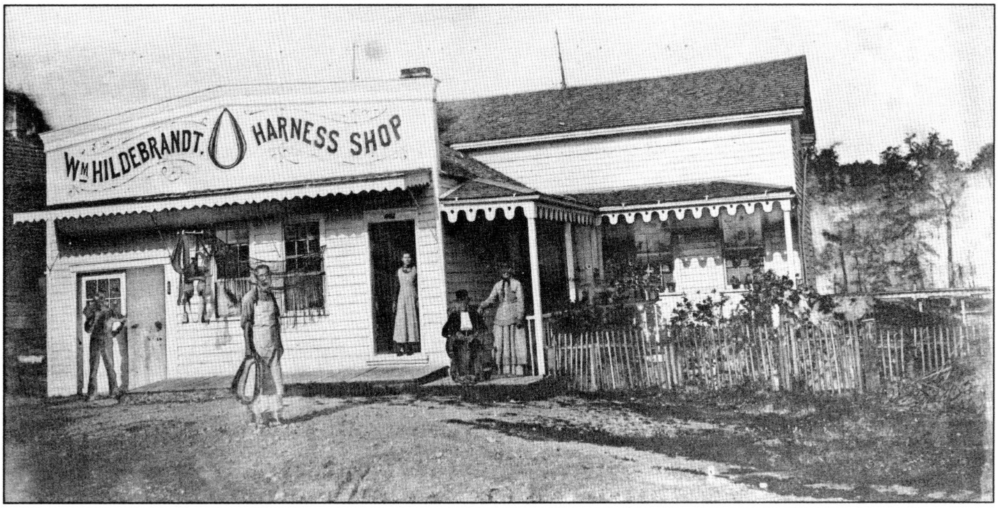

William Hildebrandt's Harness Shop and home were located at the intersection of Main Street, Kilbourn Avenue, and Poplar Street. William came to the United States from Prussia in 1856. This photograph was taken around 1880. Over the years, the building has been home to other businesses as well as to the justice of the peace. It remains a residence today.

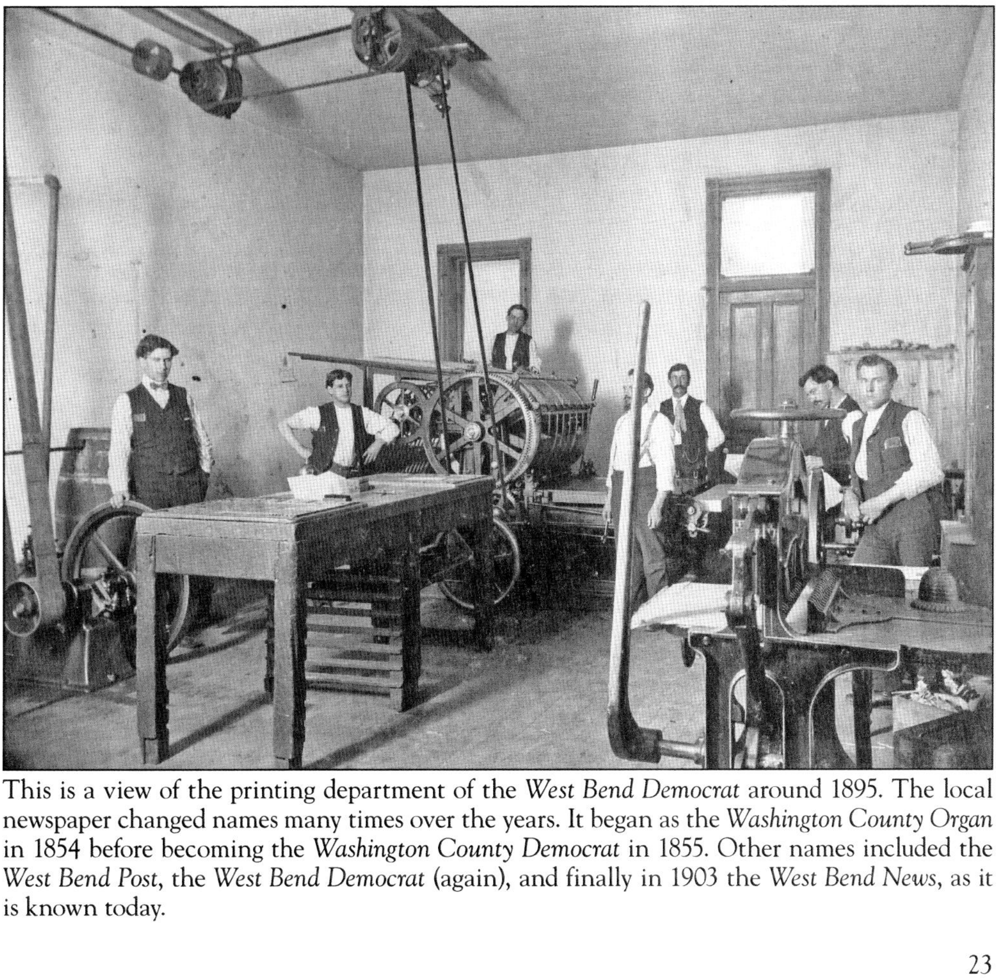
This is a view of the printing department of the *West Bend Democrat* around 1895. The local newspaper changed names many times over the years. It began as the *Washington County Organ* in 1854 before becoming the *Washington County Democrat* in 1855. Other names included the *West Bend Post*, the *West Bend Democrat* (again), and finally in 1903 the *West Bend News*, as it is known today.

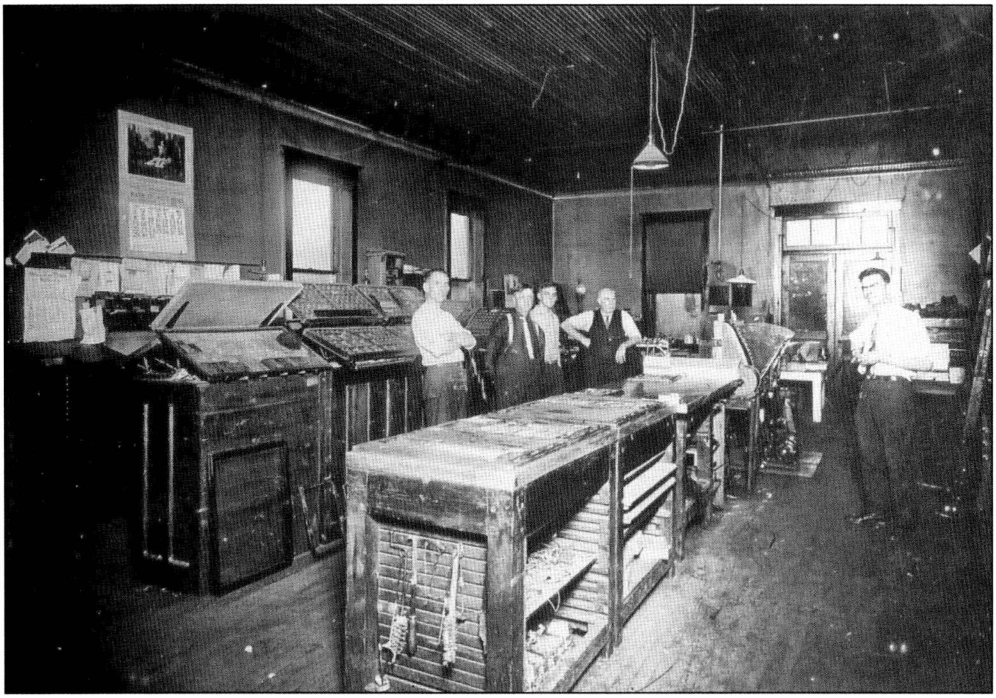

This photograph shows the typesetting department of the *West Bend Pilot* in 1915. The *Pilot* was a local newspaper printed from February 24, 1892, through June 30, 1954. The man with the dark vest is Jacob Kaempfer, and on the right is editor Henry B. Kaempfer. The other men are not identified.

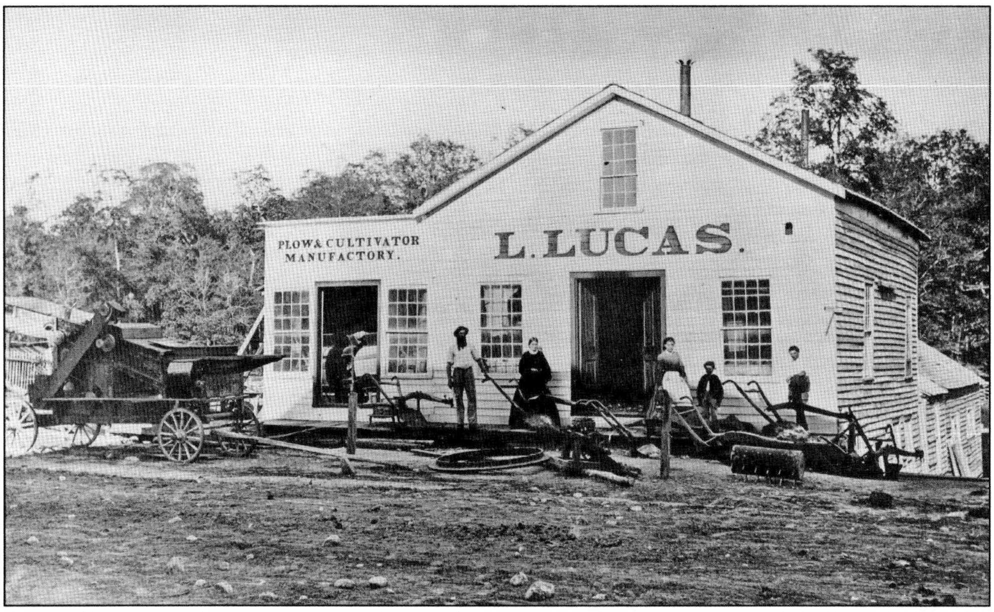

Originally a tinsmith, Louis Lucas sold his tin business in 1859 to open an iron foundry. The foundry made new farm implements and did repairs. It was located on the corner of Water Street and River Road, today named Main Street. Louis sold the business in 1879 to Jacob Young. The company changed hands to become Silberzahn Manufacturing Company and later Gehl Company.

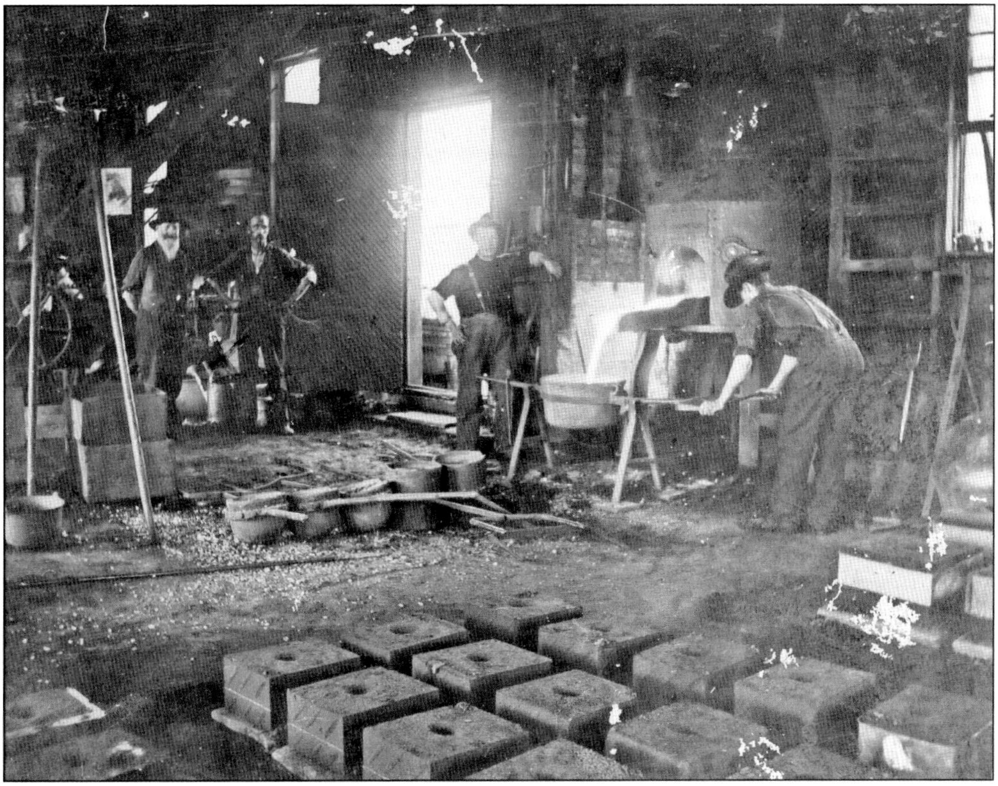

This photograph shows the Silberzahn Manufacturing Company foundry interior around 1890. Owner Charles Silberzahn is on the far left. Originally known as the Lucas Foundry, the company specialized in manufacturing farming implements. Silberzahn purchased partnership in the Lucas foundry in 1878 after selling his shares in a Sheboygan foundry, which went on to become Kohler Company.

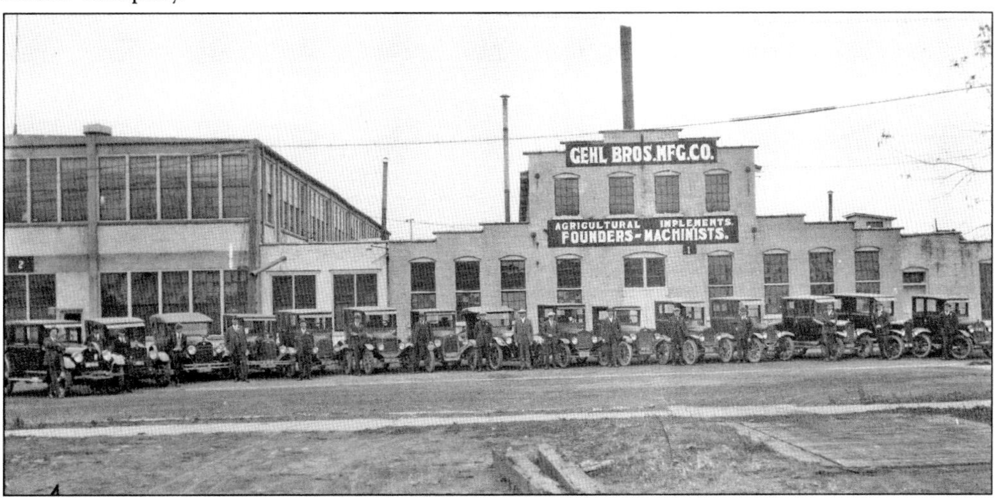

Gehl Brothers Manufacturing Company began in 1906 when Michael and Henry Gehl joined their brother John in business. They bought out Peter Berres, their then-partner in the Berres-Gehl Manufacturing Company. The company was formerly Silberzahn Manufacturing and the Lucas Foundry. This photograph from around 1921 shows the factory and fleet of company salesmen.

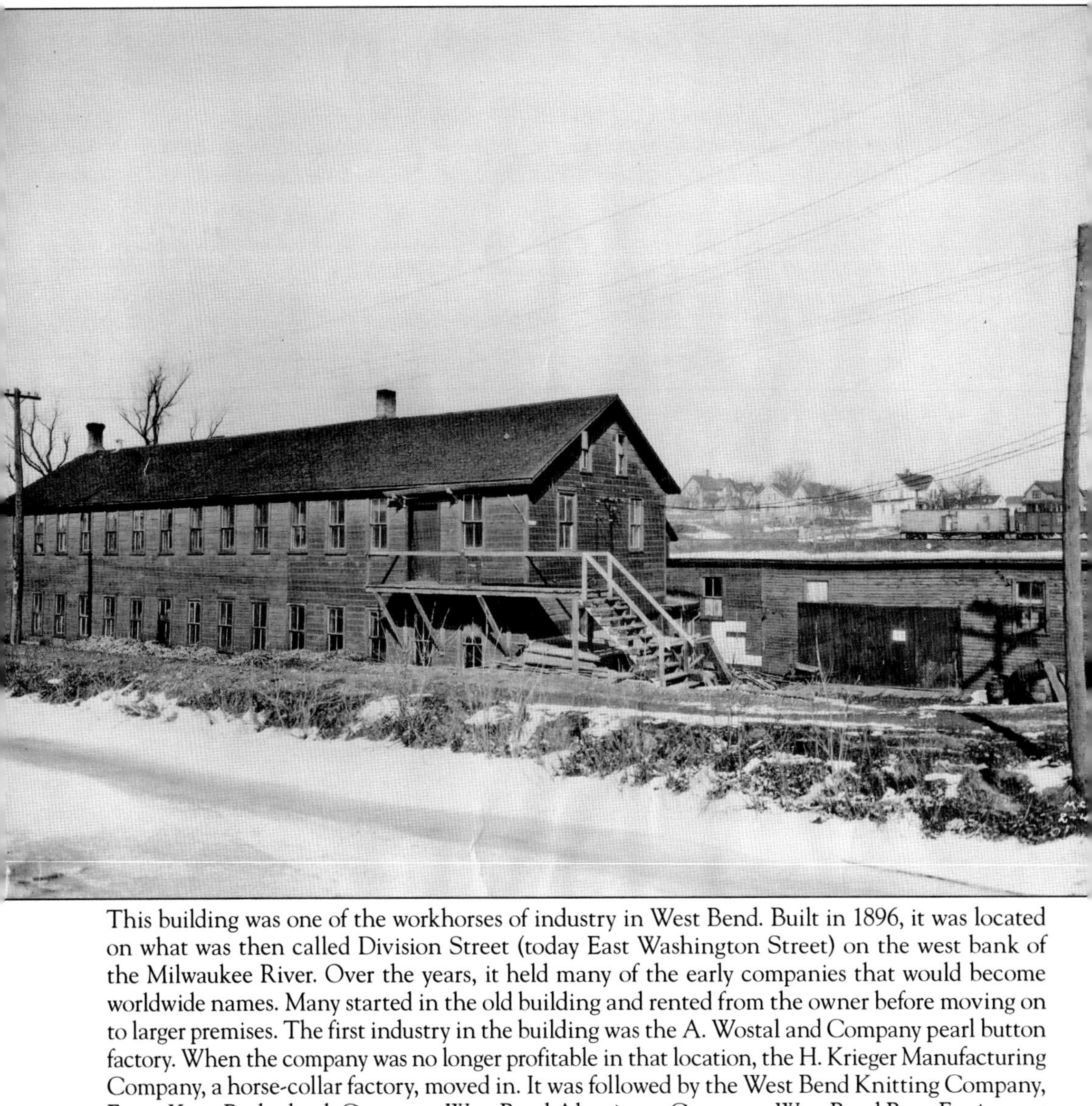

This building was one of the workhorses of industry in West Bend. Built in 1896, it was located on what was then called Division Street (today East Washington Street) on the west bank of the Milwaukee River. Over the years, it held many of the early companies that would become worldwide names. Many started in the old building and rented from the owner before moving on to larger premises. The first industry in the building was the A. Wostal and Company pearl button factory. When the company was no longer profitable in that location, the H. Krieger Manufacturing Company, a horse-collar factory, moved in. It was followed by the West Bend Knitting Company, Enger-Kress Pocketbook Company, West Bend Aluminum Company, West Bend Barn Equipment Company, Baren's Woodwork Shop, Baltus Rolfs, Inc., Carl Pick Manufacturing Company, and West Bend Plating Works, among others. The building was torn down in 1997.

The West Bend Malting Company was located on the west side of Wisconsin Street near the Chicago & North Western Railway depot. The first section of the building was erected in 1868 by the Mayer and Kuehlthau breweries to provide raw material for their beer. It changed hands, and additions were built over the years. In 1921, a fire caused considerable damage to the building. It was torn down in 1936.

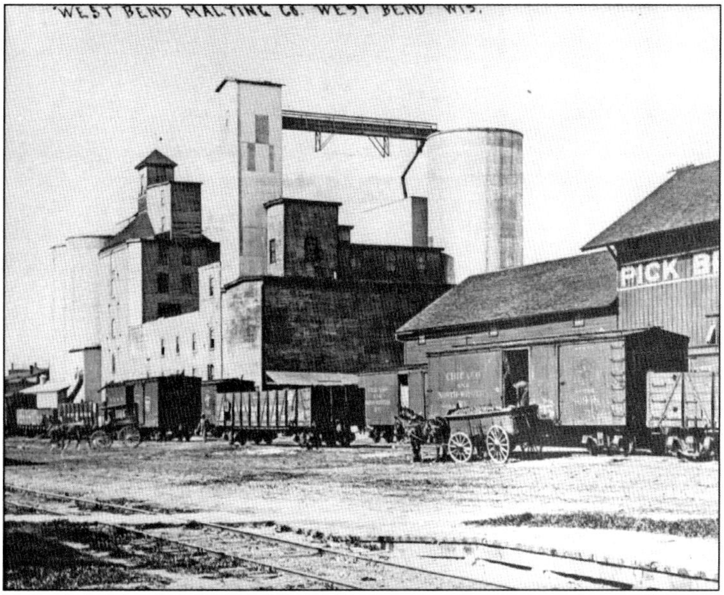

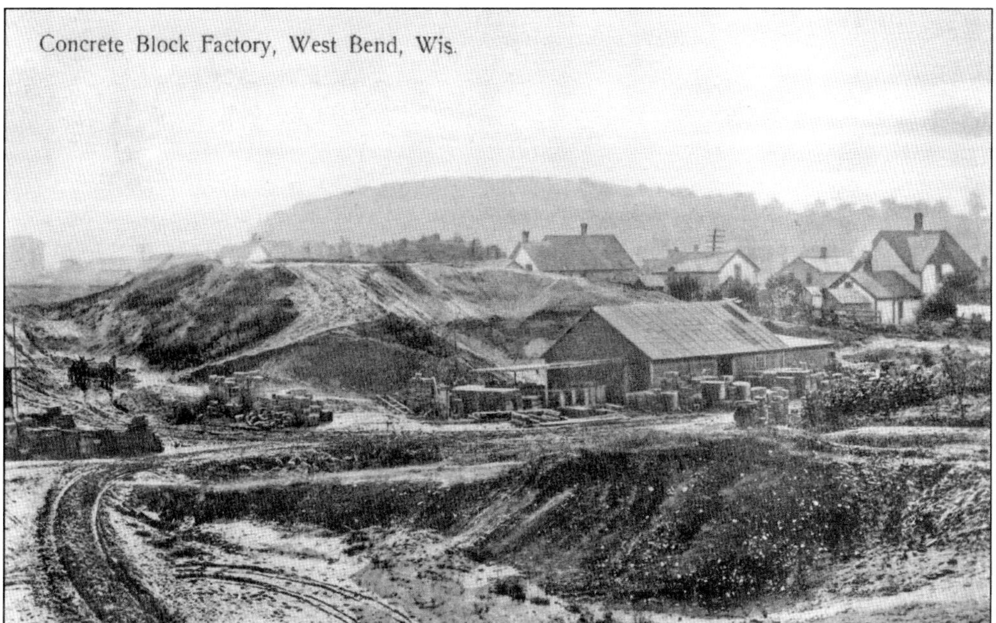

The Concrete Block Factory was located on the southeast edge of West Bend and was started shortly before this photograph was taken around 1900. It was operated by local businessmen Fuge and Kesting. Exploiting the region's natural abundance of glacial till and sand deposits, the concrete building blocks it manufactured were used in many local houses and buildings.

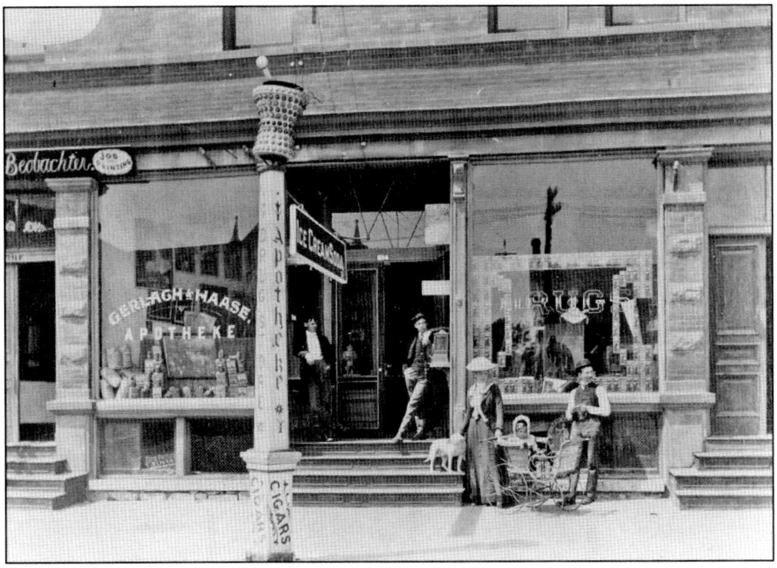

August Gerlach, his wife Agnes Haase Gerlach, and their daughter are pictured around 1900 on the sidewalk in front of the Gerlach & Haase pharmacy located on Main Street near Cedar Street. In 1899, partners Herman Gerlach and Fred Haase purchased the Eagle Drug store from Dr. Edward Wehle.

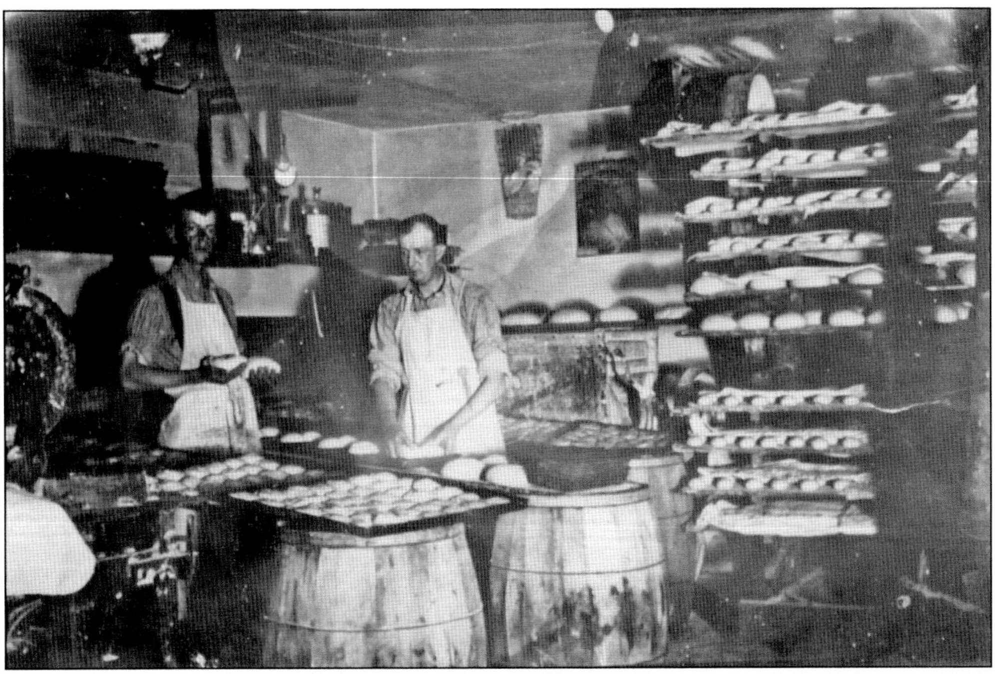

This is the interior of Bauer's bakery around 1940. Clarence Bauer opened the bakery in 1904. Not a baker himself, Clarence learned the trade by hiring experienced bakers. The business expanded to a bustling ice cream parlor. Upon his death in 1929, Clarence's wife took over before selling the bakery to her son Millard in 1936. The family sold the business in 1972. (Courtesy of Barbara Zabors.)

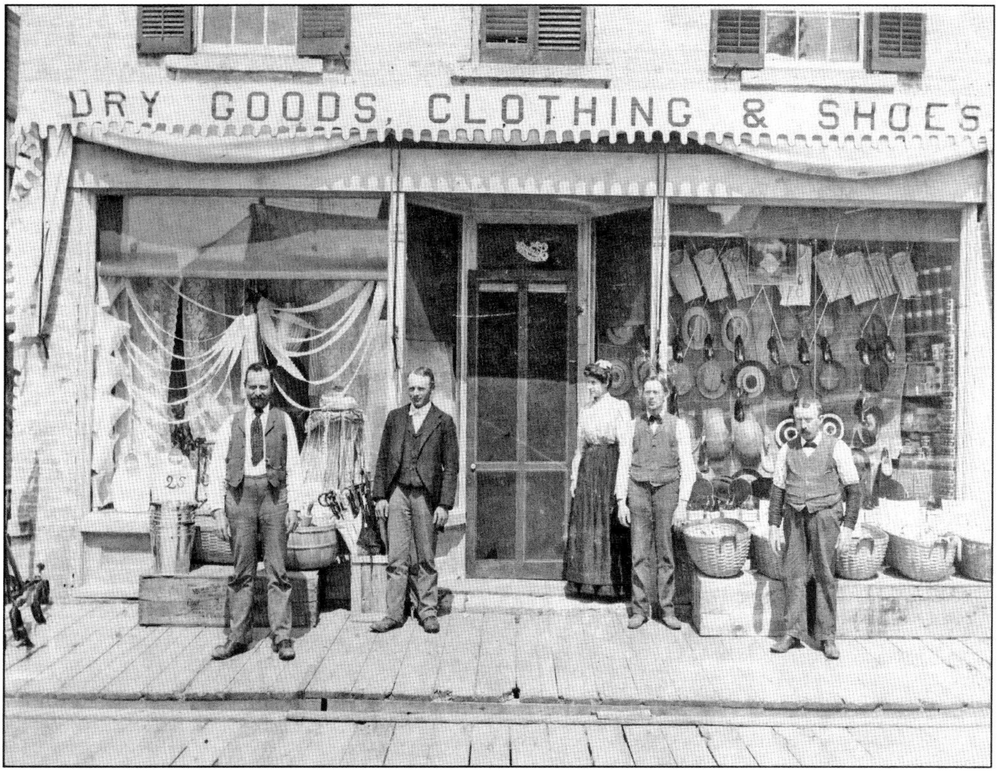

The George Kuehlthau Dry Goods and Grocery store was located on Main Street. Proprietor George Kuehlthau is on the far left of the photograph. The store sold general goods such as hats, stationary, and umbrellas, as well as groceries. The building later became the Bauer Bakery in 1904.

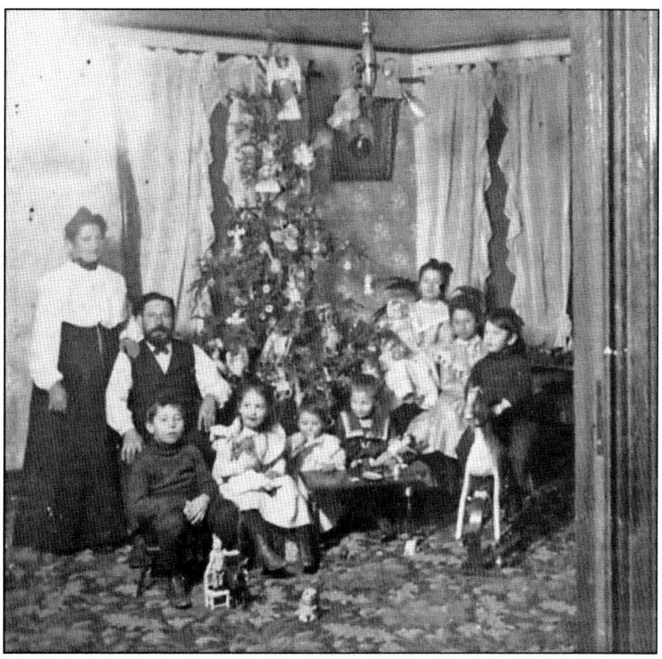

The Kress family is pictured at Christmas around 1905. August Kress was one of the owners and founders of Enger-Kress Pocketbook Company. He and his wife, Thelca, are on the far left of this photograph and are with their children, from left to right, Ferdinand, Marie, Thelca, Gretchen, Augusta, Hedwig, and Paul.

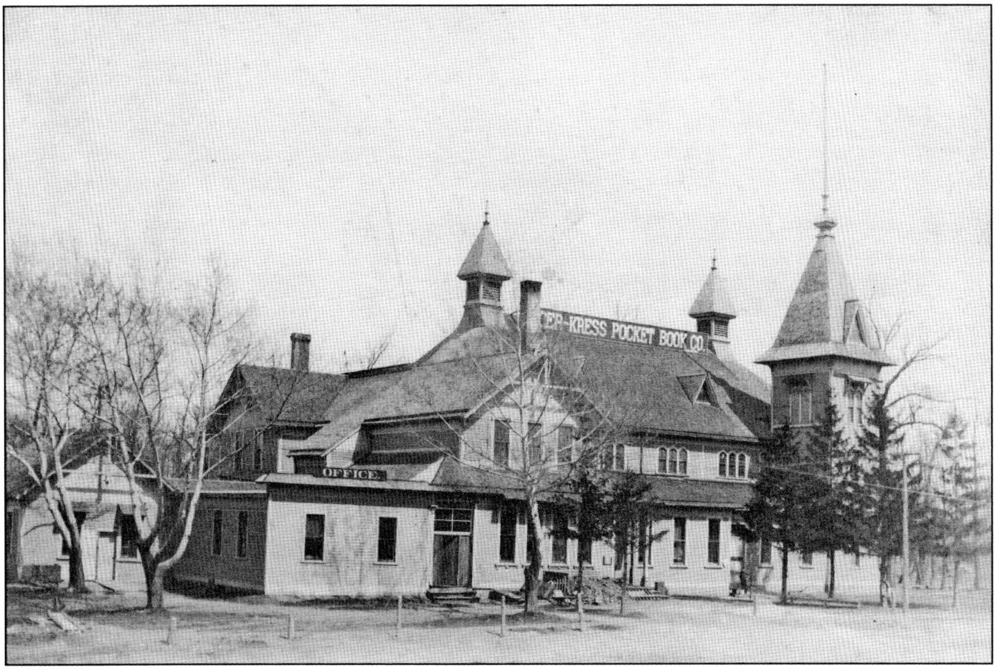

The Enger-Kress Pocketbook Company was founded in Milwaukee in 1882. After a fire destroyed the plant, the company moved to the old Fifth Avenue School in West Bend. In 1902, the company expanded to Moser Hall, pictured here. In 1911, a fire destroyed Moser Hall, and a new factory was constructed. The company used that building until 1998, when it moved to a new facility. In 2006, the company was dissolved.

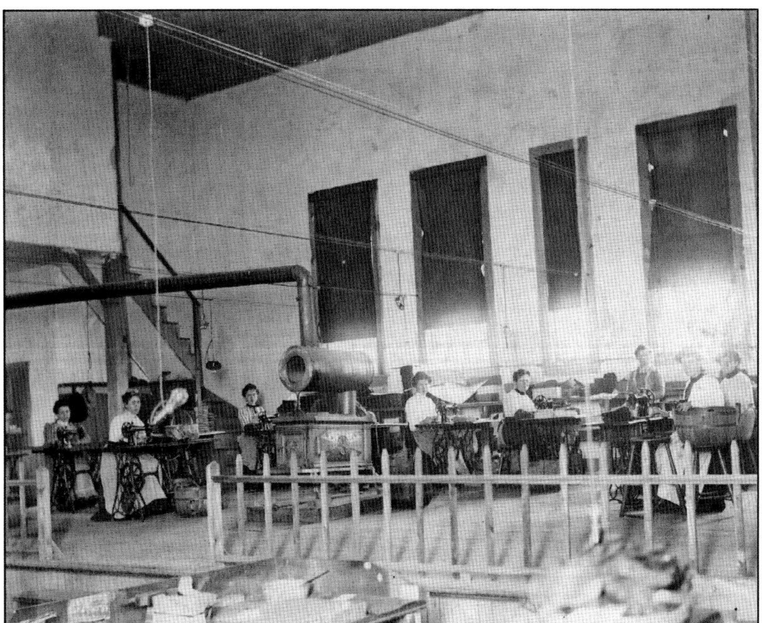

This photograph shows the Enger-Kress Pocketbook Company Sewing Department around 1906. Then housed in Moser Hall, in the old Schlitz Park pavilion, the department was located in what was the old auditorium and stage area of the building. The only person identified is the fourth woman from the right, Hannah Bastian.

B.C. Ziegler was a key player in many of the early businesses in West Bend. An entrepreneur himself, Ziegler was a founder of the West Bend Aluminum Company, president of the First National Bank of West Bend, chairman of Gehl Brothers Manufacturing Company, and president of West Bend Mutual Fire Insurance Company, in addition to funding many other businesses and individuals with loans.

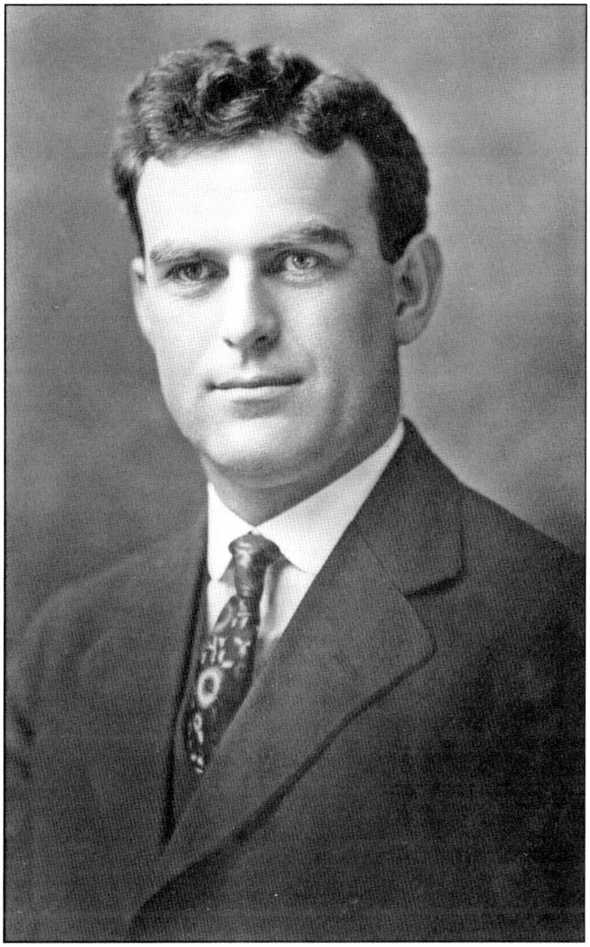

The B.C. Ziegler Company was founded in 1902 by 18-year-old B.C. Ziegler. The company specialized in fire insurance. As the firm prospered, B.C. began making small loans. It was the profits on these loans that helped found many businesses in West Bend and assisted the city though the Great Depression.

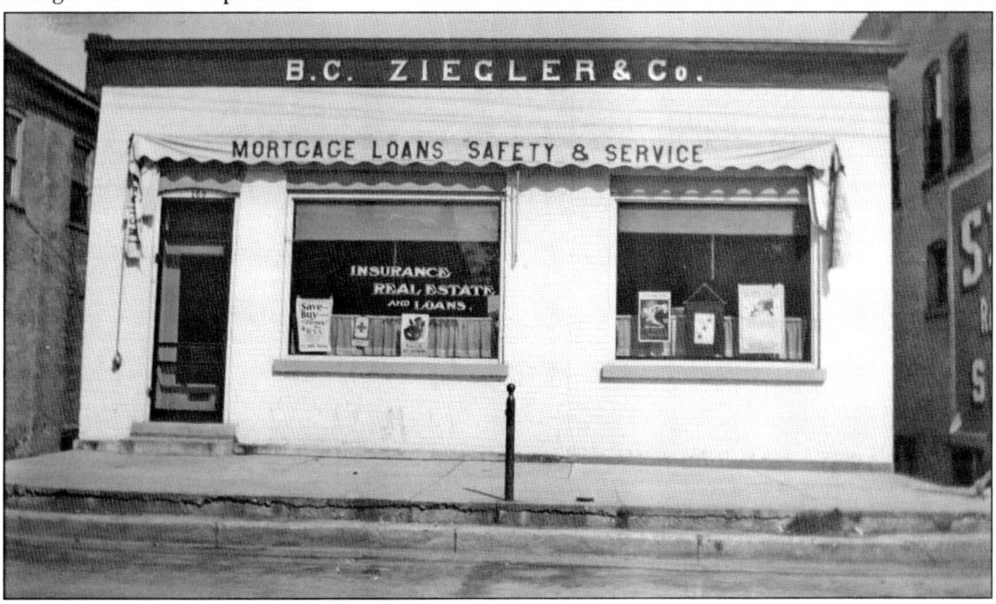

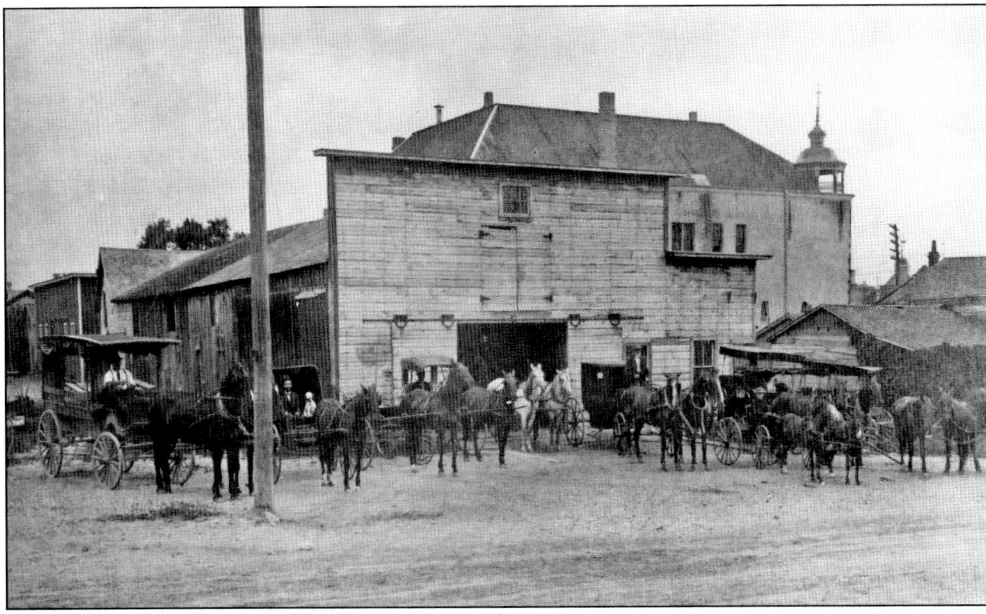

Wightman Stable was located at the corner of Hickory Street and Sixth Avenue. With several wagons, carriages, and horses available, the stables served as an early form of taxi and delivery service for the West Bend area. This photograph was taken around 1905. Today, the Slesar Glass shop is on this site.

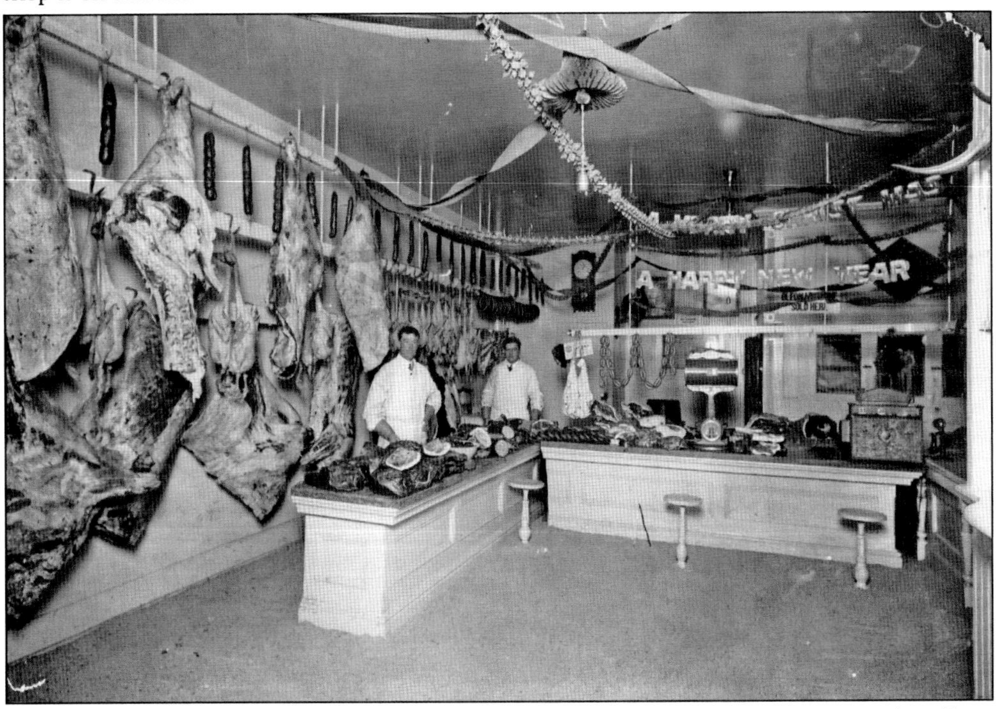

This photograph shows the interior of the Kortendick Meat Market shortly after it opened. William Kortendick (left) and this brother owned a joint butcher shop outside Washington County. In 1906, William decided to go out on his own and opened this store in West Bend. The store was located on Main and Hickory Streets.

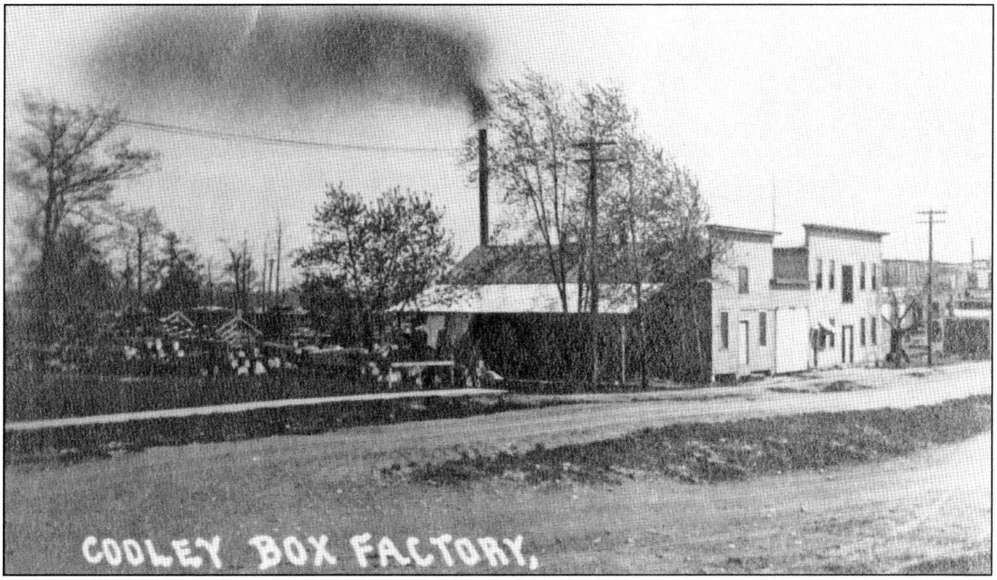

The Cooley Box Factory is one of West Bend's unique industries. Located on Wisconsin Avenue, the company started in 1910 and made round boxes for local dairies' cheese and butter. Raw material for the boxes is seen stacked behind the factory. Wood was originally locally sourced from recently cleared land. Eventually, it was purchased from farther afield.

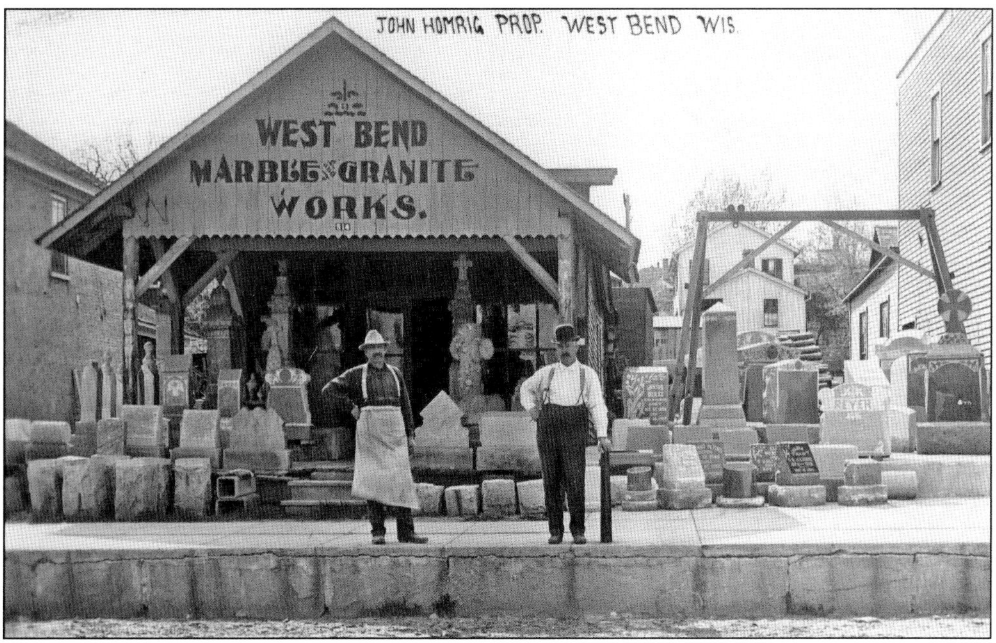

West Bend Marble and Granite Works was owned by John Homrig when this photograph was taken around 1910. When he became the superintendent of the Washington County Insane Asylum in 1912, he sold the business to Erier and Weiss, competitors from the north side of the city. The business was located in what is now the parking lot on Fifth Avenue near Tennies Ace Hardware.

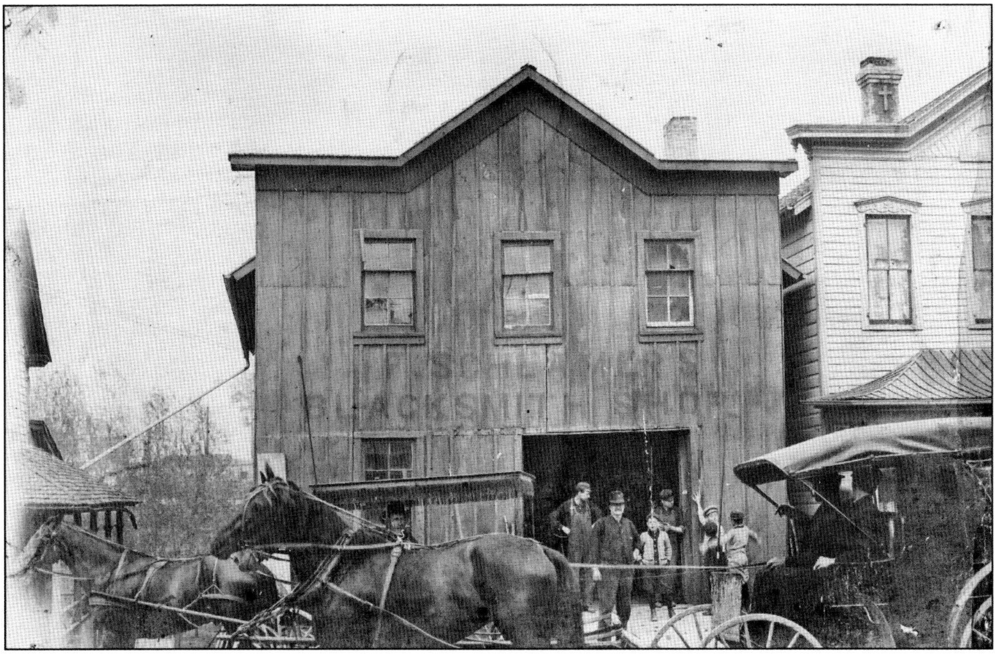

Fred Schloemer, former Washington County sheriff, purchased this blacksmith shop from Herman Wagner in 1883. The building was originally at the corner of Walnut and Main Streets. It was moved across the street in 1907. In 1913, Schloemer sold to his sons Fred and Oscar Schloemer. The business operated as a blacksmith, general metal-repair, and welding shop until the 1950s. The final owner was William Luedeke. The exterior photograph of the shop (above) was taken around 1913. The interior (below) was taken earlier, around 1905.

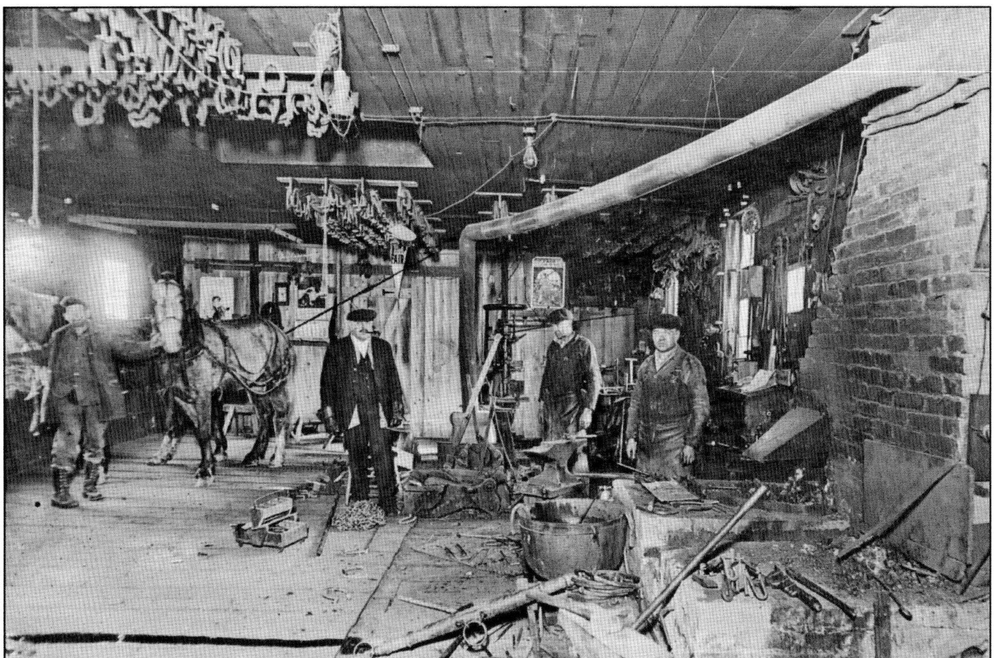

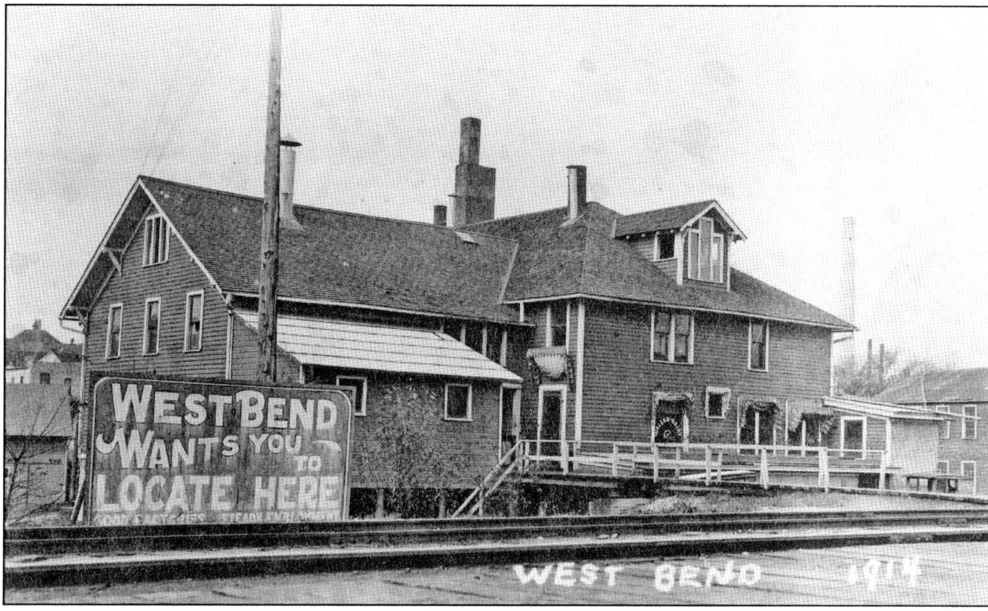

The Wallau Dairy Company and the sign inviting people to relocate to West Bend were located along the railroad tracks across from the depot. This photograph was taken around 1914 during West Bend's industrial boom. There was a shortage of skilled workers to fill the newly created jobs, and the sign was placed to encourage people to relocate.

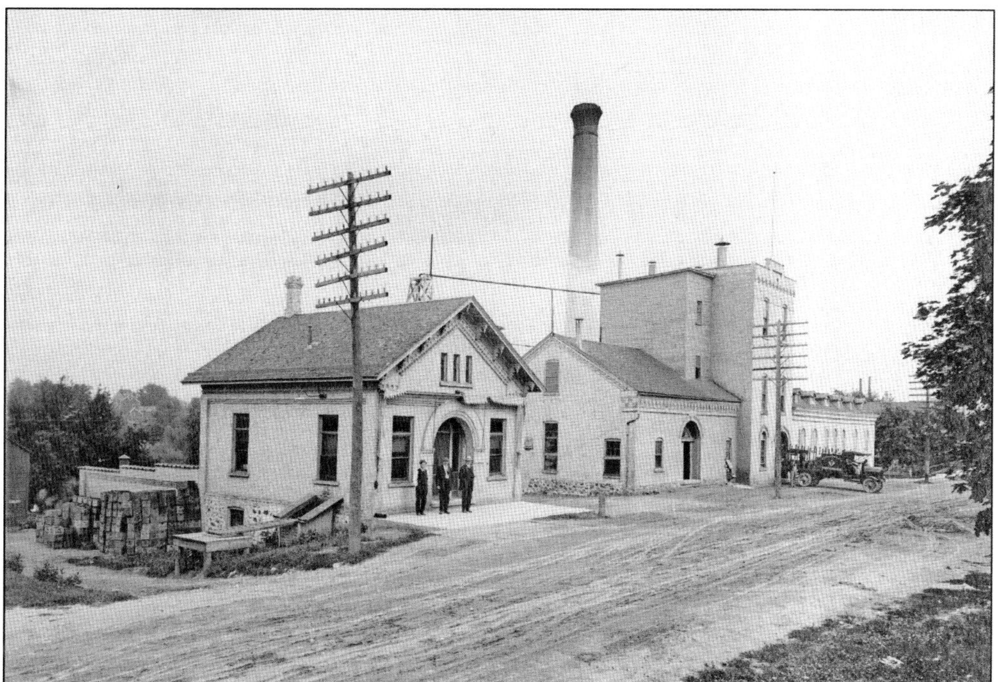

This view is of the West Bend Brewing Company around 1920. Originally the home of Eagle Brewery, the Eagle and West Bend Breweries operated across the street from each other until they merged in 1882. The former Eagle Brewery became the new company's home. In the 1920s, after the arrival of Prohibition, the company changed its name to West Bend Lithia Company.

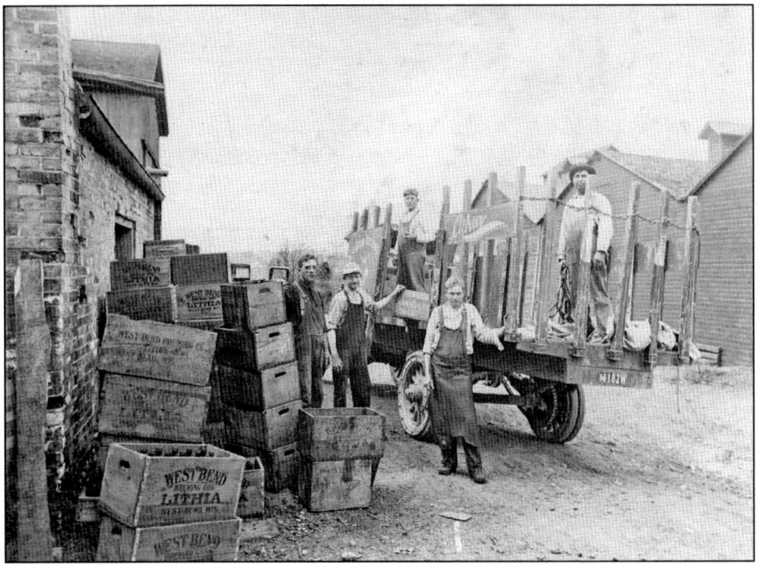

Taken at the rear of the West Bend Brewing Company around 1912, this photograph features brewery workers posing for the camera. The beer the company produced and advertised on the crates and trucks was called Lithia, named after the lithium salts found in the local water used in the brewing process.

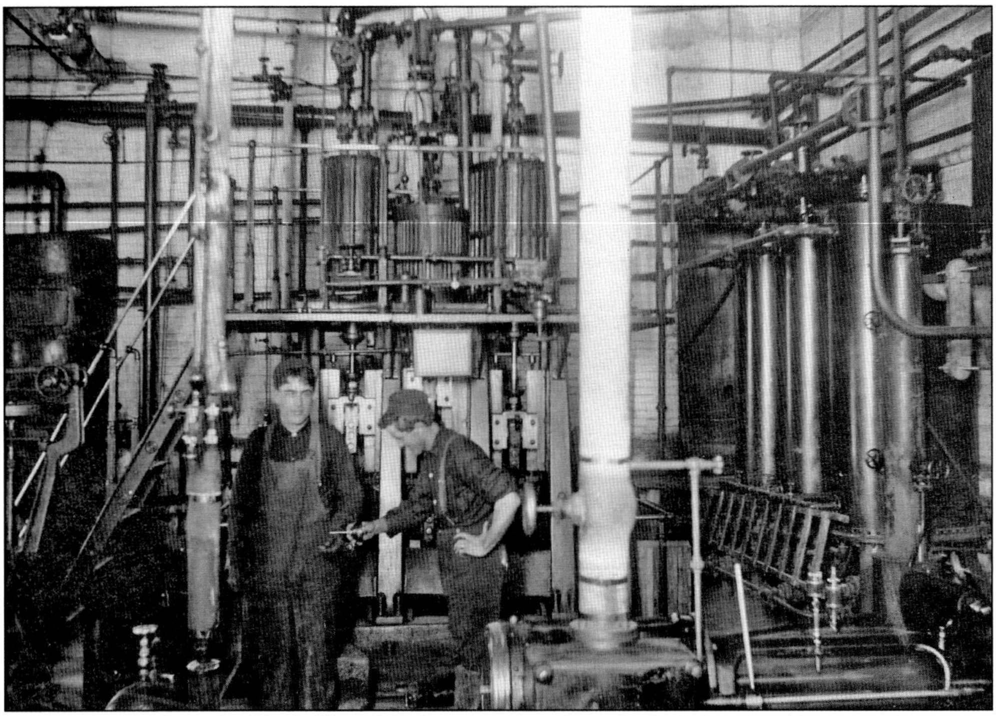

Here, Joseph Schneider (the left) and Seth Meyer stand inside the West Bend Brewing Company around 1915. In 1972, the company was purchased by the Walter Brewing Company of Eau Claire, Wisconsin, which continued to produce Lithia until 1986. In 2008, local businessman Gunther Woog, who owns the rights to the Lithia name, revived Lithia Beer with a slightly modified ingredient list.

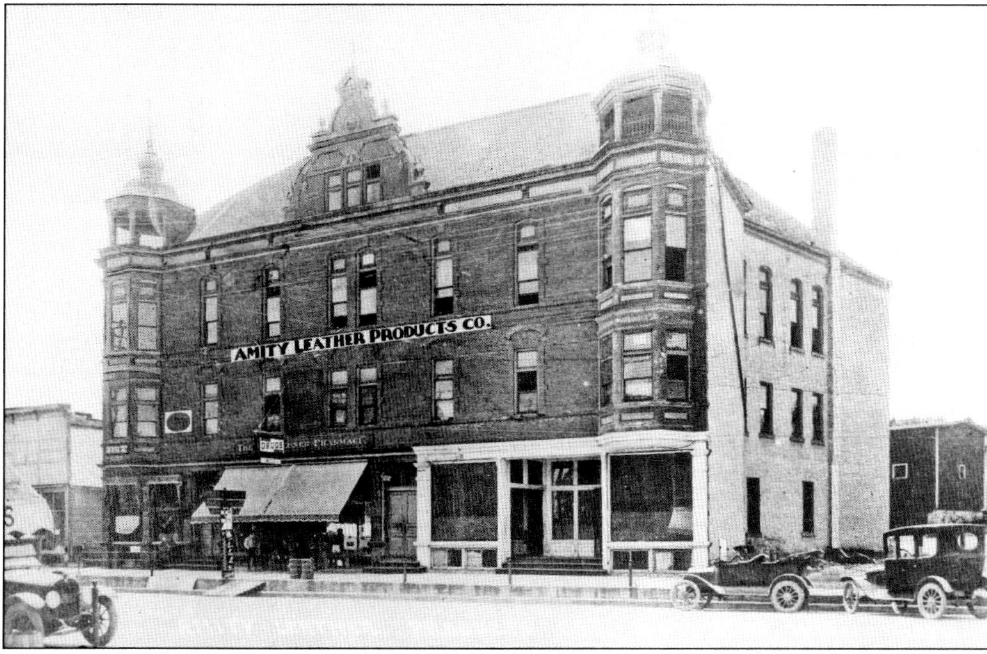

Constructed in 1893, the Hargartner Building was home to many businesses through the years. In 1918, when this photograph was taken, Amity Leather Products Company occupied the upper floor of the building. This was the second home for the company, which started in 1915. A new factory and office building on South Fourth Avenue, now Main Street, was built by the company in 1924 when it outgrew the Hargartner space.

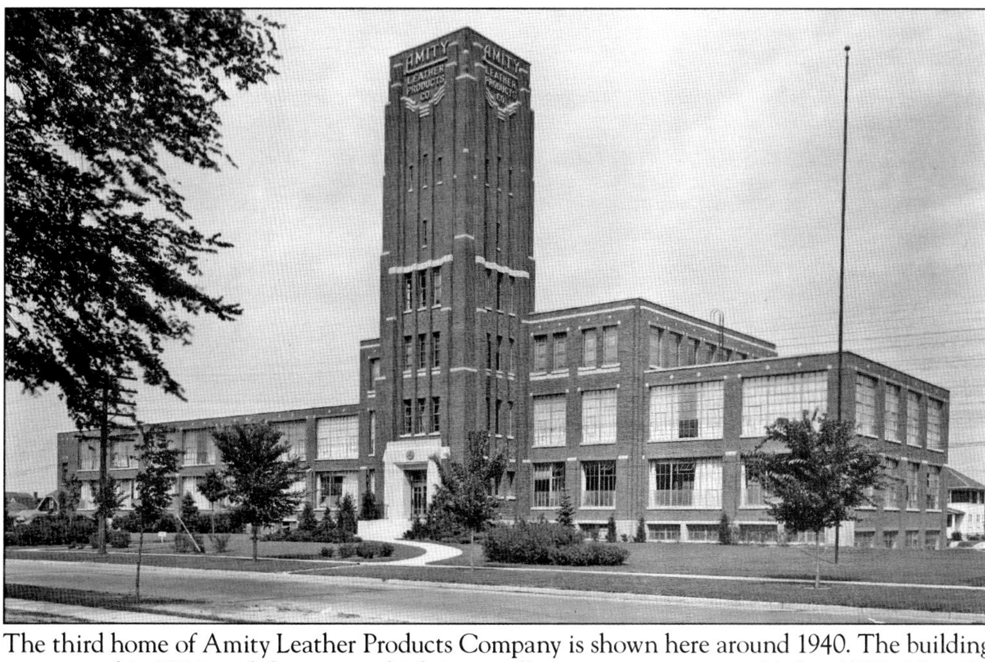

The third home of Amity Leather Products Company is shown here around 1940. The building was erected in 1924, and the tower, which is actually a water tower, was added in 1929. After the company moved offices and manufacturing out of West Bend in 1996, the structure was used for small businesses before being renovated into income-based apartments.

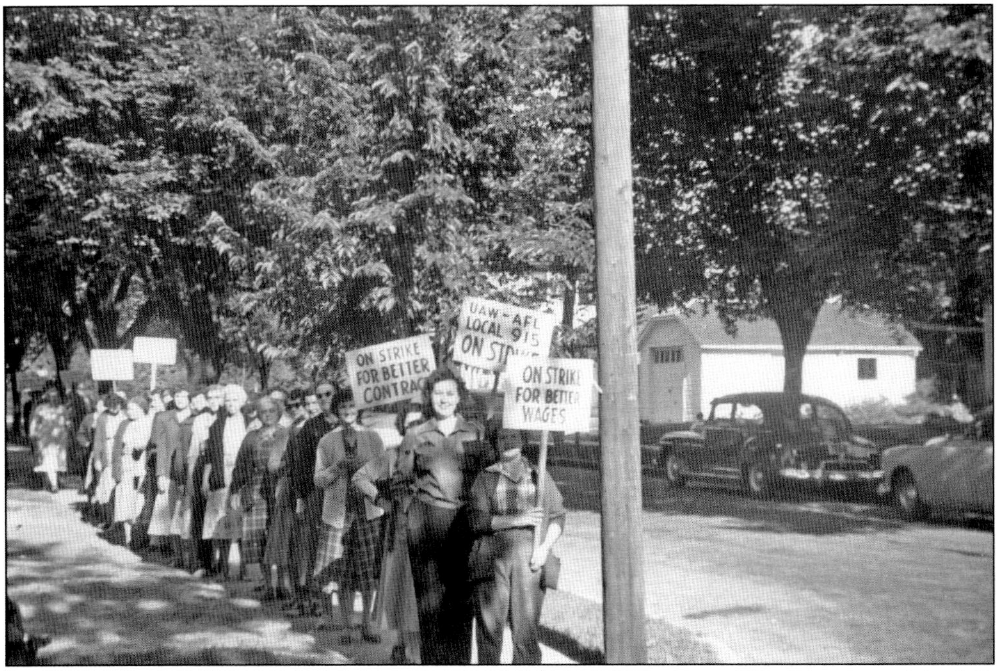

Amity Leather Products workers went on strike in July 1952 over wages. Here are some of the 300 striking workers picketing outside the company. Members of the UAF-AFL Local 915 wanted wages increased by 15¢ per day and 12¢ per piece for piecework. At the time of the strike, the company was the third-largest purse manufacturer in the country and made around 6,500 billfolds each day.

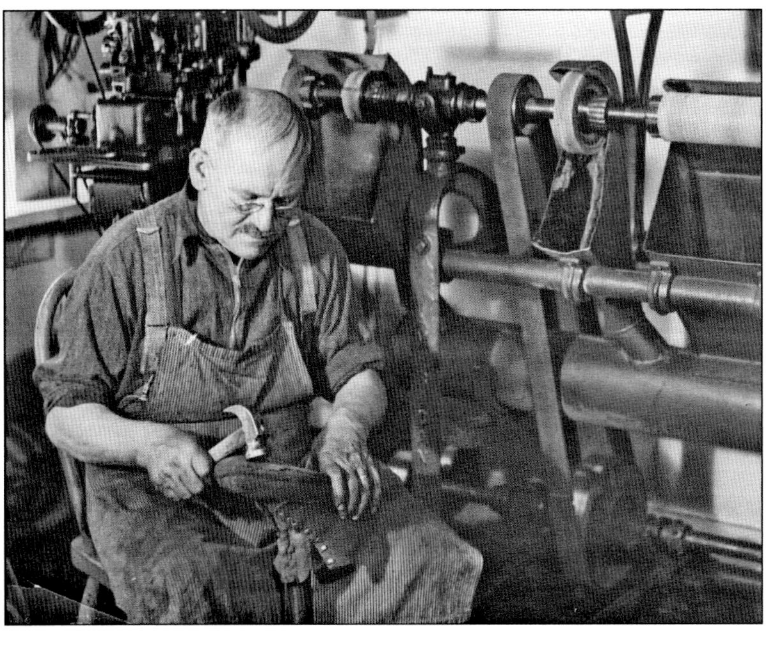

Here, Joseph Stangle practices his craft of shoe repair in his shop in West Bend. Born in Austria-Hungary in 1883, Joseph immigrated to the United States in 1906 and lived in several locations before making his way to West Bend. He spent 25 years there as a shoe repairman before his death in 1939.

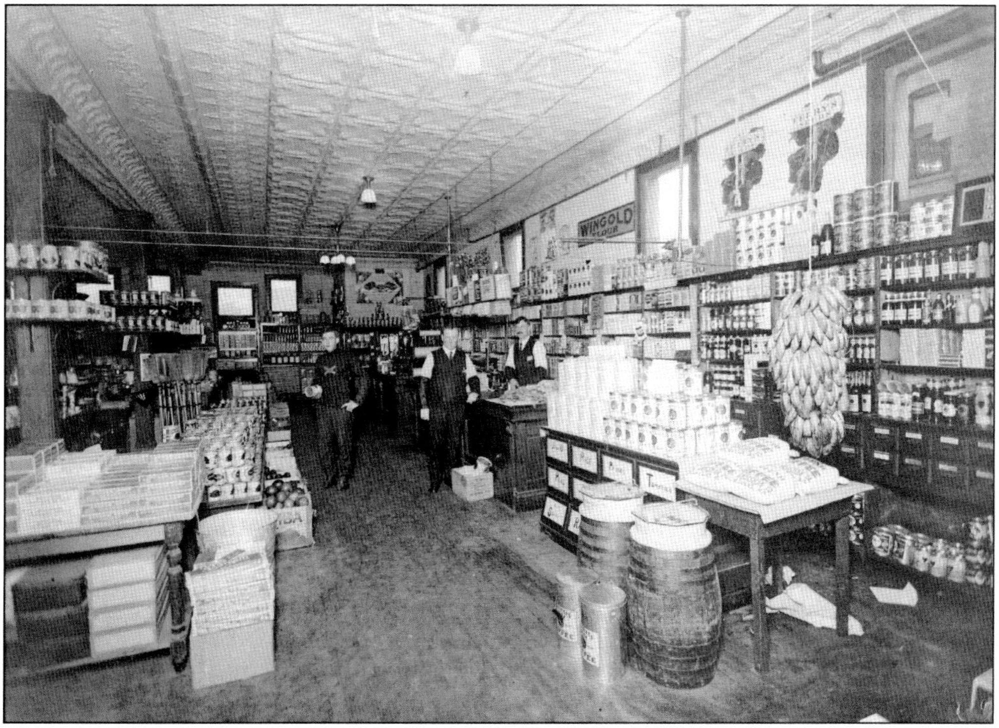

These two photographs show the interior of the Nagel-Bloedorn Store on Main Street in downtown West Bend. The grocery part of the store was operated by Albert Bloedorn, seen at the center of the image above. The man on the right is Matt Goeden, and the other man is unidentified. The photograph below shows the clothing area of the department store, which was operated by Henry Nagel. Pictured are, from left to right, Manny Kirsch, Albert Bloedorn, Lucille Bloedorn, Lulu Eberhhardt, and Matt Goeden. Both images were taken around 1920 before the building was purchased by the B.C. Ziegler Company.

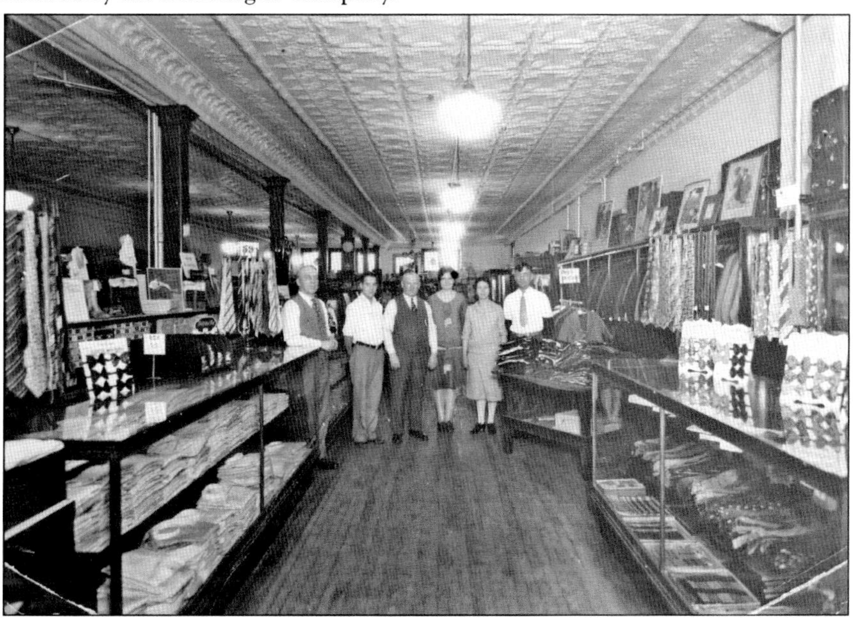

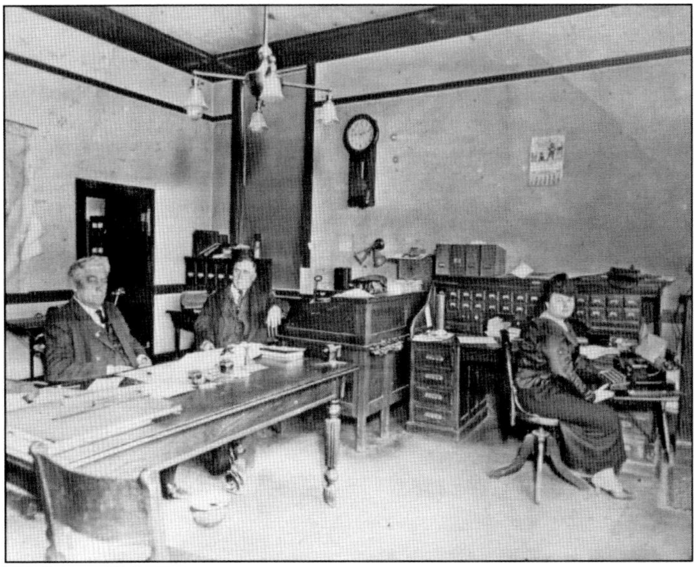

This photograph shows the office of the West Bend Limited Mutual Insurance Company around 1915. Beginning with fire and lightning insurance, the company slowly expanded to include a full line of policies. Pictured are, from left to right, founder and Washington County superintendent of schools C.F. Leins, John Homring, and Josephine Niebler. The company is still in existence and has seen significant expansion in recent years.

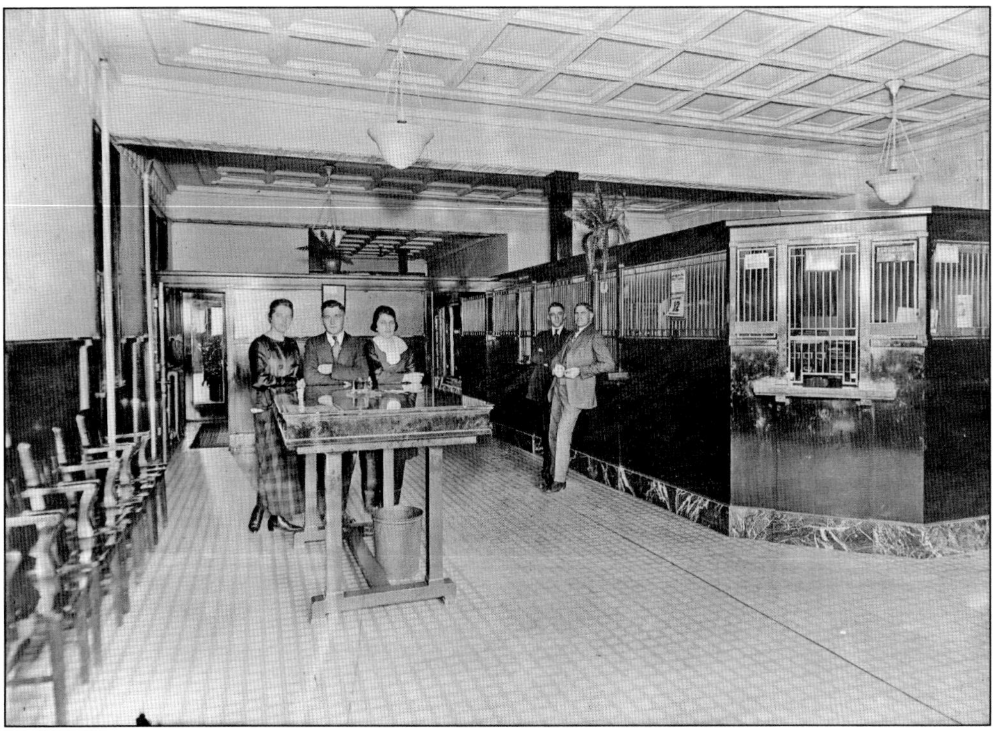

This interior view of the First National Bank of West Bend was taken around 1919. The Bank was founded in 1917 by local businessman Bernard C. Ziegler and was located on Main Street. It was originally intended to be a community bank. There have been several mergers over the years, and it is now part of BMO Harris Bank.

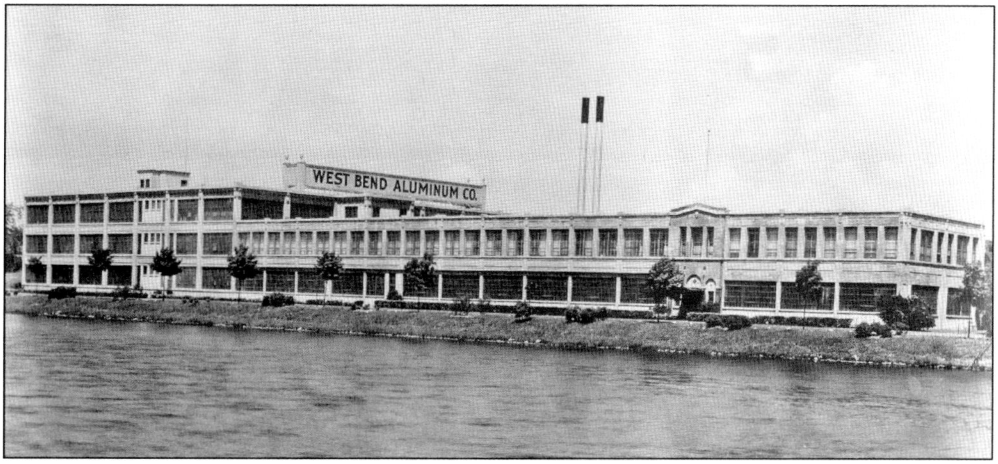

The West Bend Aluminum Company was founded in 1911 in an effort to bring more jobs to the area. Bernard C. Ziegler was one of the instrumental men who brought the industry to West Bend. Until 2002, when the company was dissolved, it was one of the largest employers in the area with a multinational presence. This photograph, taken in 1927, shows newly completed office and factory additions.

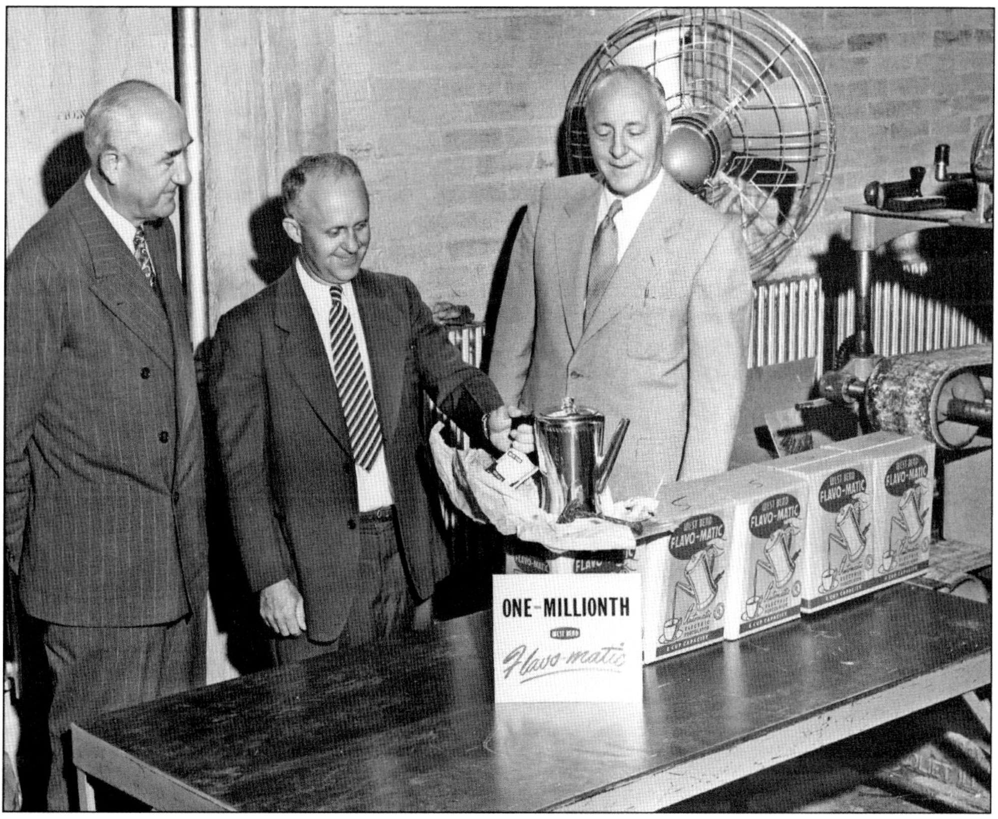

Here, A.C. Kieckhafer, president of the West Bend Aluminum Company, poses with the millionth Flavo-Matic coffee pot manufactured at the West Bend factory. Also present are A.R. Finch, director of manufacturing, and E.A. Kraemer, vice president in charge of sales. The Flavo-Matic was one of the company's most successful products.

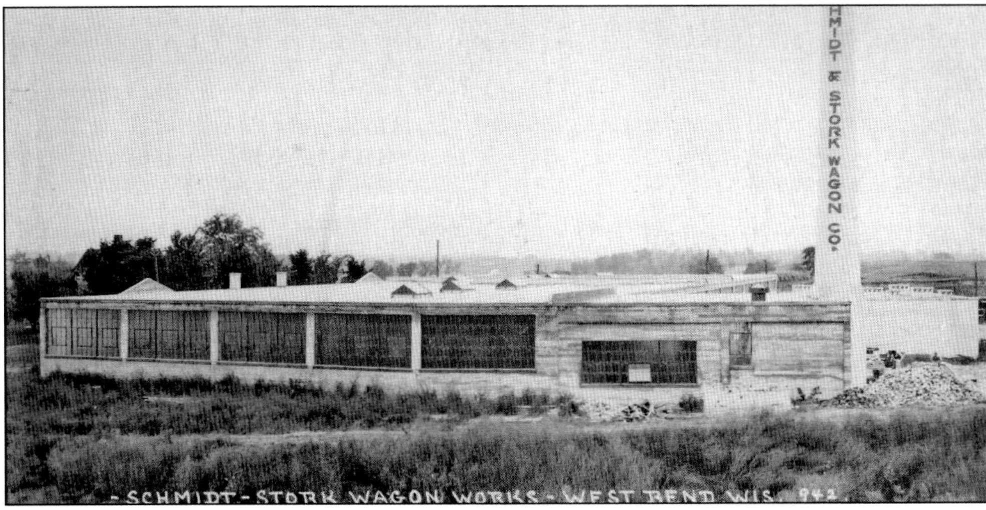

In 1892, the Schmidt and Stork Wagon Company moved to West Bend from nearby Young America. The company made wagons, carriages, and sleighs. As cars replaced horse-drawn vehicles, the company diversified to include display cases, coffins, tables, truck bodies, and fruit presses. The factory in this photograph was built in 1921.

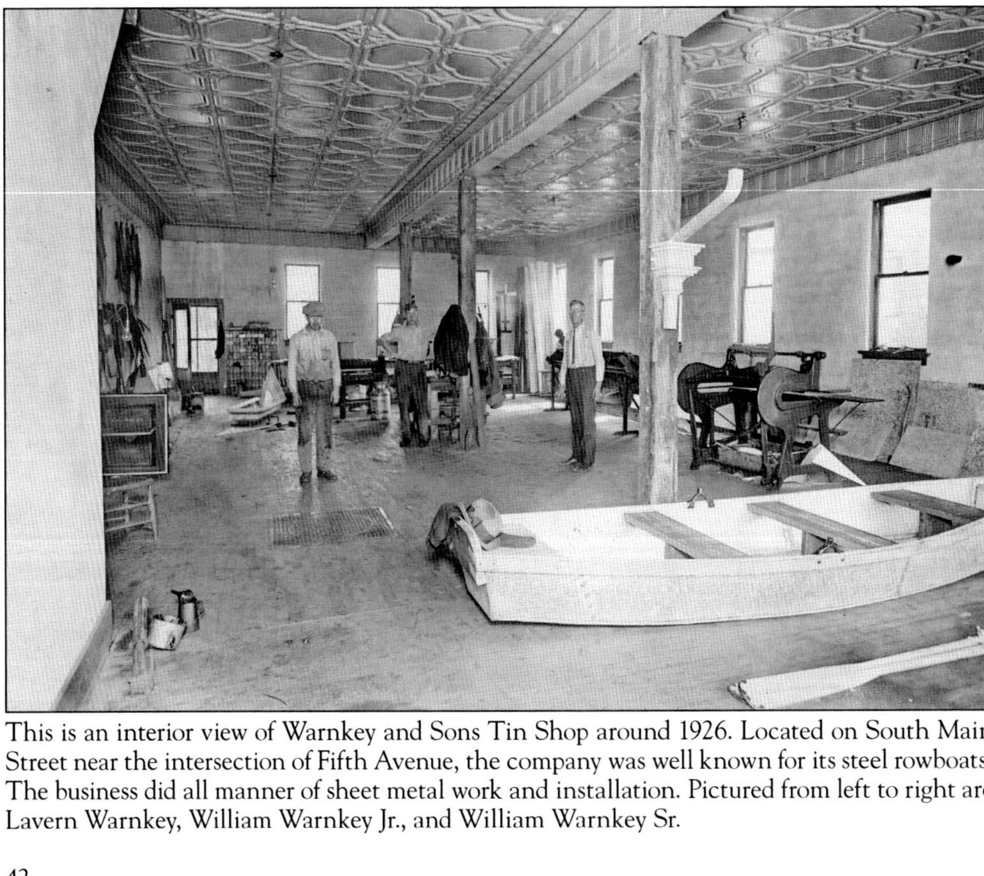

This is an interior view of Warnkey and Sons Tin Shop around 1926. Located on South Main Street near the intersection of Fifth Avenue, the company was well known for its steel rowboats. The business did all manner of sheet metal work and installation. Pictured from left to right are Lavern Warnkey, William Warnkey Jr., and William Warnkey Sr.

The White House Milk Company was located along what is today Veteran's Avenue, just south of the passenger train depot. The company hit peak production in the late 1920s, with a record of processing 1.25 million pounds of milk in one day. The plant was demolished in 1976. These are the large furnaces in the plant around 1930.

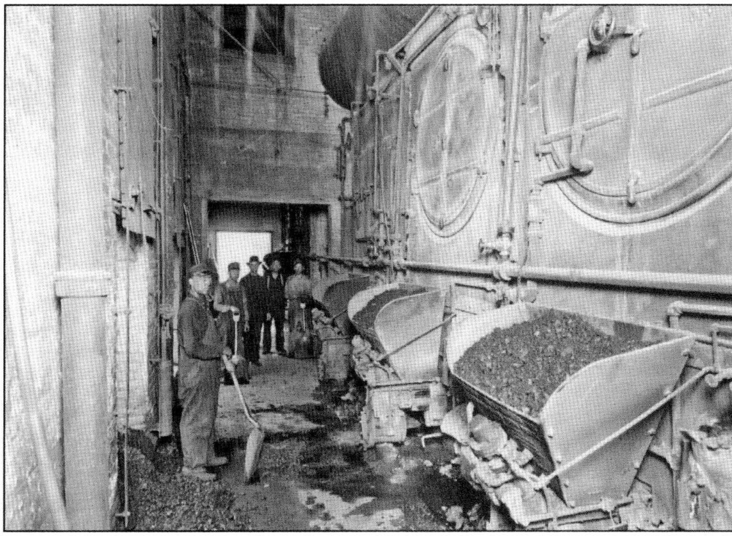

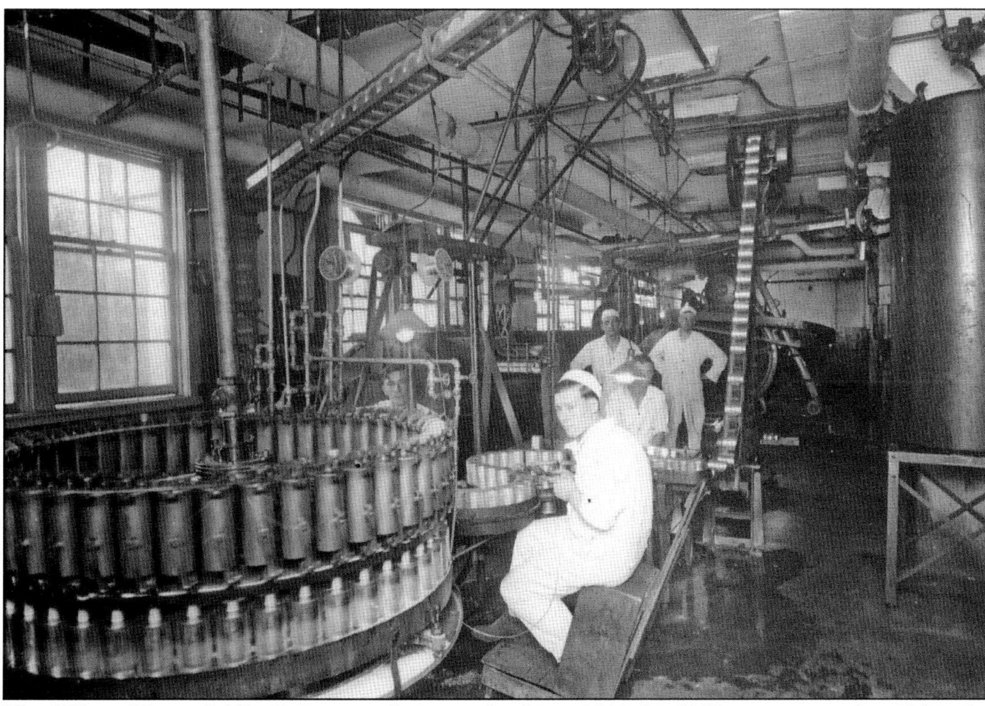

The White House Milk Company plant was built in 1918. In 1922, it was purchased by the Great Atlantic and Pacific Tea Company. The company condensed and canned milk from local farmers. Seen here are the machines that fill the cans and seal them. This photograph was taken around 1930.

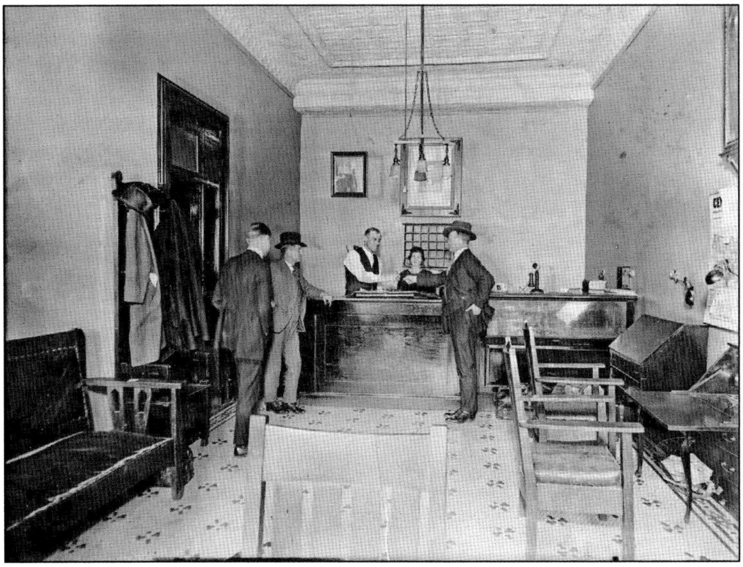

The first Washington House Hotel was a wooden structure built by Balthasar Goetter in 1852. It was reconstructed in 1864 after a devastating fire. The new building was the first brick structure in West Bend. This photograph was taken in the hotel lobby around 1925. The Washington House still stands on Main Street today as a restaurant and bar.

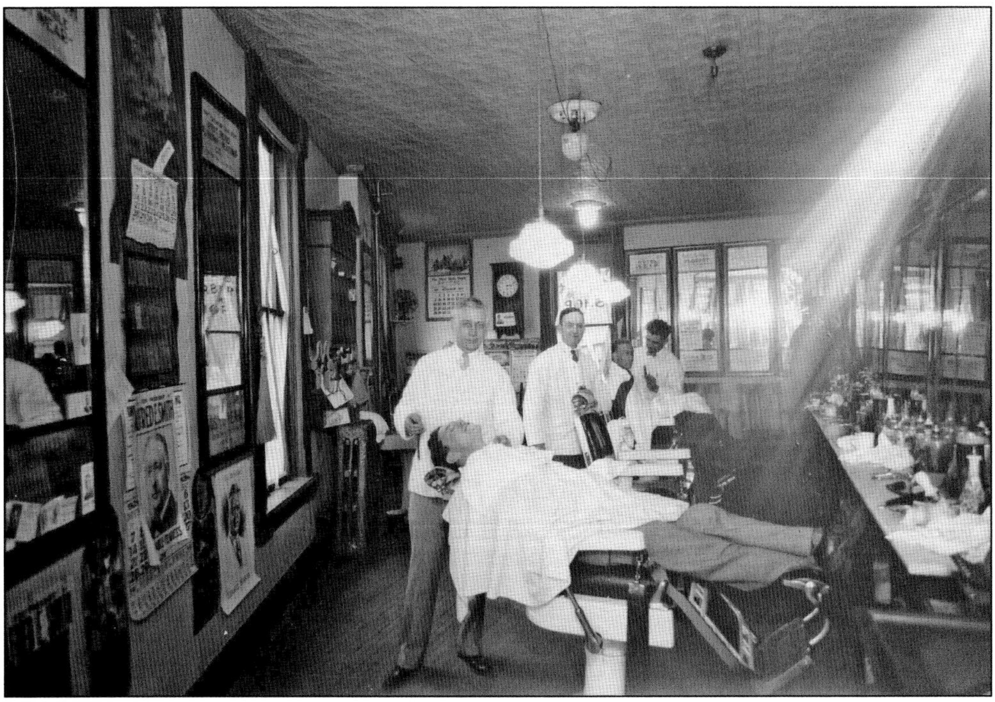

Knipple Brothers Barber Shop was located on the first floor of the O'Meara Law Office on Main and Elm Streets, now the Old Settlers' Park. Joe and Bill Knipple purchased the business in 1905. This interior view of the shop was taken in October 1928. The nearest barber is Joe Knipple, the center barber is Bill Knipple, and the farthest barber is thought to be Frank Valliere.

John Ernst, a deliveryman for the Ott Coal Company, worked for the company for 35 years. The company began in 1918 and supplied heating coal and wood to the West Bend area. In 1923, the company expanded its capacity to 700 tons of coal. In 1929, it expanded to include heating oil. This photograph was taken around the time of the oil expansion in 1929.

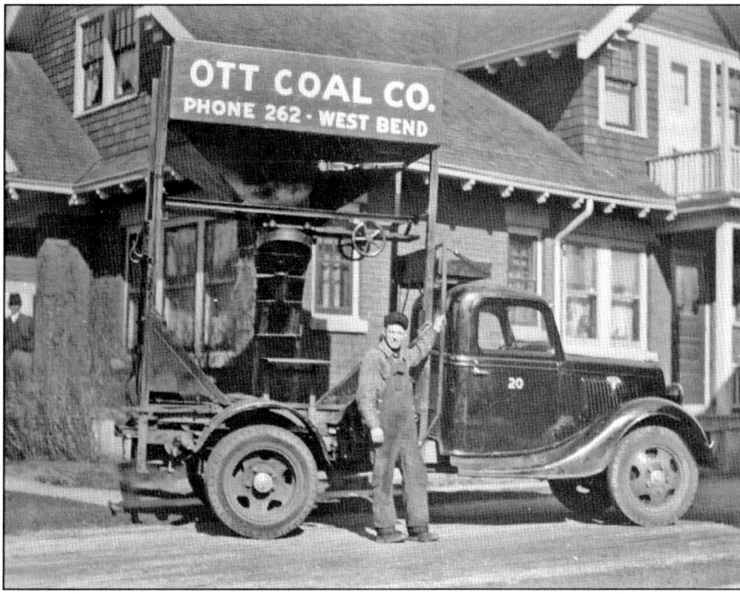

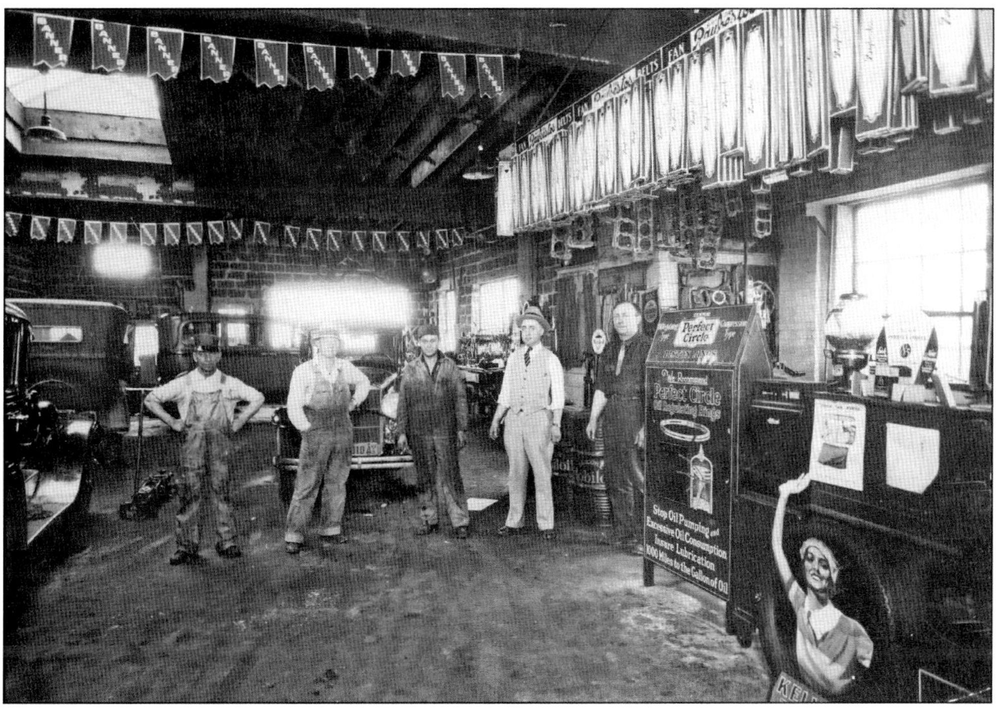

This photograph shows the interior of Klinka's Garage around 1930. Located on Main Street, it was also the local Oldsmobile dealer for many years. Pictured are, from left to right, Art Fike, Reuel Gerach, Carl Gerhardt, an unidentified salesman, and owner John Klinka. In 1969, the business was sold to Elmer Schwartzburg and became Schwartzburg Oldsmobile.

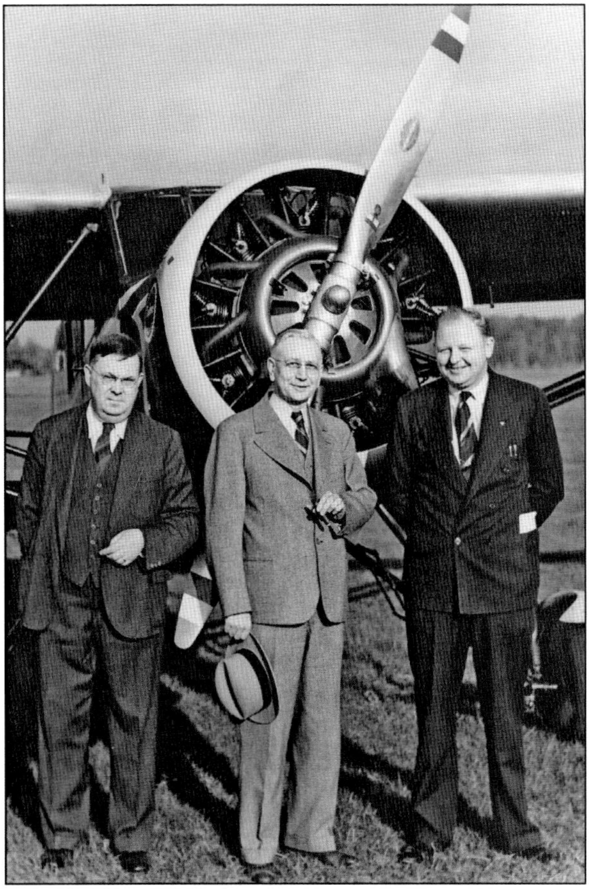

In 1929, the US Department of Commerce came to West Bend to establish an airport. The airport would be for government use unless the city decided to purchase the land. In that case, the government would set up the airport, but it would be available for use by the public. On May 25, 1930, the public West Bend Municipal Airport was dedicated. Pictured from left to right are Joseph O'Meara, Joseph Knipple, and unidentified.

On May 25, 1930, the West Bend Municipal Airport was dedicated. Located west of the city on Highway 33, land for the airport was purchased in 1929 by B.C. Ziegler, Dr. William Urkart, and Frank Groom. The 96 acres were then leased back to the federal government, which maintained the airport. Pictured here at the dedication are several of the planes that attended the ceremony.

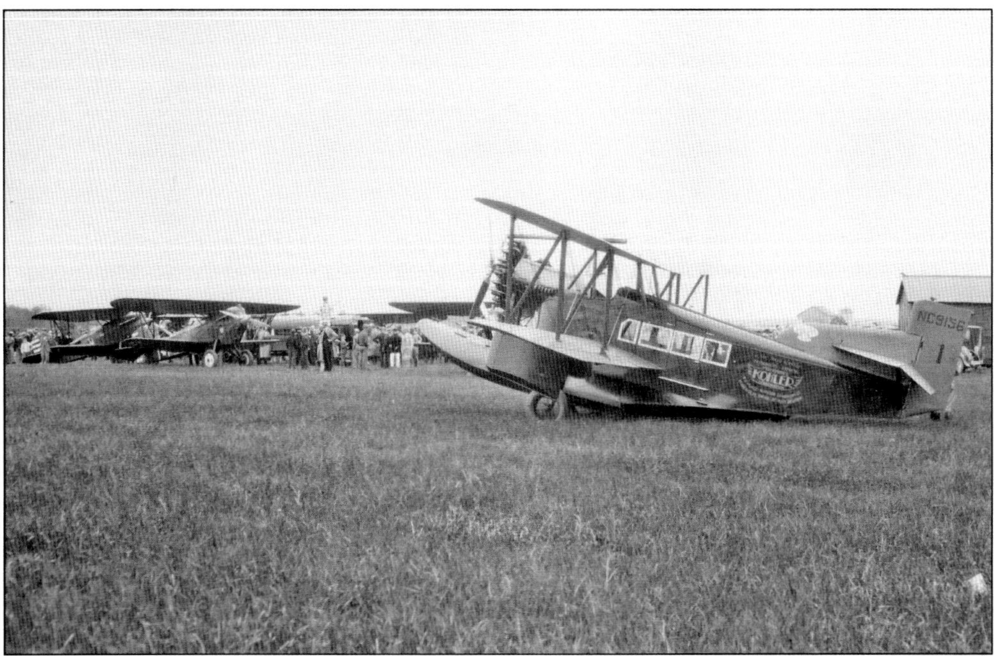

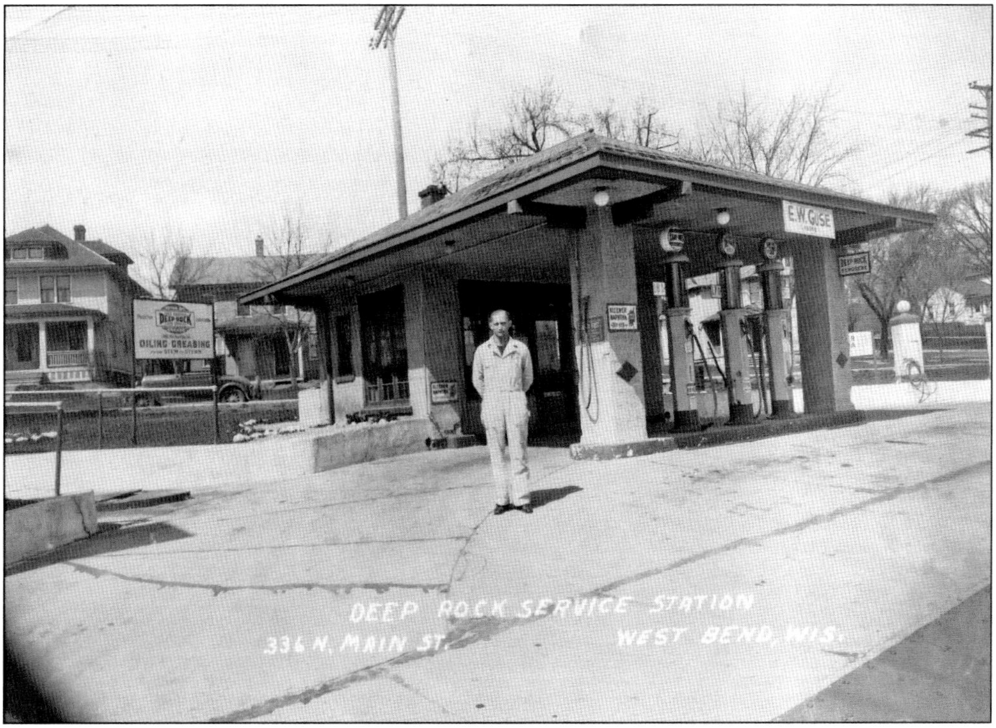

The Deep Rock Service Station was located at the corner of Seventh Avenue and Main Street and was built in 1921. It was owned by the United Consumers Corporation but was managed by several West Bend natives over the years. Here, Ernst Guse, who took over management in 1935, stands outside the station. This photograph was taken shortly after he took over the lease.

West Bend youths lounge by the Works Progress Administration (WPA) sign around 1935. The only one identified is Earl Baer (left). The WPA was a federal government program intended to help put people back to work during the Great Depression doing skilled and unskilled labor for useful projects, such as improving parks and building roads.

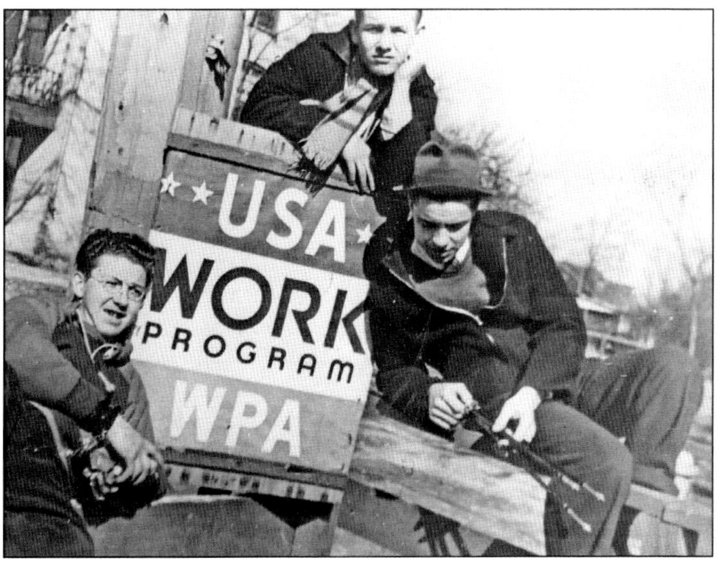

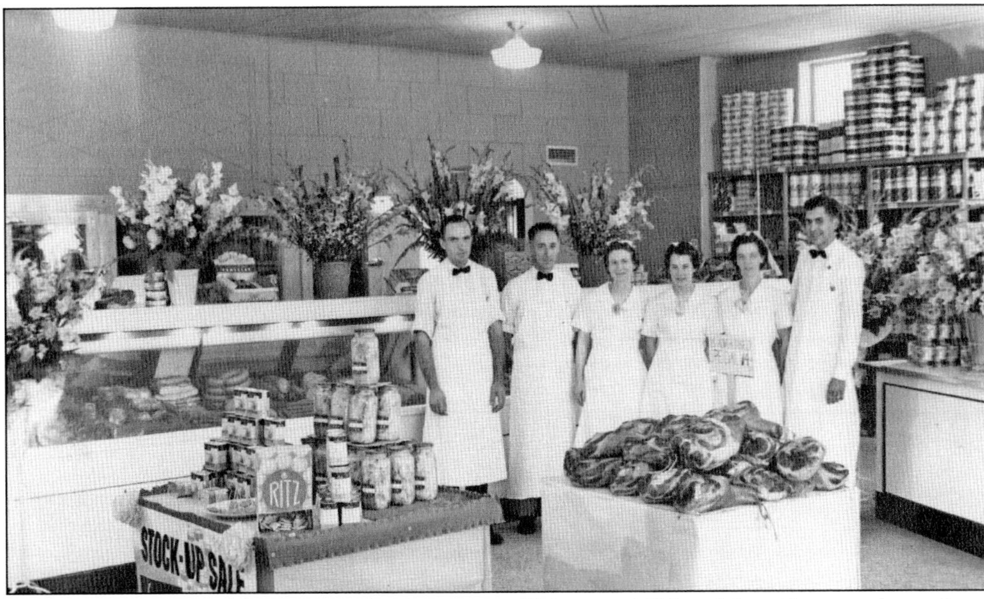

The grand opening of the new Naab's Grocery and Meats in 1939 on Main Street is shown here. The store was started in 1932 by Arthur and his wife. Employees shown from left to right are Herb La Buwie, Arthur Naab, Alma Naab, Helen Blome, Ruth Gritzmacher, and Carl Gritzmacher.

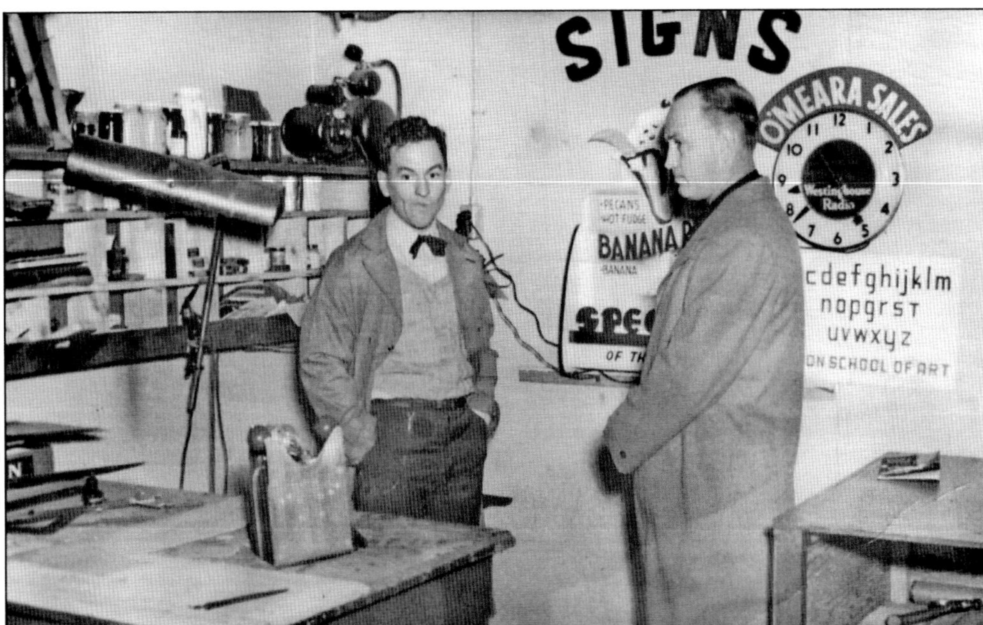

This photograph is of the interior of the Weiss Sign Shop. Owner Fredrick Weiss is on the left. Weiss went to the Layton School of Art in Milwaukee before returning to his hometown of West Bend and opening his shop on Poplar Street. Sign painting was a part-time job for Weiss, who also was on staff at the *West Bend Pilot* newspaper.

The WBKV-AM radio station was originally located near the intersection of Decorah Road and Sand Drive. WBKV began broadcasting in 1950, its call letters standing for West Bend Kettle Moraine Valley. The total cost to build and equip the station in 1950 was around $35,000. The station moved to new, larger quarters in 1992.

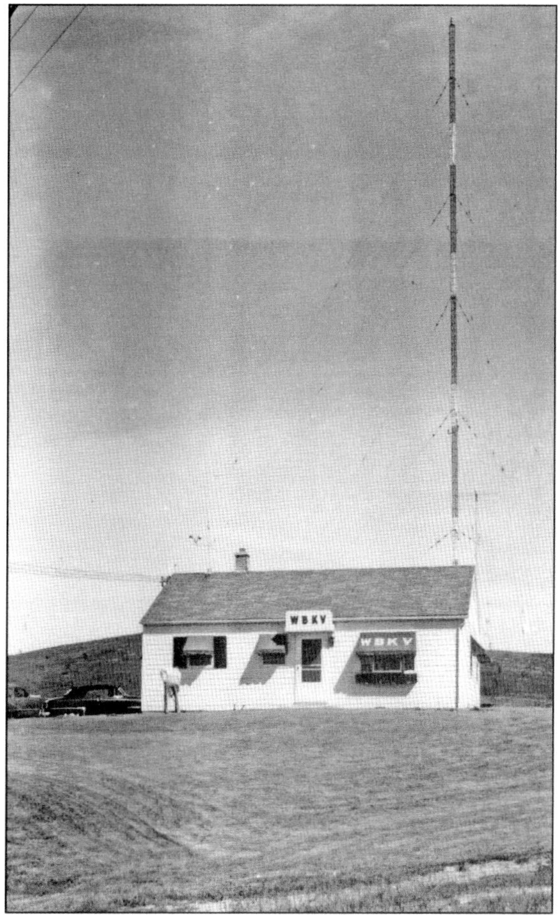

The Beacon Restaurant was located in the Hargartner Building on Main Street. During World War II, it was owned by the Poull family and served as the West Bend USO headquarters. After the war, the restaurant was owned by Joseph Zager. In the 1970s, Zager retired, and it became a Chinese restaurant. At one point, the Beacon was open 24 hours and advertised juicy steaks, chops, shrimp, and even oysters.

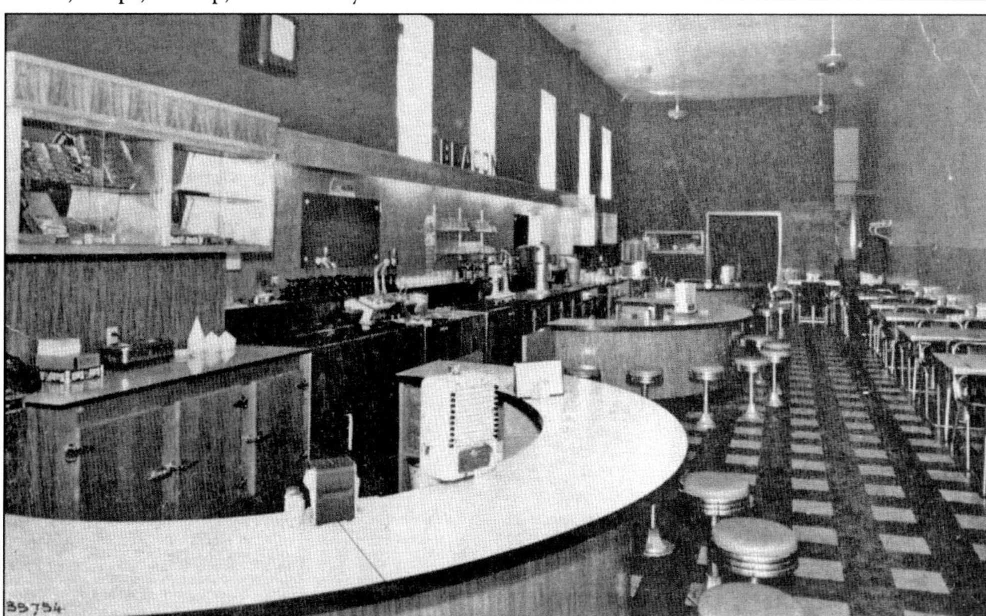

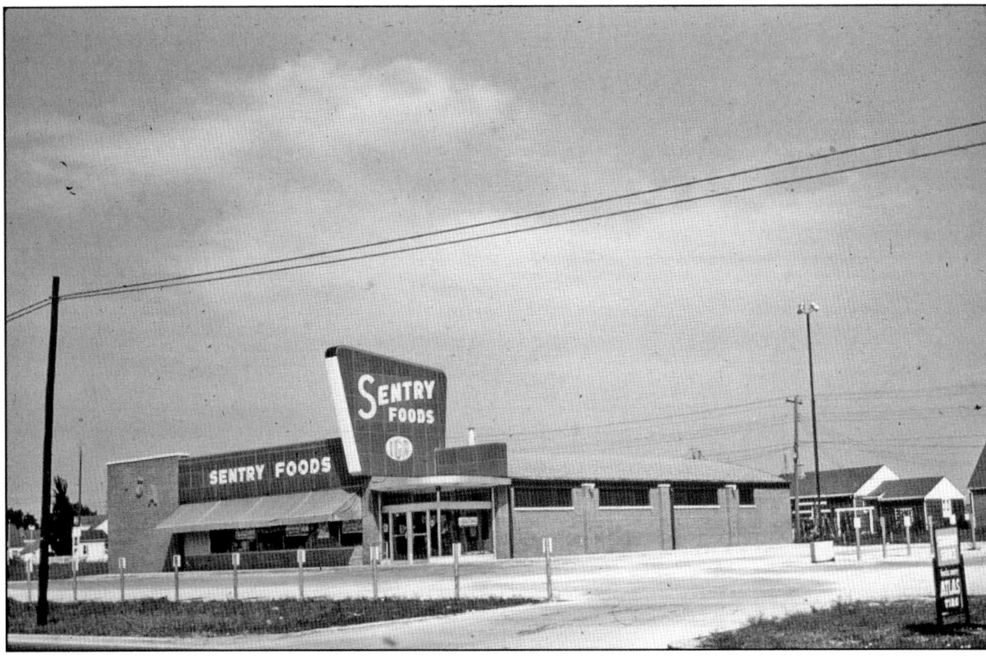

Sentry was one of the first chain grocery stores in West Bend. This photograph was taken around 1955. The grocery portion of the store was owned by John Plout, while the meat department was owned by Fred Lange. A second Sentry was opened at a different location in following years, but was not associated with Plout or Lange. Today, this structure houses the Sherwin-Williams Paint Store.

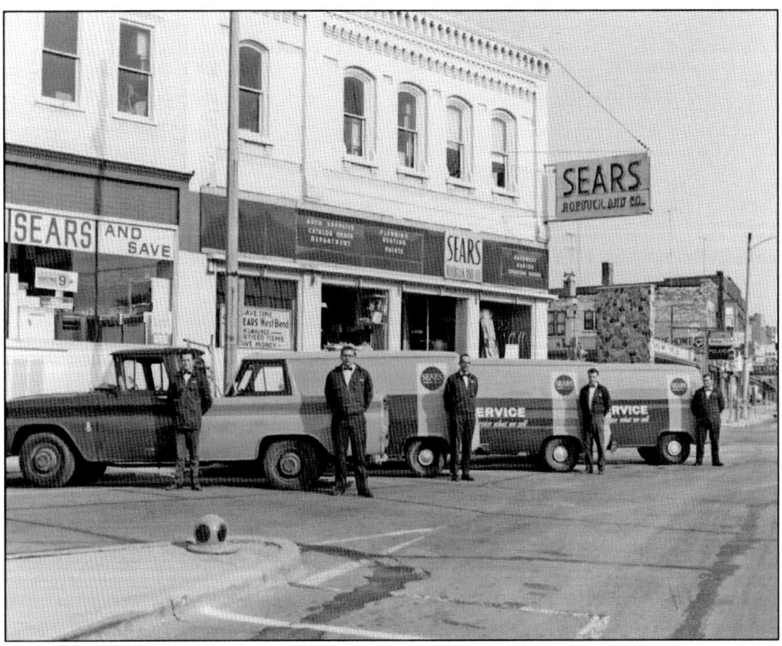

Sears servicemen stand with their trucks outside Sears, Roebuck & Company on Hickory Street and Fifth Avenue around 1960. The Sears store was in that location for over 50 years before closing in May 1993. When Sears halted catalog sales, the West Bend store was forced to close as the majority of their business came from these sales.

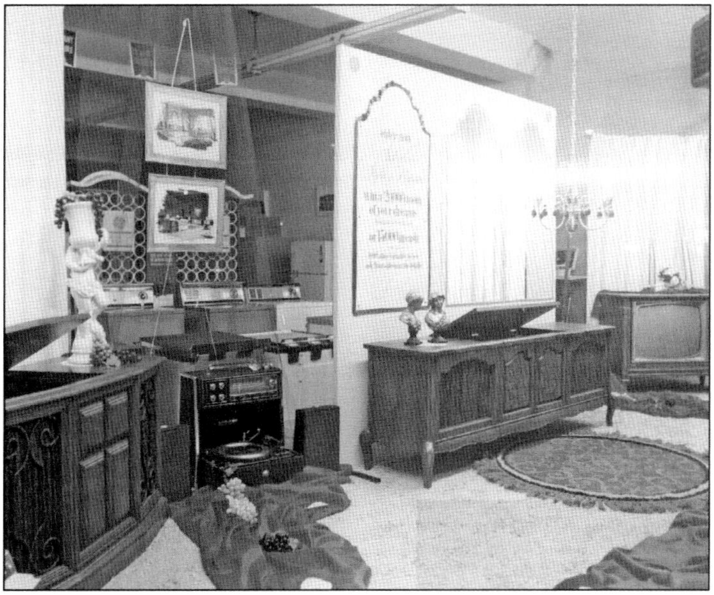

This is the center display window at Burkhardt's TV and Appliance store in downtown West Bend around 1965. Begun by William Burkhardt in the early 1930s, the business offered gas and electric home appliances and light fixtures, as well as residential and commercial electrician services. The business was later sold to Bob Steiner and became Steiner TV and Appliance. (Photograph by Bob Boltz.)

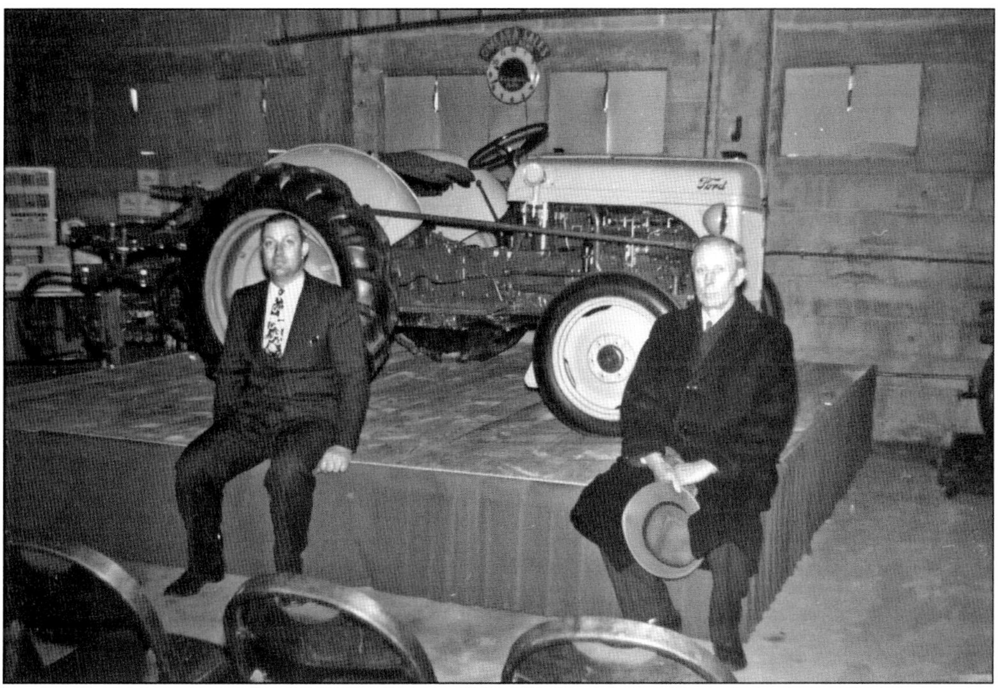

Ray Schmidt (left) and Ralph Hansen (right) are founders of the West Bend Implement Company. The business was primarily a Ford tractor dealer, but also sold farming equipment and did excavating work for sewers and building footings. Hansen acted as president for the company and Schmidt was the sales manager. This photograph was taken around 1965.

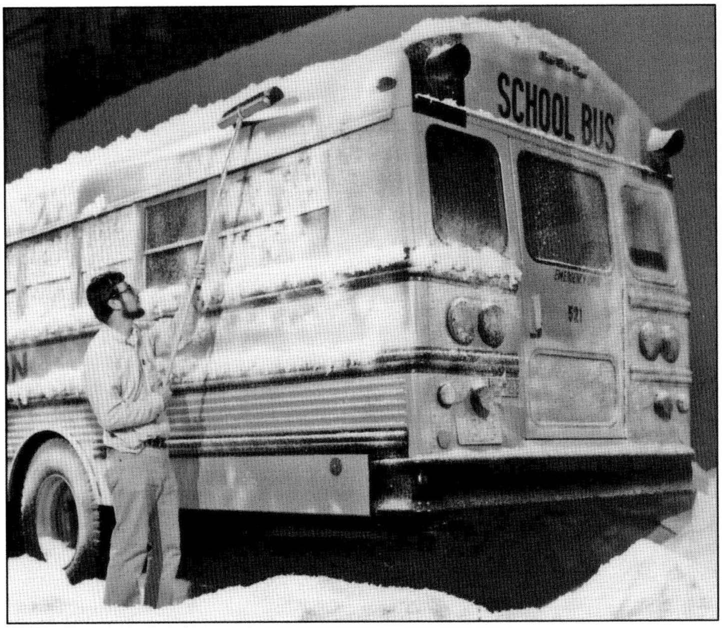

A Johnson Bus employee cleans snow from the windows around 1985. Established in 1942 by Aaron Johnson, Johnson Bus Company is headquartered on West Washington Street. Initially, the company provided school bus service, but it quickly expanded to charter and now also offers medical and specialized transportation services. The company is still owned by the Johnson family and continues to expand.

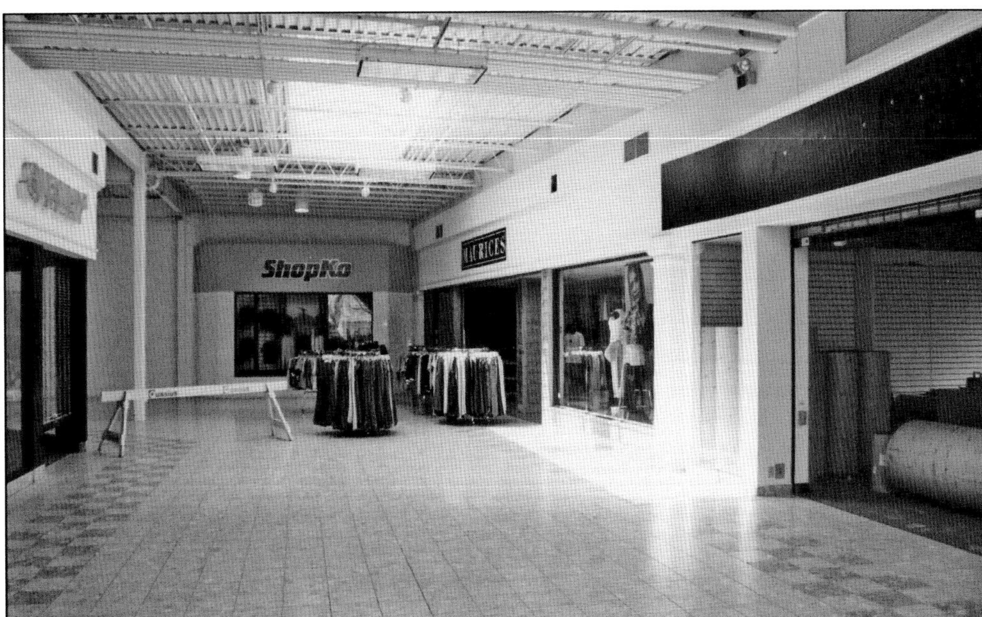

Paradise Mall opened in 1987 as an indoor facility. This photograph, taken in 1998 just before the mall closed, shows the south end of the mall. Paradise Mall was plagued with monetary problems from the start, and in 1999 the owners renovated it into a strip mall. Many of the businesses remained in the new facility. Today, the former site is called Paradise Pavilion.

Three

Churches and Parochial Schools

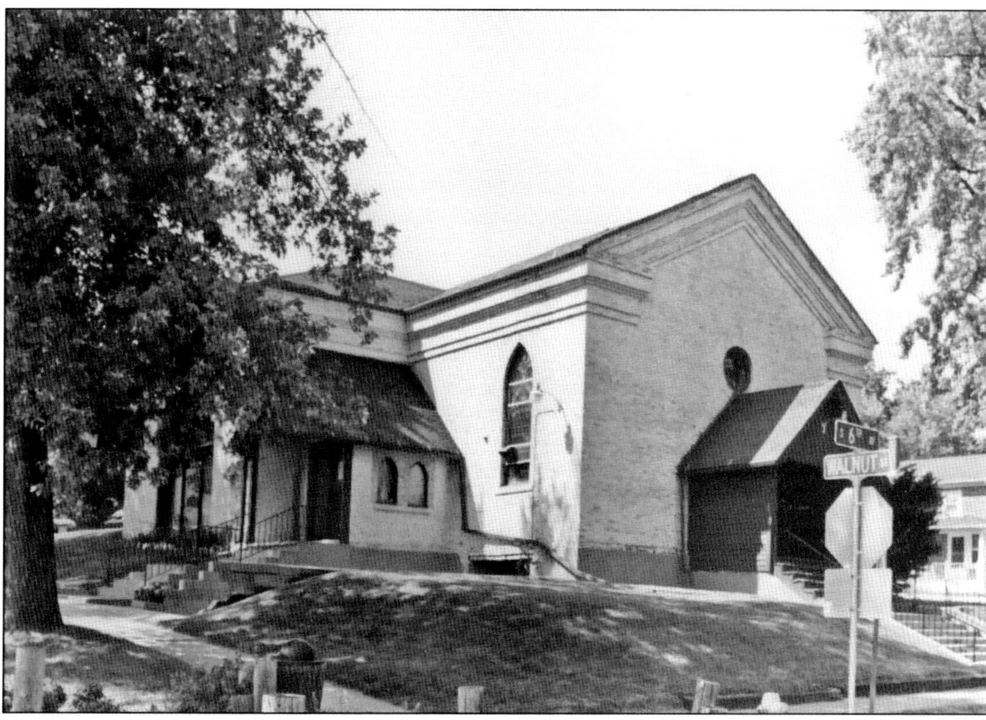

In 1850, one of the earliest recorded churches in West Bend was organized, the congregation of St. John's Evangelical Lutheran Church. They began services at a school before building a small log church. In 1864, the congregation built the church pictured here on the corner of Walnut Street and Sixth Avenue.

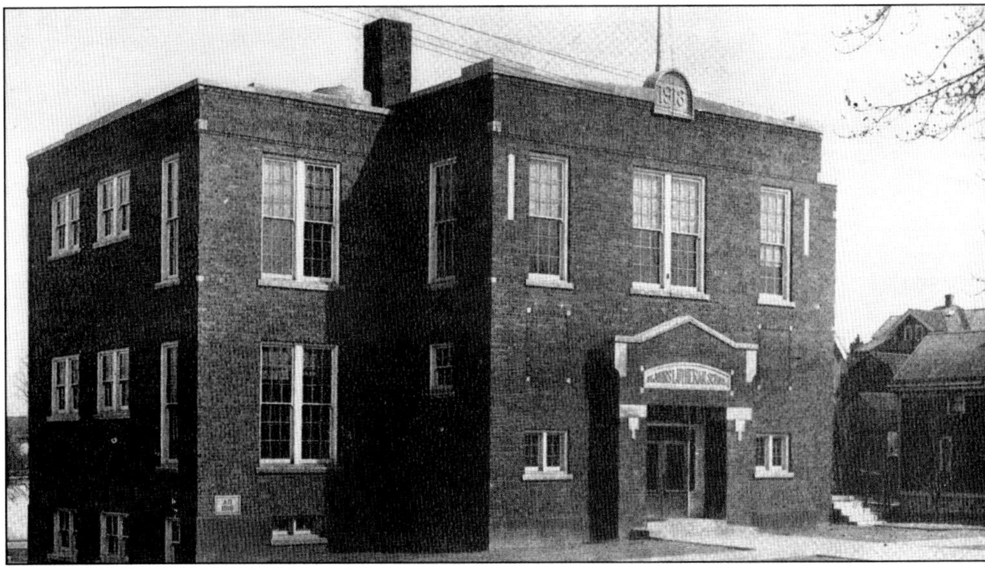

In 1891, St. John's Evangelical Lutheran Church began a school in a building near the church. Over the years, the school had several homes. This photograph shows the third St. John's Evangelical Lutheran School around 1919. It was located on the corner of Sixth Avenue and Walnut Street and was razed by Immanuel Evangelical and Reformed Church, which purchased the property for a parking lot.

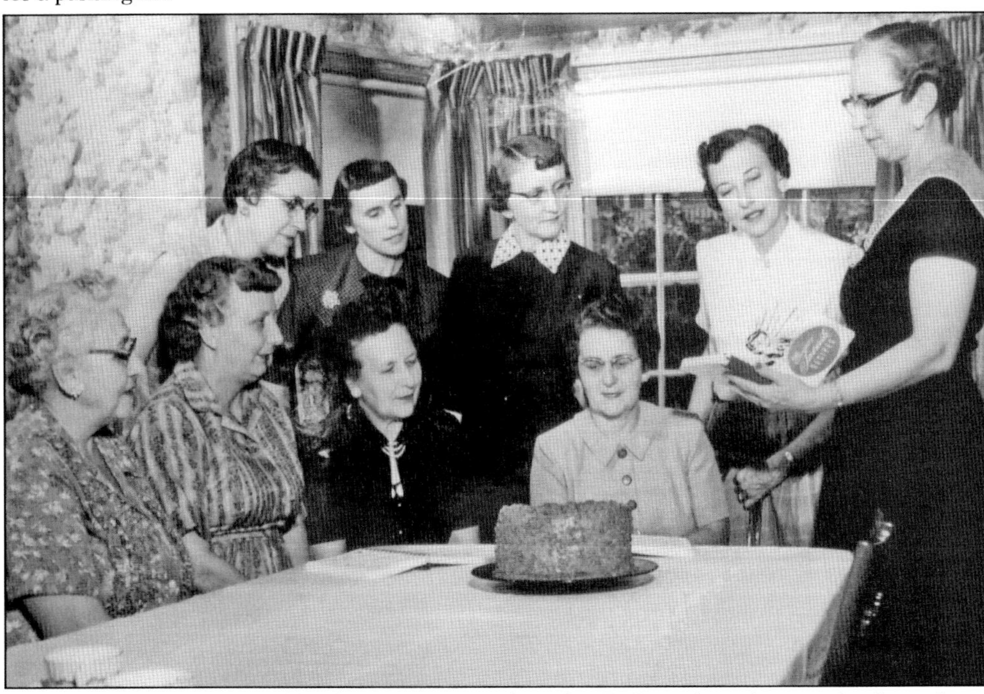

The original St. Johns Cookbook Committee gathered at Esther Klein's home. The first edition of *Our Favorite Recipes* was published in 1949 as a fundraiser. Since then, there have been 24 printings, which have raised over $140,300. Pictured from left to right are (seated) Frieda Lange, Edna Schloemer, Esther Daly, and Esther Klein; (standing) Emily Sauer, June Spielman, Rose Justman, Maybell Nimmer, and Cloris Sager.

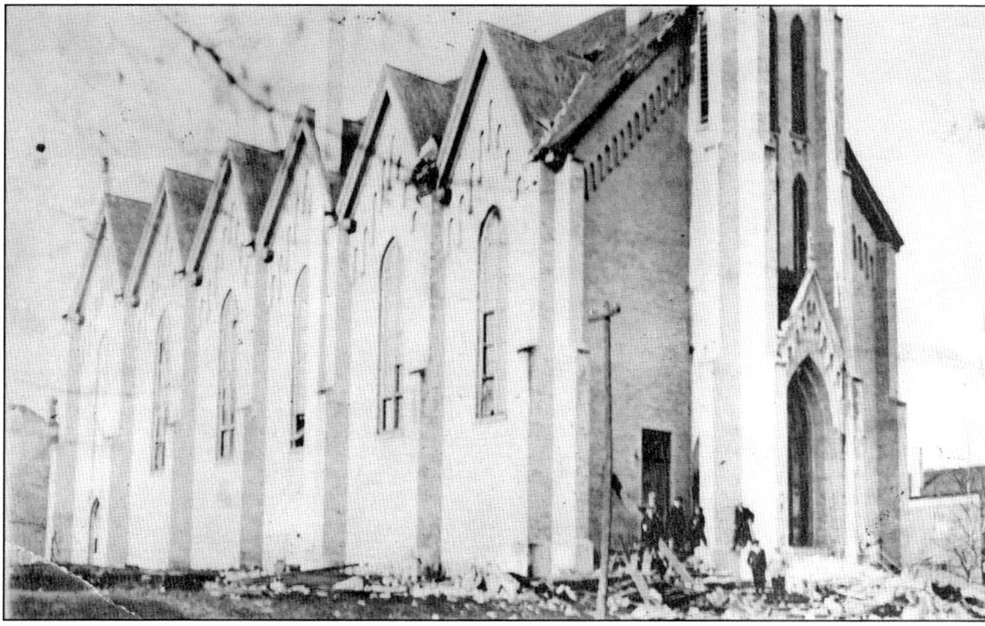

The second Holy Angels Catholic Church is shown here around 1913 and was located at Seventh Avenue and Elm Street. This was the second home of the congregation and was built in 1866. In 1928, the original wooden church was converted to be the first Holy Angels School. Trinity Lutheran Church now stands on the same location that this first church occupied. (Photograph by Herman Trakat.)

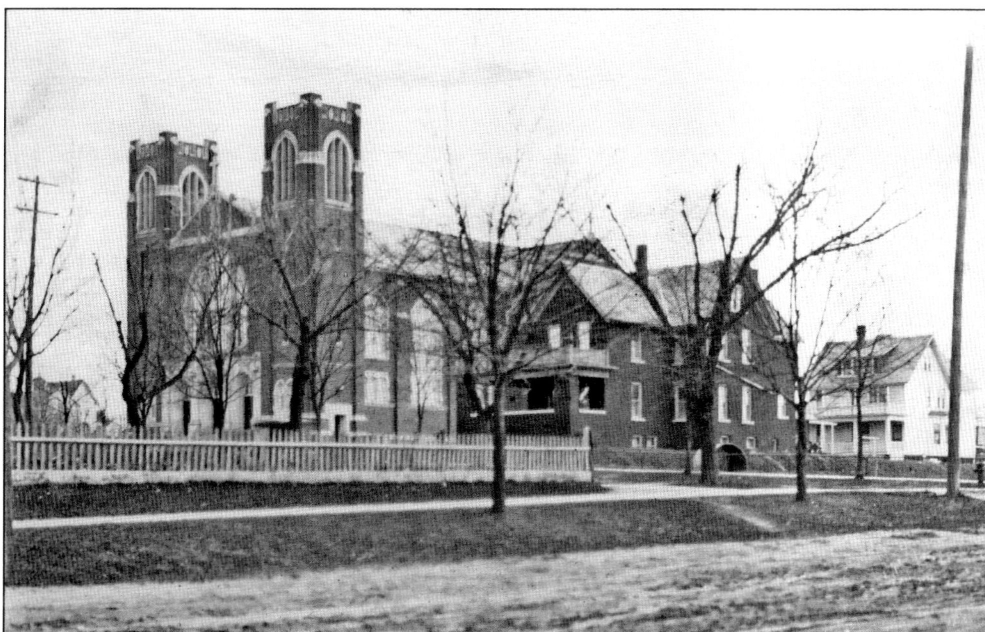

This structure, the current Holy Angels Catholic Church, is located at Eighth Avenue and Hickory Street and was built in 1914. The house next to the church was the parsonage, built in 1894, and has since been torn down. After moving to several locations, a new school was erected next to the church in 1963.

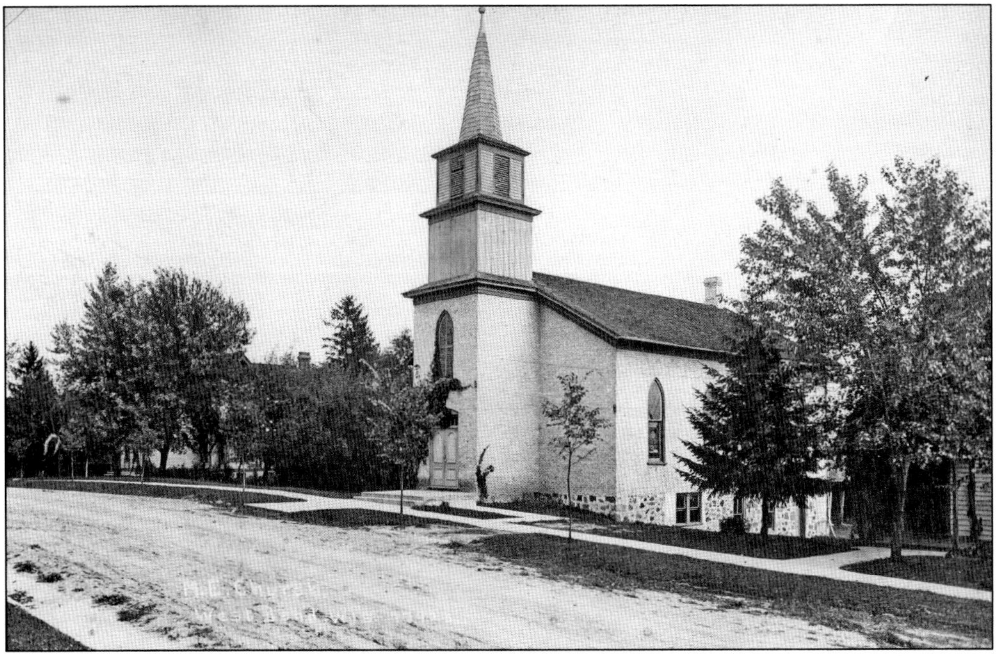

This photograph is of the first Fifth Avenue Methodist Church building, constructed in 1872. Founded in 1853, the early congregation was served by a circuit pastor. The current church was built on the same site in 1950. Over the years, the congregation absorbed several smaller groups who were disbanding.

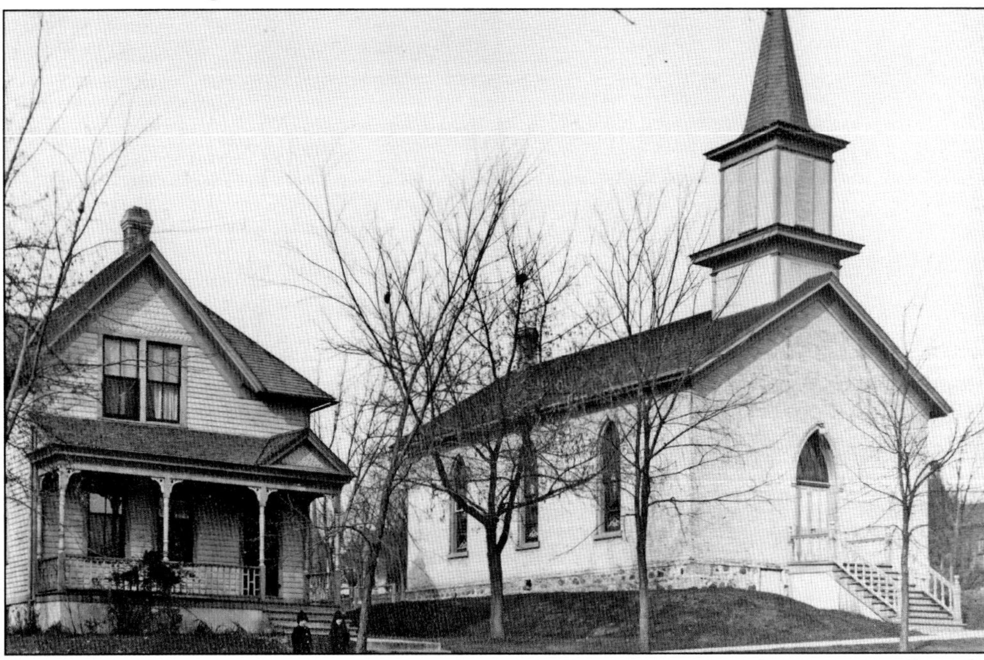

This is the German Methodist Episcopal Church and parsonage around 1916. Located on the corner of Seventh Avenue and Walnut Street, it was the second home of the congregation. Services were held in German as opposed to the English Methodist Church, which held English services; the two eventually merged. Today, the building is home to the Kettle Moraine Bible Church.

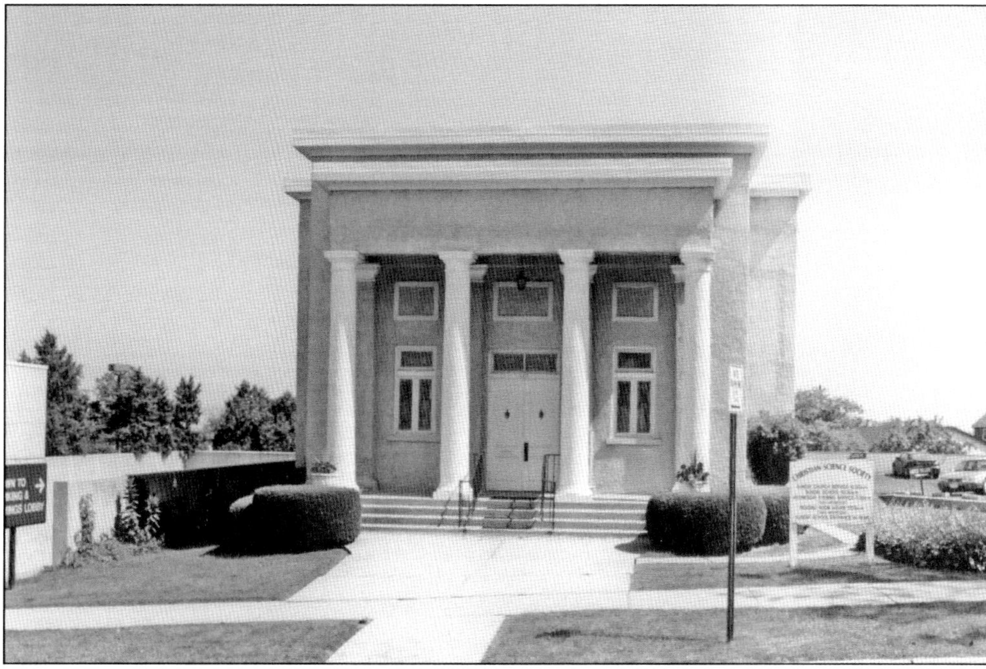

Christian Science began in West Bend in 1907 when an ill girl was miraculously healed. Her parents recruited friends, and the congregation met informally until 1921, when this church was built. Located on Fifth Avenue near Poplar Street, this photograph was taken around 2000, just before the church disbanded. The building is now used as a bar.

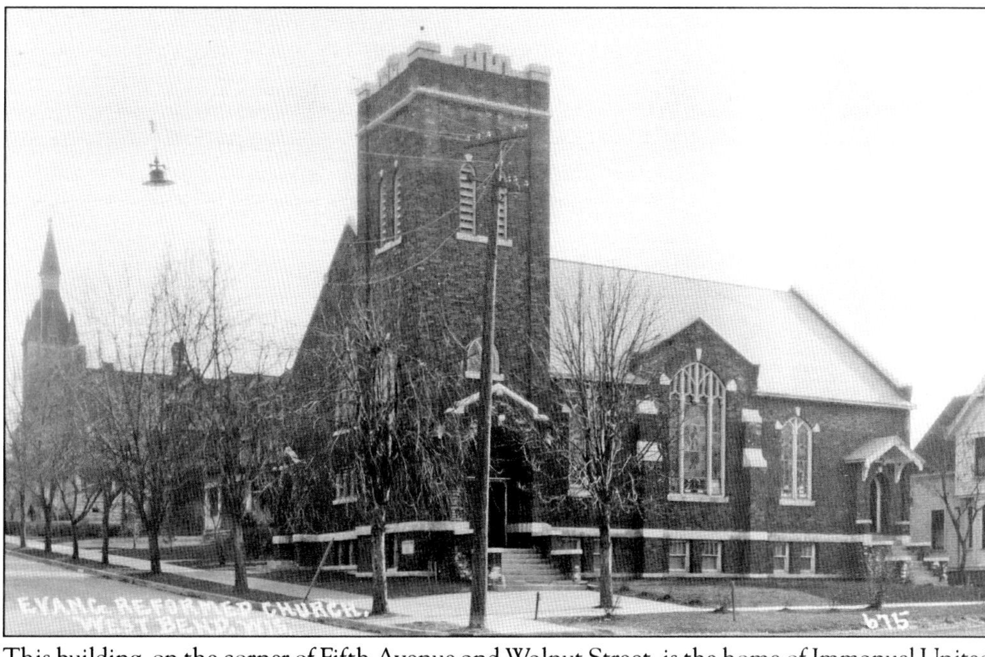

This building, on the corner of Fifth Avenue and Walnut Street, is the home of Immanuel United Church of Christ. The second building on the site, this brick structure was erected in 1923, replacing a smaller wooden church. Several additions have been made though the years. This photograph was taken around 1925, shortly after the current building was completed.

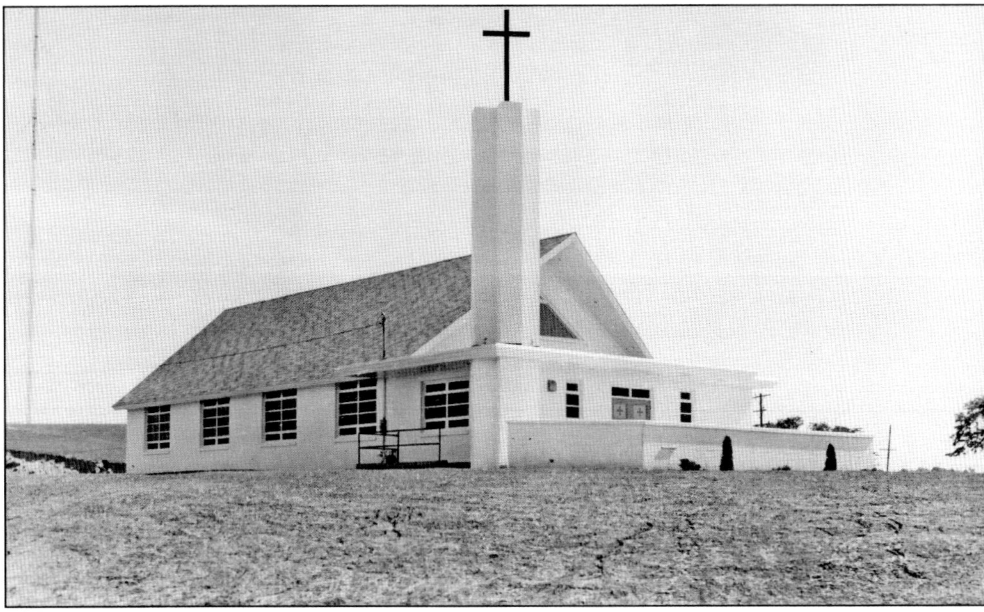

The Good Shepherd Evangelical Lutheran congregation was formed in 1951 and held services at Peterson's Restaurant until a church could be built in 1953. Located on Indiana Avenue, the church cost $25,000 to build and served the church until 1978, when a new facility was constructed on the same site.

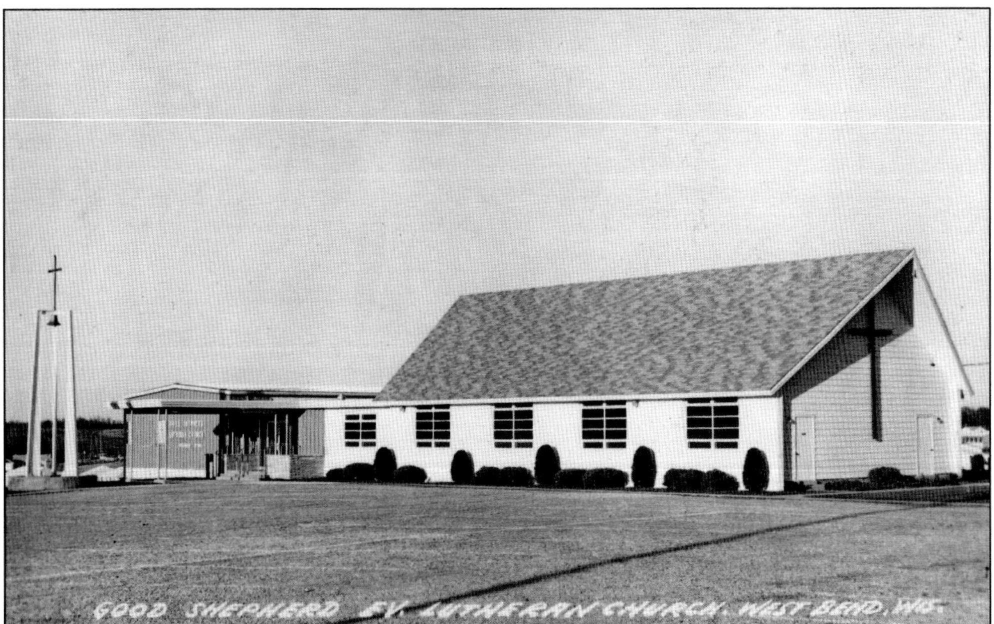

This photograph is of Good Shepherd Evangelical Lutheran Church and School. Good Shepherd School was opened in 1963 with 35 students. Today, it has grown to 190 students and holds classes from prekindergarten through eighth grade. The school partners with Kettle Moraine Lutheran High School in Jackson for students wishing to stay in the parochial school system.

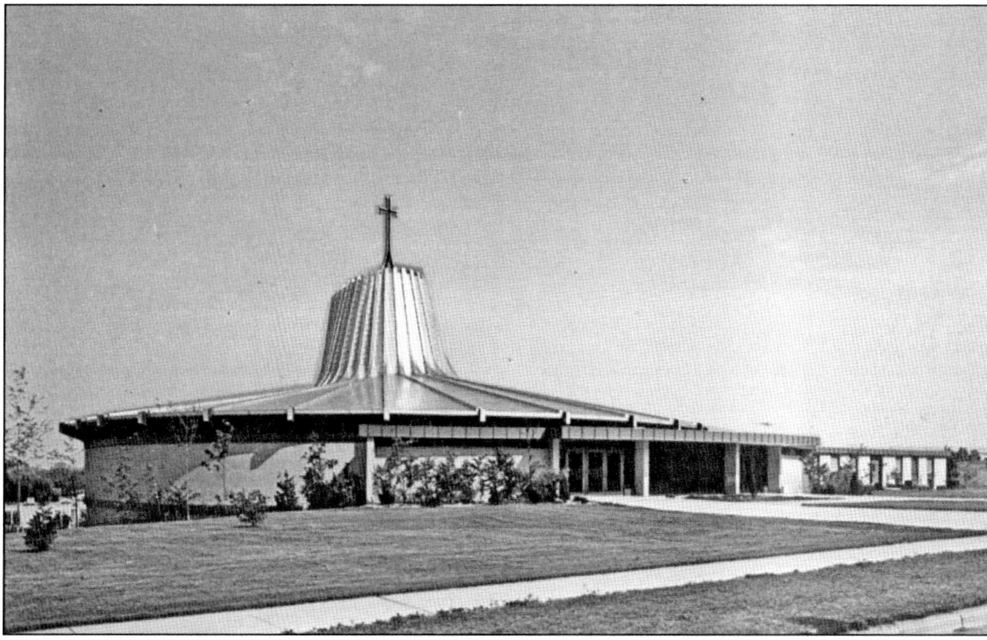

St. Francis Cabrini Catholic Church was established as a parish in 1955 when it divided from Holy Angels Catholic Church. The archdiocese decided the Holy Angels congregation was becoming too large for one parish. Until a new building could be finished, the congregation held Mass in the gym of McLane Elementary School. The new church and school were completed in 1957.

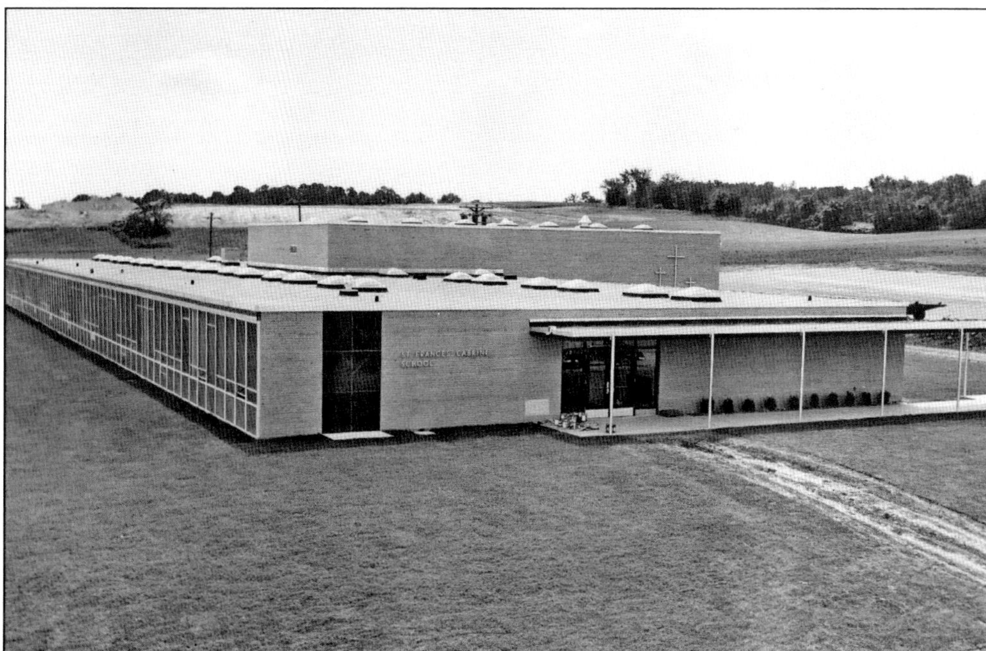

St. Francis Cabrini Catholic School was established in 1957 with the building of the church and began classes in the fall of 1957. The first year, the school had 250 elementary-aged children enrolled, with four Catholic sisters and three lay teachers. Today, the school teaches kindergarten through eighth grade.

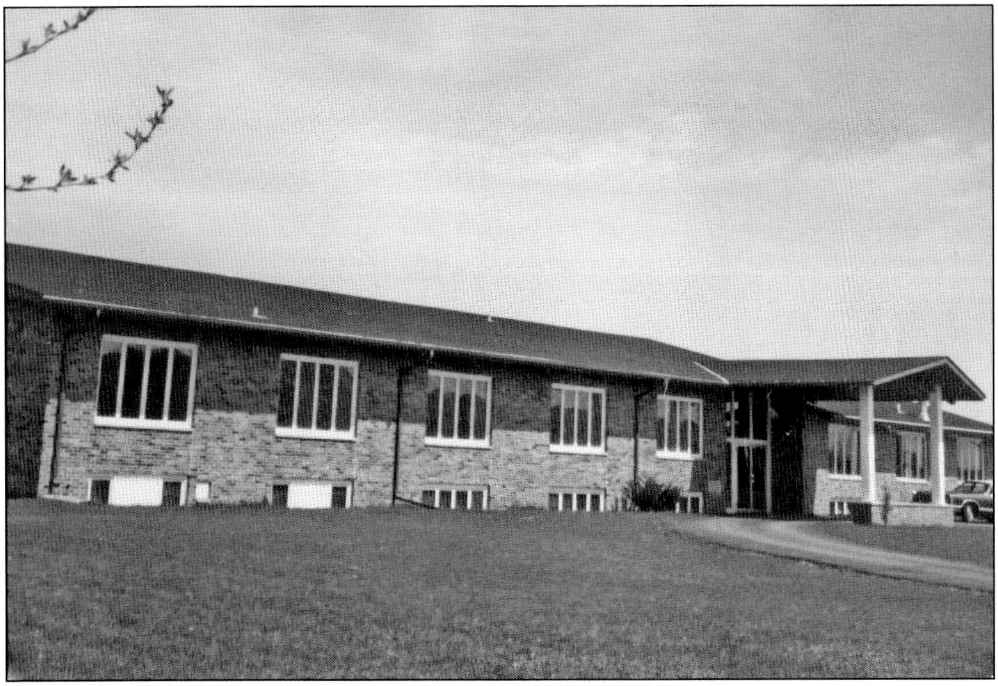

Calvary Assembly of God congregation was organized in 1948 and used the West Bend Moose Lodge for services until it purchased the old German Methodist Church in 1951. In 1969, the congregation was able to build this structure on East Decorah Road. The church also runs a school, Calvary Life Academy, on the site.

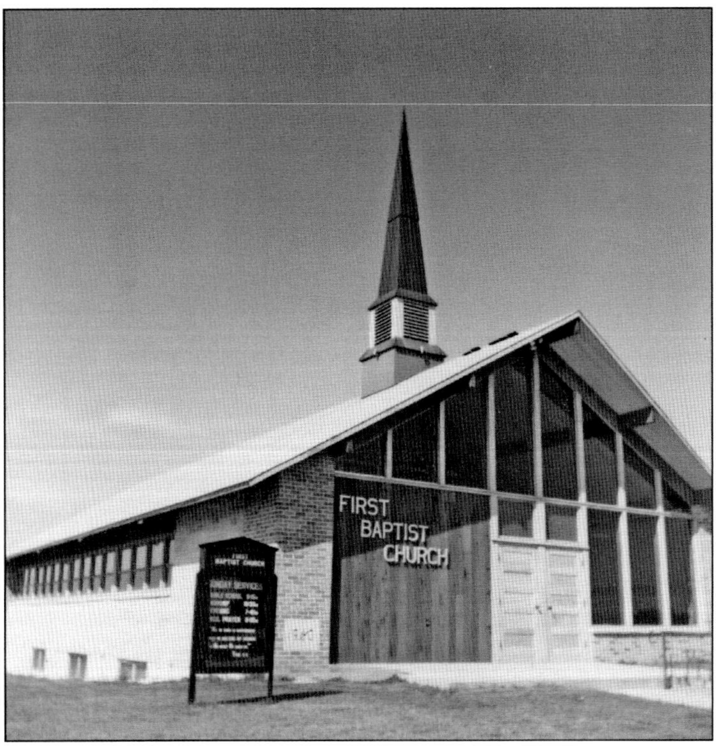

The First Baptist Church was founded in 1955 and met in members' homes or at public schools until they were able to build this church in 1960. The congregation remained at this site on Butternut Street until 2007, when they relocated. Since 2010, the Bend City Church, a nondenominational congregation, has occupied the building.

Four

Civic Organizations

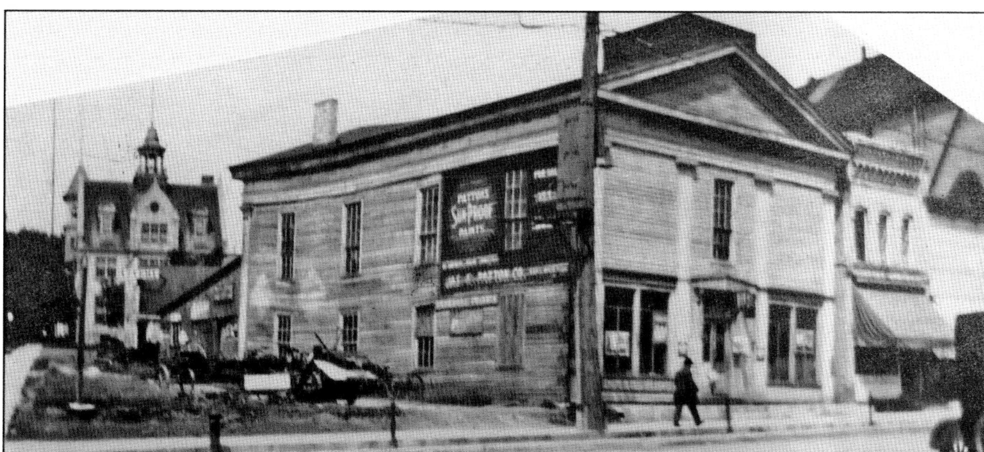

The building on the left is the original Washington County Courthouse. First located on the hill where the Old Courthouse Museum now stands, this wooden building was moved to the other side of the property in 1889 before the brick structure was erected. Shortly after, it was relocated downtown to the corner of North Main and Hickory Streets. It was demolished in the 1920s to make room for a filling station.

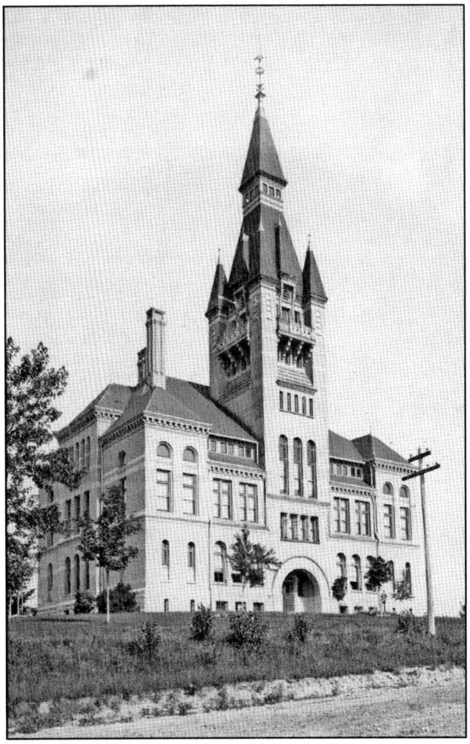

The Old Washington County Courthouse was built in 1889. It was used as a courthouse until 1962, when a new facility was built. At that time, Social Services, University of Wisconsin-Extension, and other departments added drop ceilings and cubicles to divide the large circuit and probate courtrooms into manageable office spaces. These were restored to their original glory in the 1990s when the building was taken over by the Washington County Historical Society.

Since early in Wisconsin's history, gambling laws were a controversial topic. During the 1930s, gambling in unlicensed facilities was illegal. Here, Sheriff Leo Burg and District Attorney Milton Meister sort though a pile of confiscated slot machines around 1938. These were probably confiscated from various Washington County taverns running illegal gambling operations.

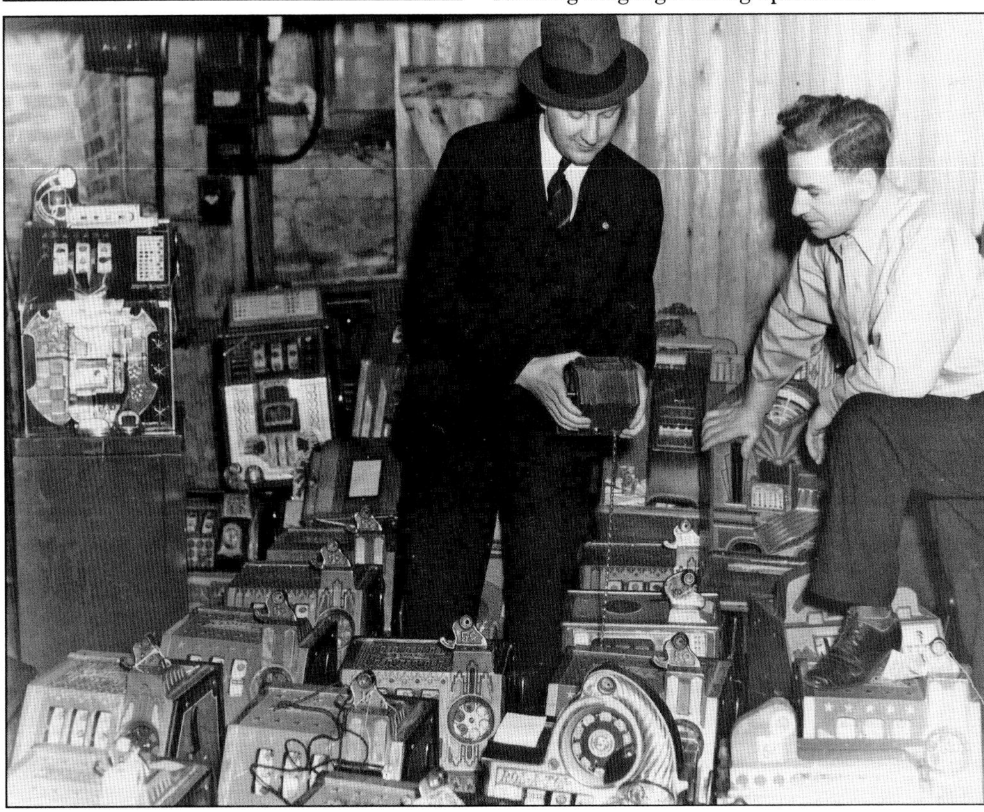

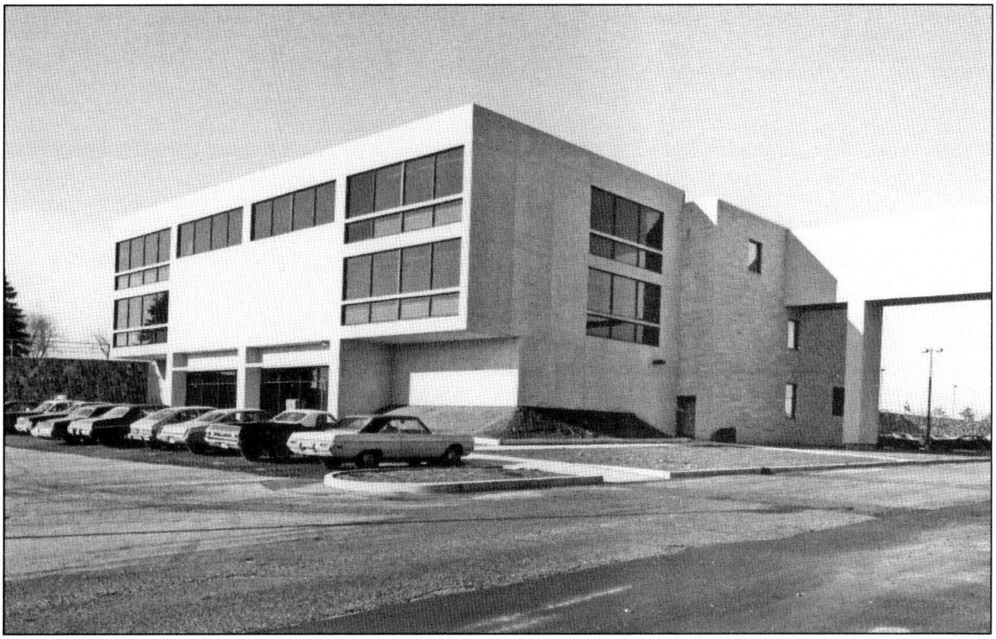

The need for a new county courthouse was dire. Among other things, there were no facilities for the jurors, no conference rooms for attorneys, and no private office for the judges. Other departments were overcrowded, and storage was overflowing. The lack of an elevator meant those with disabilities could not access the facilities. The new Washington County Courthouse was completed in June 1962 at a cost of $1.7 million.

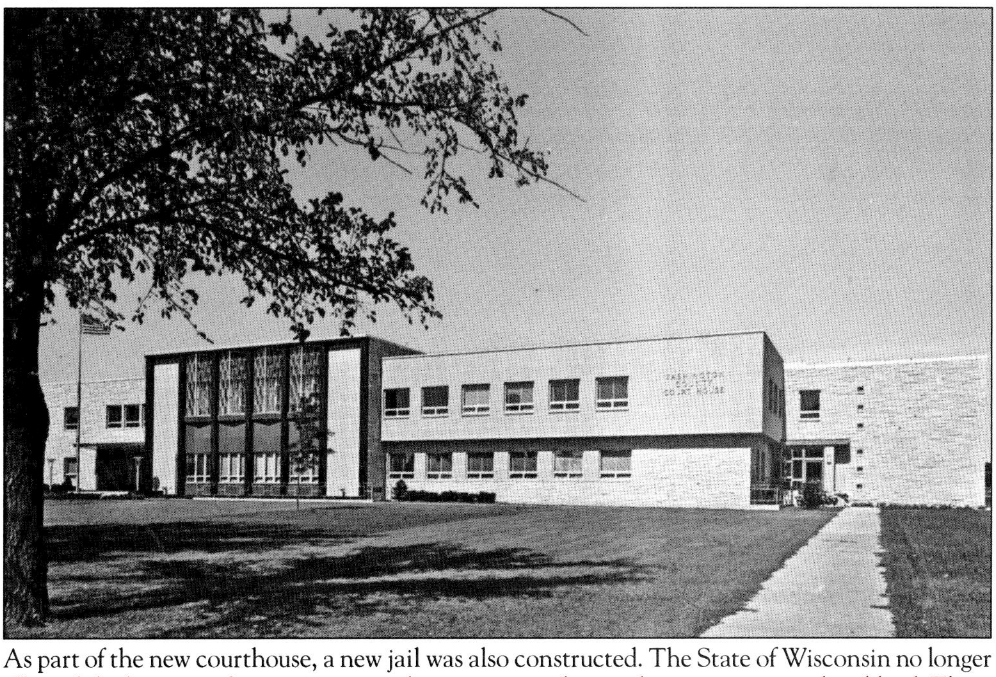

As part of the new courthouse, a new jail was also constructed. The State of Wisconsin no longer allowed the housing of women or juvenile prisoners in the conditions present at the old jail. There were no facilities for interrogations, and the radio room was located in the private section of the building designated for the sheriff's family.

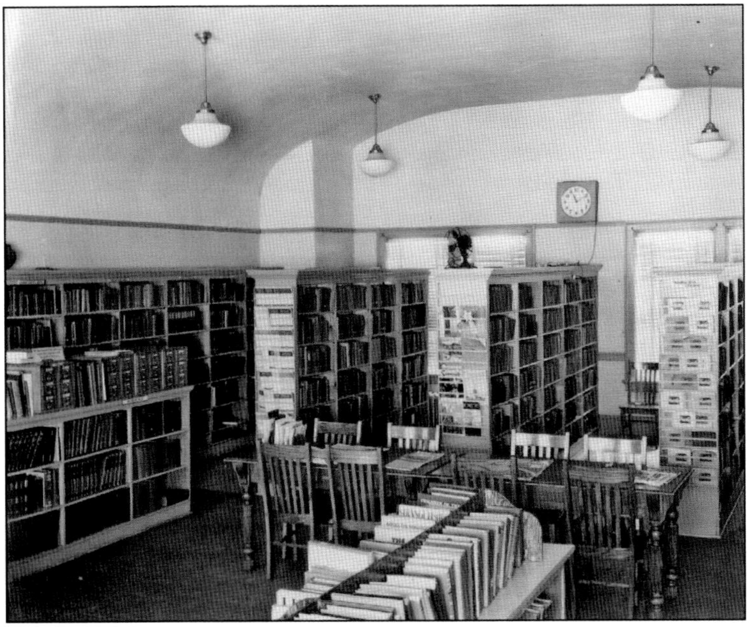

The first public library in West Bend opened on the second floor of city hall on September 13, 1901, and held between 700 and 800 volumes. It was organized by the Women's Club of West Bend, and it took several years to raise the funds needed for furniture and books. It was one of the club's first efforts after organizing in 1899. In November 1940, the library moved to a new location.

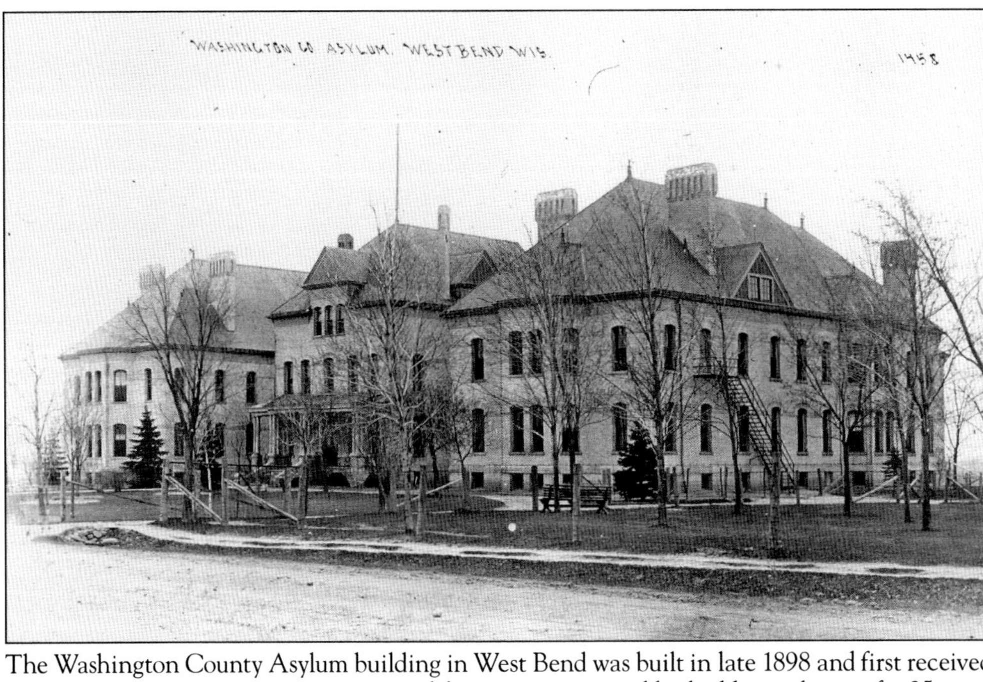

The Washington County Asylum building in West Bend was built in late 1898 and first received residents in January 1899. It was equipped for 100 patients and had additional room for 25 more if needed. The first residents were not local and were transferred from nearby facilities such as Fond du Lac, Wisconsin.

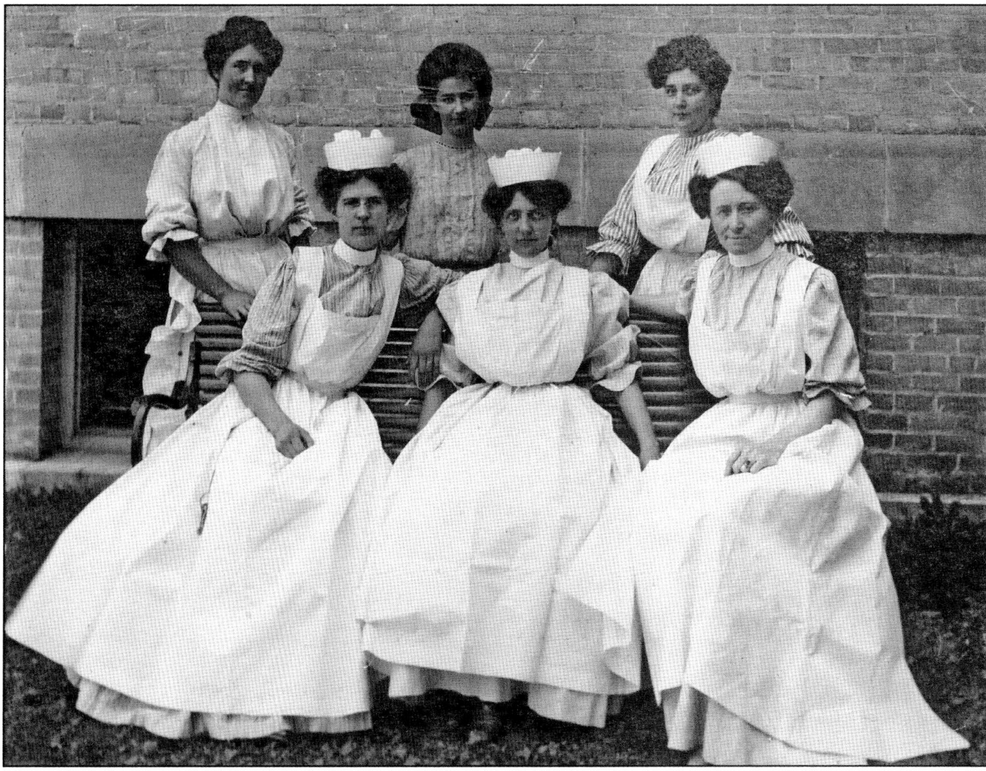

These ladies were the staff servers, cooks, and attendants at the Washington County Asylum. The only person identified is Margaret Hausmann (center). The attendants were required to be on overnight call every other night and had to stay in dormitory rooms at the asylum. They were expected to treat their patients with respect and to follow a strict set of rules.

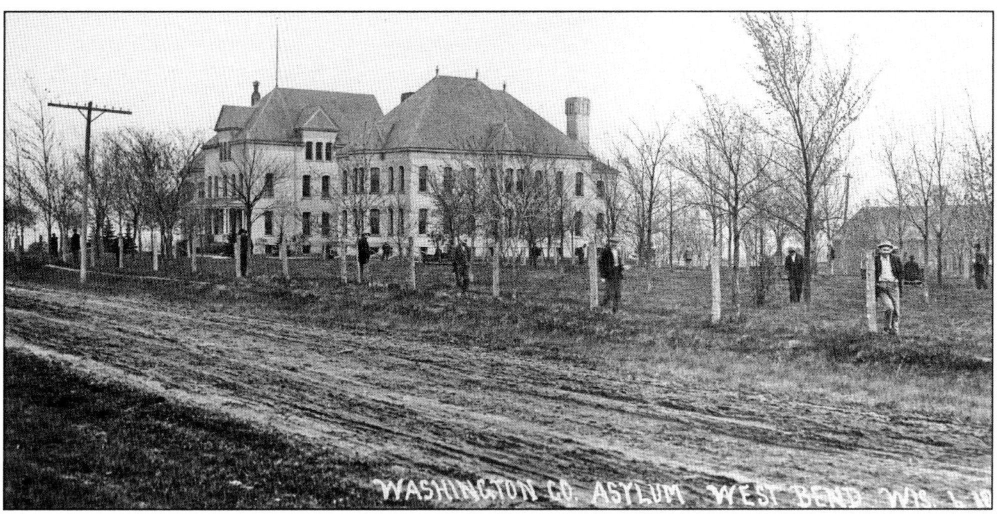

The original Washington County Poor House, located in Jackson, Wisconsin, had been built in 1850. By the end of the century, there were problems with overcrowding. It was decided to relocate the home to county-owned property next to the Washington County Asylum in West Bend. This building was constructed in 1912 and included a large farm worked by residents.

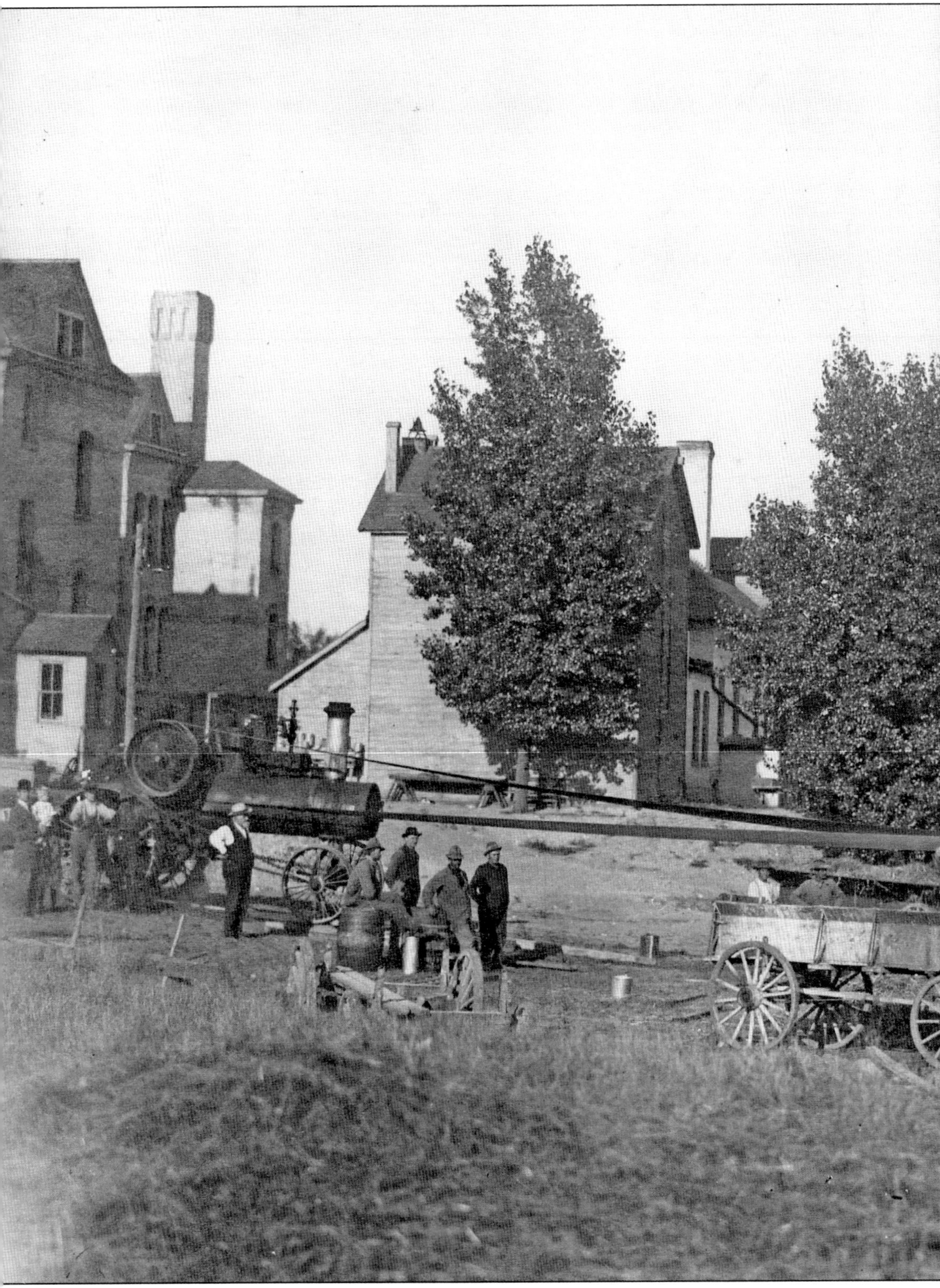

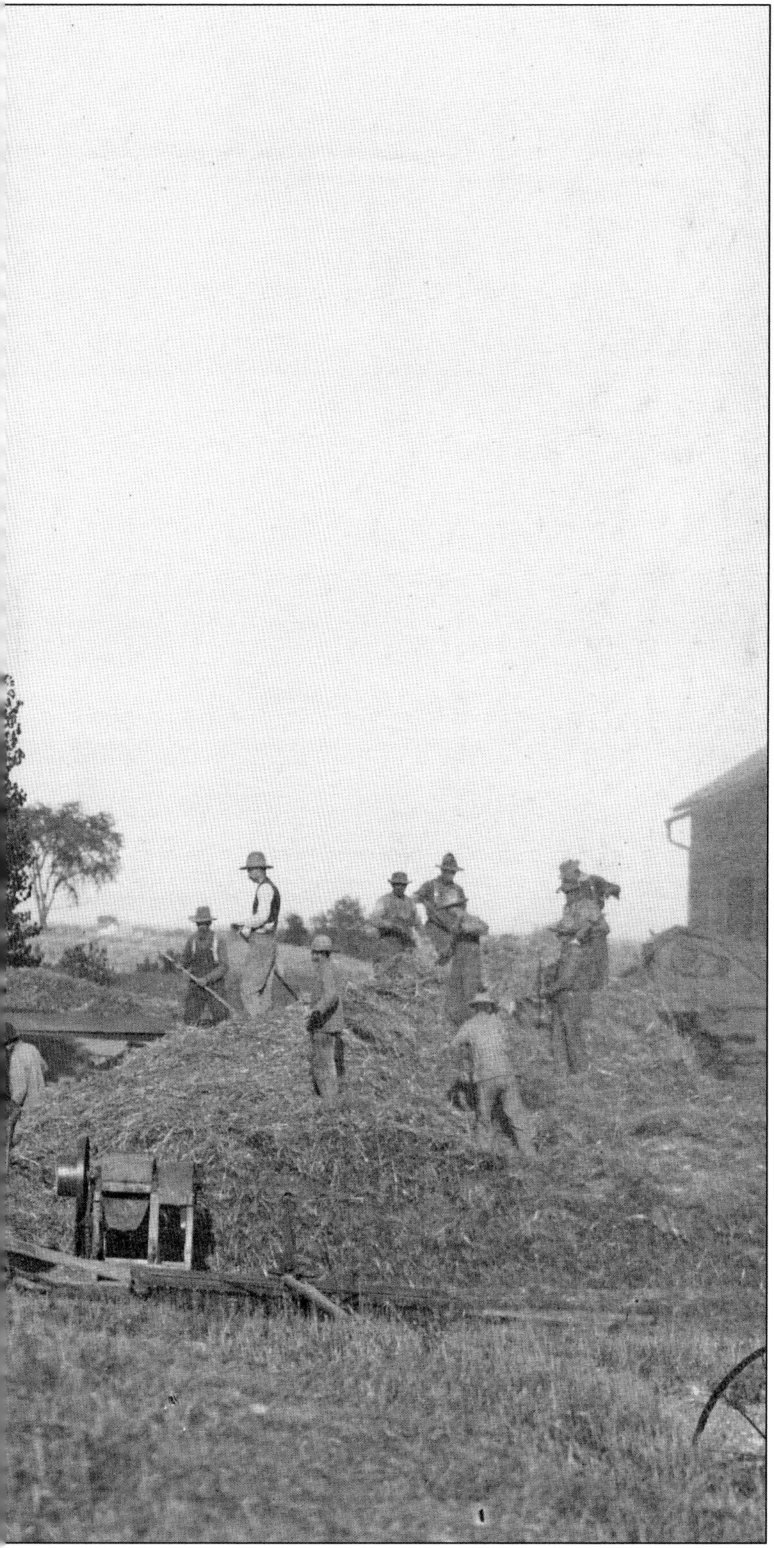

Taken around 1910, this photograph shows threshing operations on the Washington County Farm grounds. The farm was part of the county health facility, which was home to the Washington County Asylum, the County Home, and the Old People's Home and Alms House. Residents from these facilities worked the farm, which not only had arable land, but cows and pigs as well. Farmland was on either side of present-day Highway 33, and a tunnel under the highway allowed for safe passage of livestock and workers. The farm provided income from sale of produce, as well as food for residents. Operations ceased, and the livestock and equipment were sold at auction in 1963 when the farm was no longer profitable.

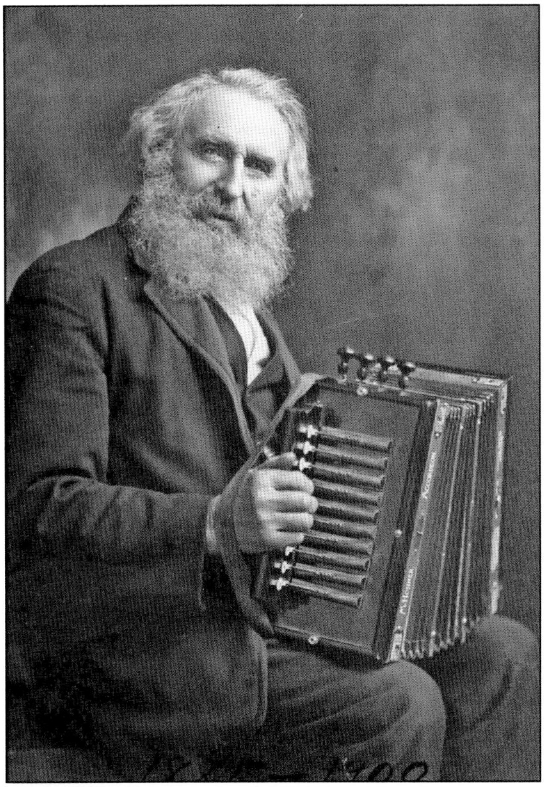

John Stein was West Bend's first police chief, serving from 1885 to 1890. He was born in Mecklenburg-Schwerin, Germany, in 1832 and came to West Bend in 1852. In addition to being police chief, Stein ran a stagecoach service to Fond du Lac, Wisconsin, and served as the city's street commissioner. This photograph was taken around 1900 when Stein was about 68 years old.

The police department is pictured here during Homecoming in July 1913. From left to right are (first row) Edward Morawetz and unidentified; (second row) Fred Schloemer, Mr. Hron, Adam Held, John Ryan, and unidentified; (third row) John Eder, Herman Mueller, Ferdinand Nehrbass, Henry Lemke, and unidentified.

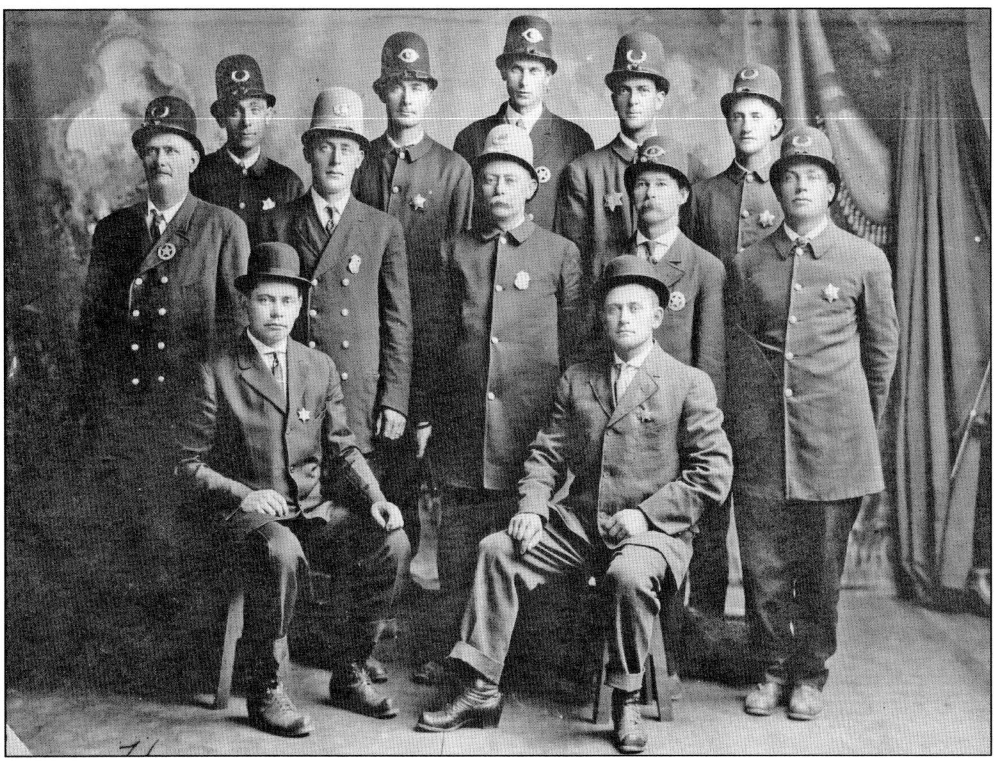

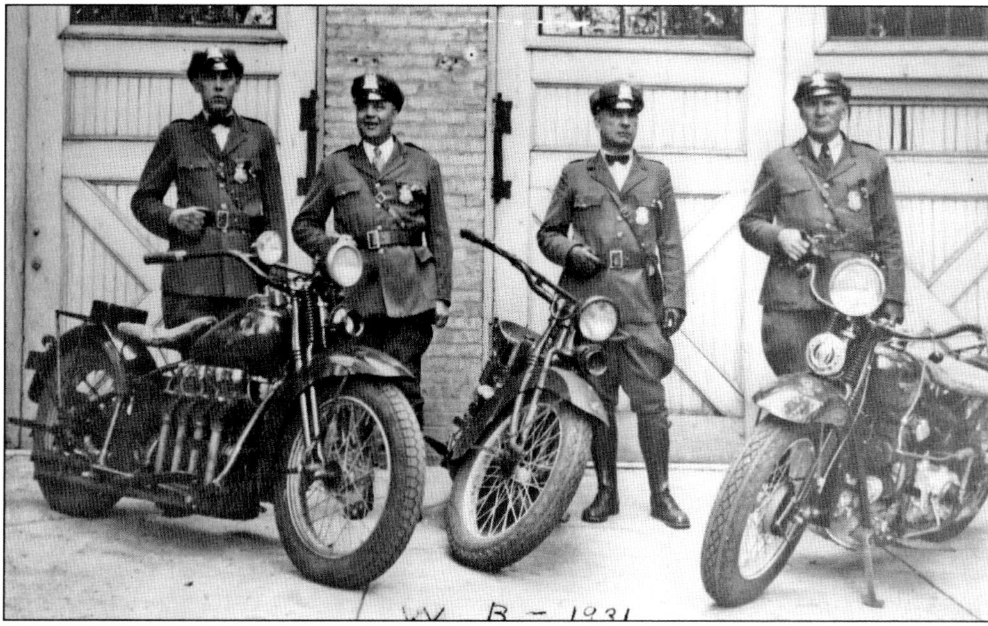

Around 1917, West Bend Police Department officers began using motorcycles. The officers in this 1931 image are, from left to right, Harvey Lemke, William Scott, Peter Steiner, and Chief Arthur Juech. This photograph was taken outside the police department when it was located at the old city hall on Sixth Avenue and Hickory Street.

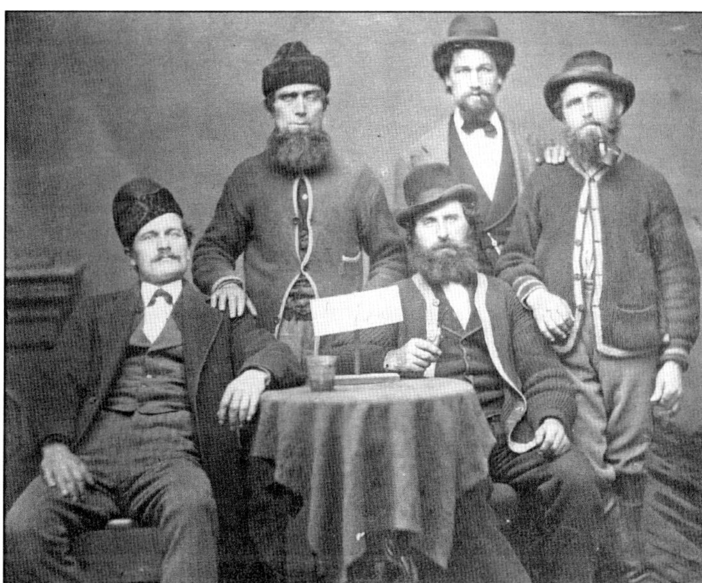

This photograph of the Neptune Engine Company organizers was taken around 1869. The Neptune Engine Company was the first-known organized fire company in West Bend. The company owned a used hand-pulled water pump, which had been purchased by the Village of West Bend. From left to right the men are Albert Semler, George Suerr, Henry Lemke, F. Duetsch, and Peter Wetenberger.

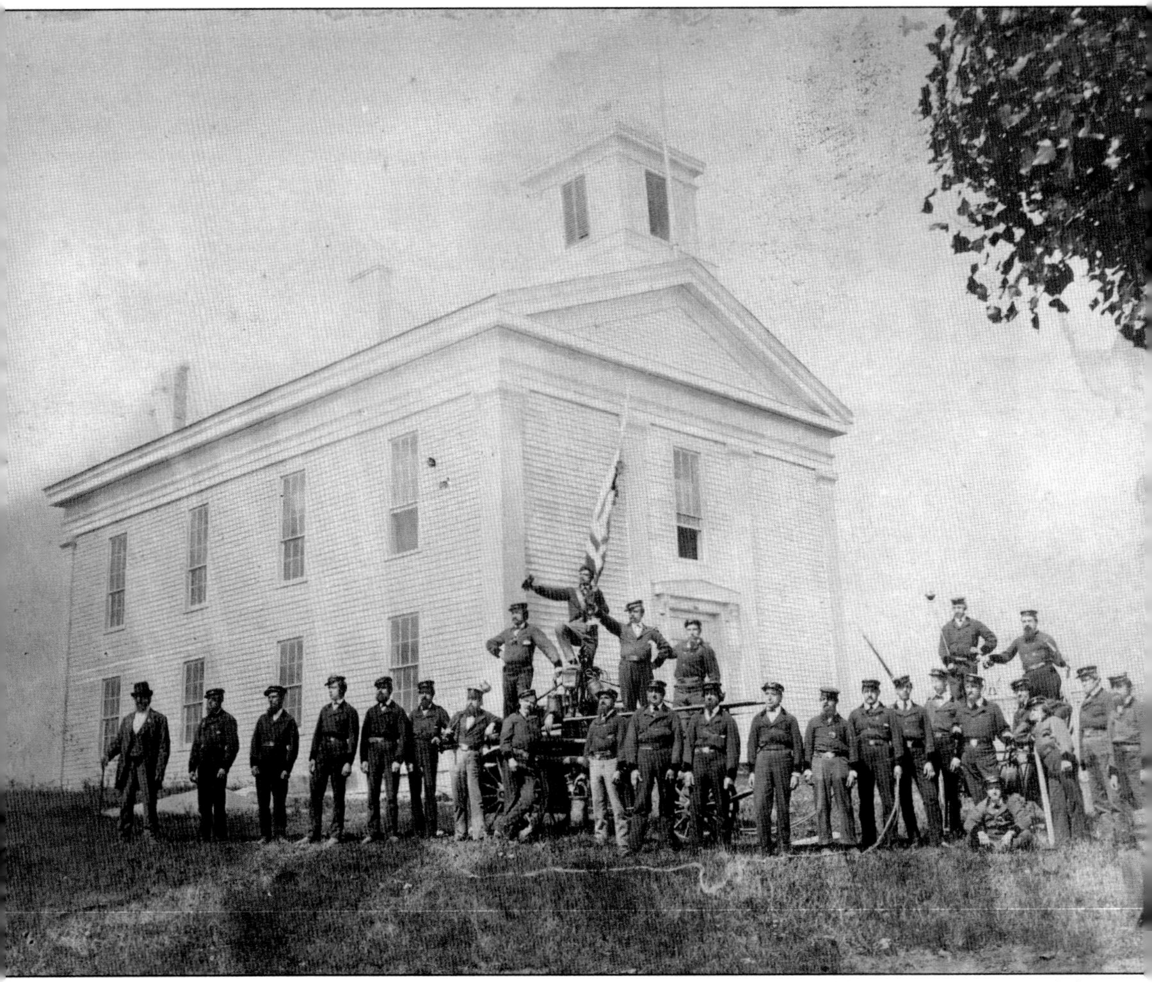

The West Bend Neptune Engine Company poses with its engine and hose cart in front of the first county courthouse around 1870. The Neptune Company, formed in 1869 and composed of volunteers, owned the first fire engine in West Bend. Rival companies supplied hook-and-ladder and hose services. Identified members of the fire department are, from left to right, (first row) "Schnabel" Haase, William Karsten, Henry Voss, William Kreibohm, two unidentified men, George Kleffler, unidentified, Carl Troedel, unidentified, Leonard Lambert, Louis Heisse, William Klatt, two unidentified men, Robert Gottsleben, Albert Semler, Dave Meyer (seated), Poli Meyer, John Fick, two unidentified men, and Fred Althaus; (second row) Mr. Konrad, Wenzel Wachter, Peter Boden, Pete Westenberger, unidentified, and Mr. Geier. The volunteers of the department had a wide range of jobs, from stonemason to cigar maker.

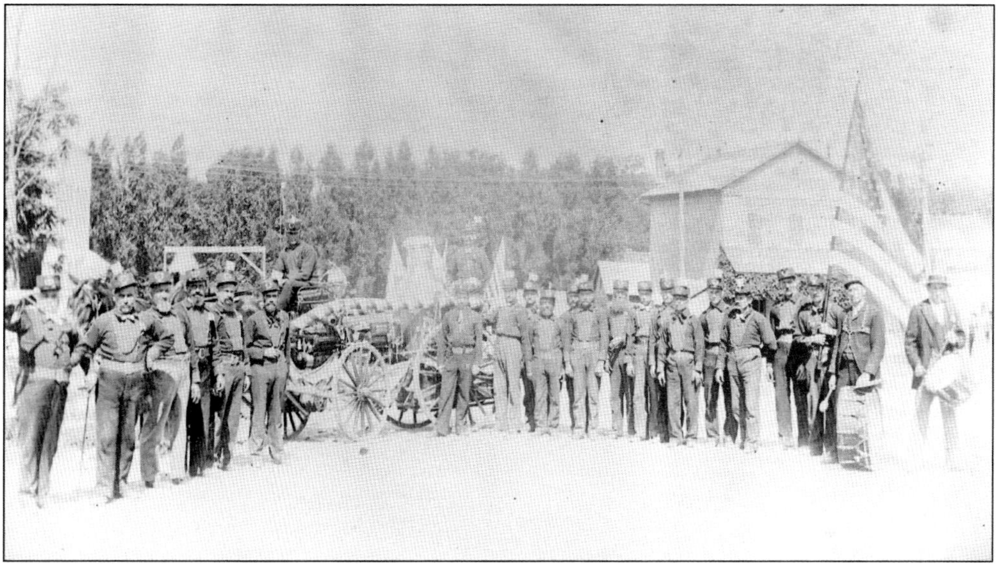

The entire Neptune Engine Company is pictured here around 1896. Standing from left to right are Chief Peter Boden, Capt. Peter Heindl, Mathias Regner, Anton Roeckel, Ben Berger, William Schmidt, engineer Charles Silberzahn, Jac Mertin, Herman Weinert, John Karsten, Ernst Hiller, Herman Voss, August Nicolaus, Fred Manthie, Herman Warnkey, William Macholz, Herman Warnkey, George Groeshel, Steve Lang, Christ Troedel, William Kahl, and John Weil. On the engine are Herman Kuester (driver) and John Romas (fireman).

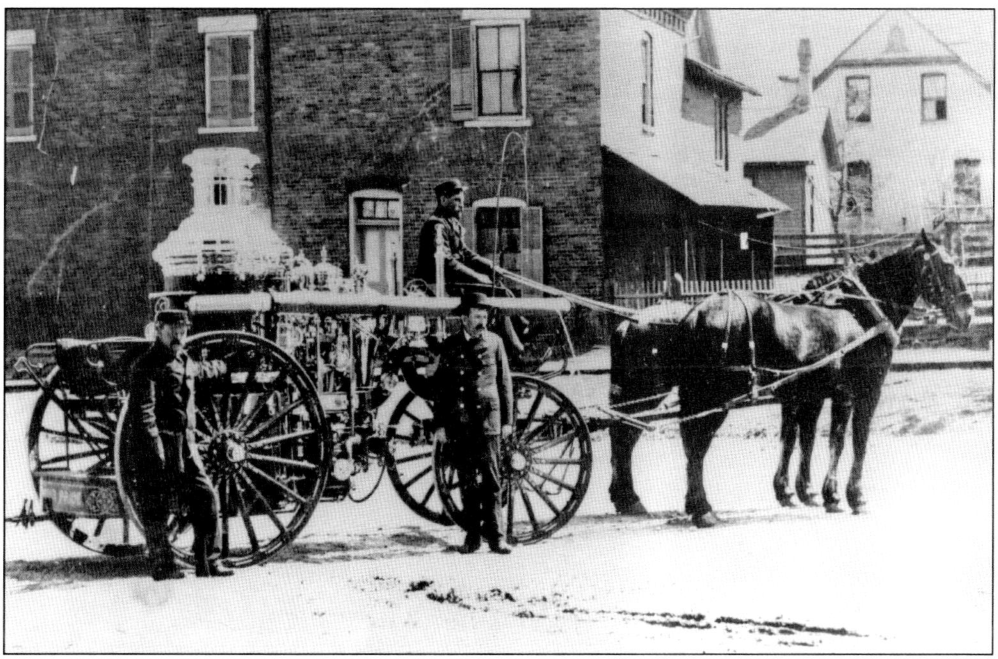

Taken around 1902, this photograph shows the horse-drawn 1902 Metropolitan Steamer Engine used in West Bend until 1923. At this time, the fire department was divided into four rival companies. Each specialized in a different aspect of fire control, from water control to pulling down burning parts of the building. The driver is Jacob Bastion, and the standing firemen are Charles Silberzahn (left) and Charles Koelle.

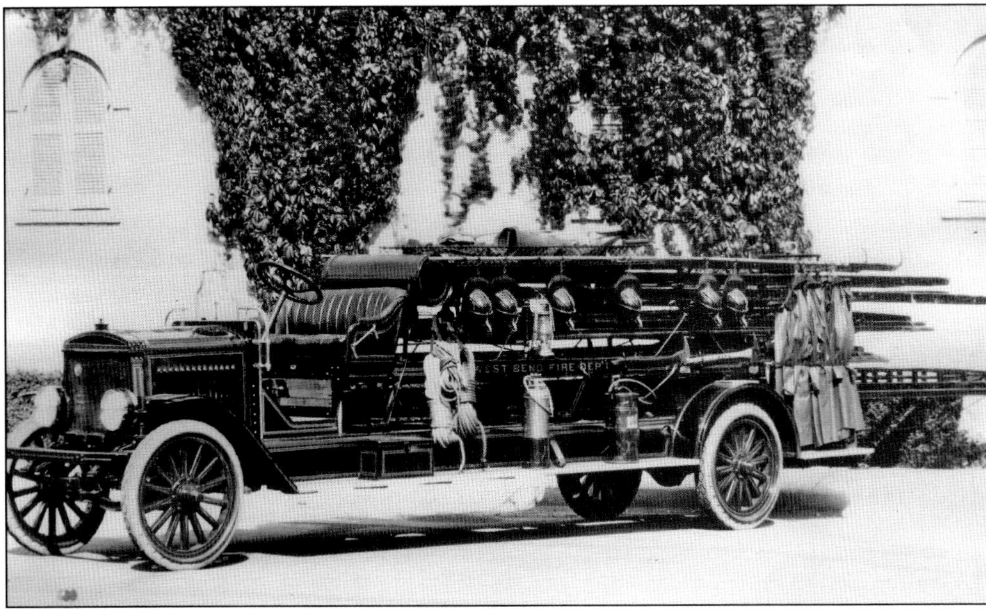

By 1917, the four rival fire companies were consolidated into one company of 50 to 60 members. They were paid 50¢ per hour of service. This photograph shows the first motorized hook-and-ladder truck purchased by West Bend in 1923, which replaced the Metropolitan Steamer Engine.

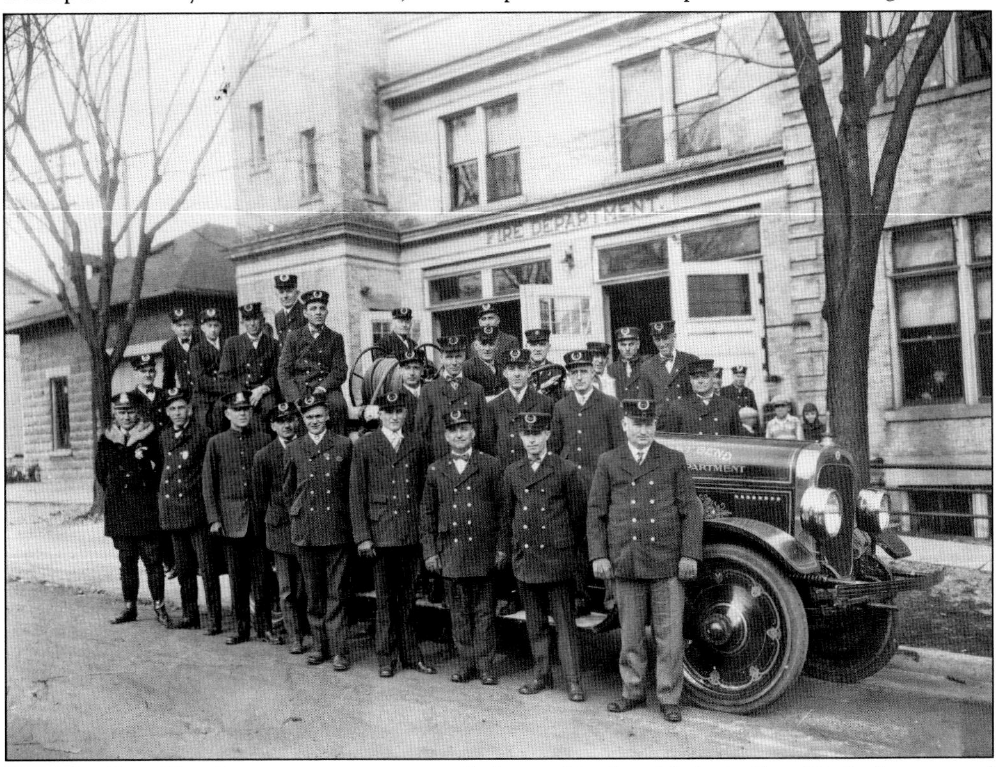

The West Bend Fire Department was originally located in the old city hall on Sixth Avenue and Hickory Street. This photograph was taken around 1925 in front of the department garage on Hickory Street with the first motorized hook-and-ladder truck in the city.

Five

Public Schools

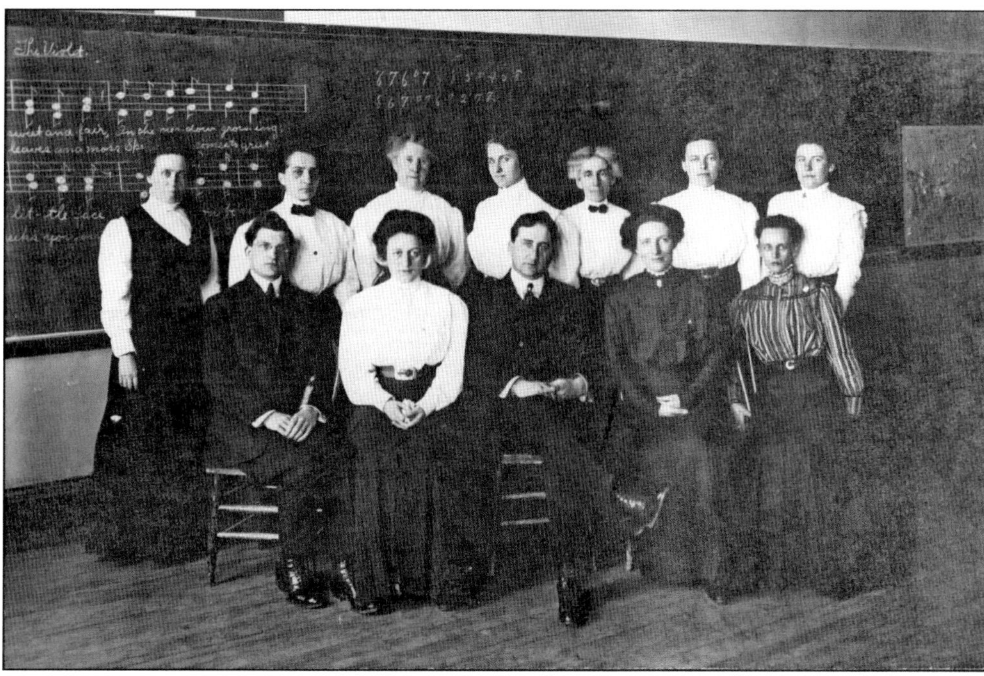

This is a photograph of a group of public schoolteachers from 1908. From left to right are (first row) Irvin Coates (high school), Tessa Hickish (high school), D.E. McLane (high school principal and superintendent), Bella Mac Arthur (high school English), and Lola Woodford (eighth grade); (second row) Roxanna Knapp, Marie Weller (second grade), Margaret O'Connel, Anna Gossel, Elisabeth Dunham, Barbara Mueller, and Mary Mueller.

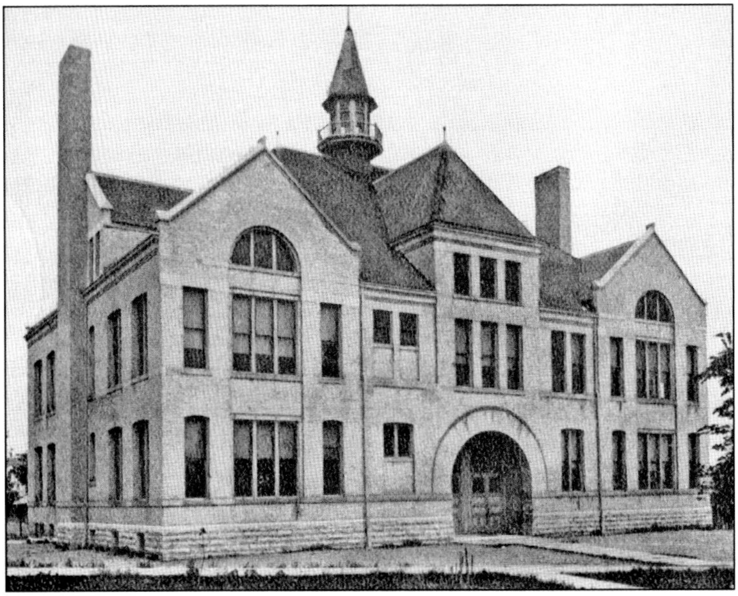

The West Bend Grade School was located at the corner of Elm Street and Eighth Avenue. As the city population grew, the school became too crowded, and McLane Elementary School was built in 1939. This school was closed and became Holy Angels Catholic School. When the church built a new school building in the early 1960s, the old facility was torn down.

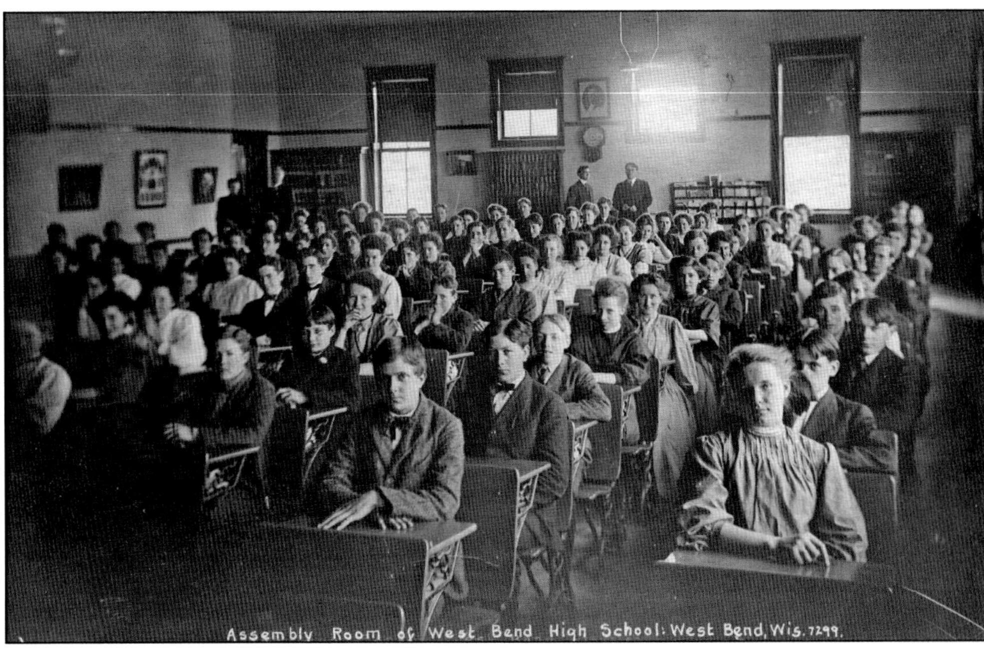

This photograph of West Bend High School students was taken in the school's assembly room around 1909. That year, five teachers were on staff, including the principal and vice principal. The student body consisted of 12 seniors, 22 juniors, 25 sophomores, and 33 freshmen.

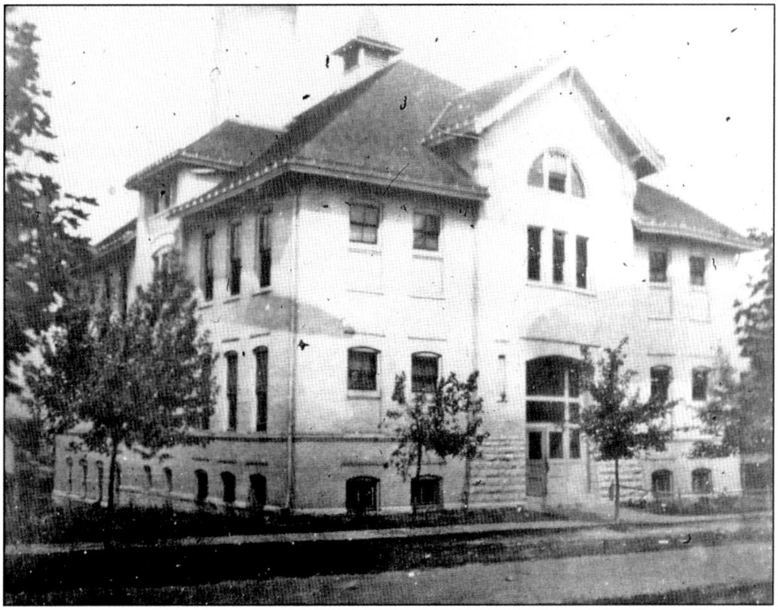

The second high school built in West Bend was located on the corner of Eighth Avenue and Elm Street. The old school was converted to an elementary school and later used for city services, such as the library, and department offices. Today, it houses a private law firm.

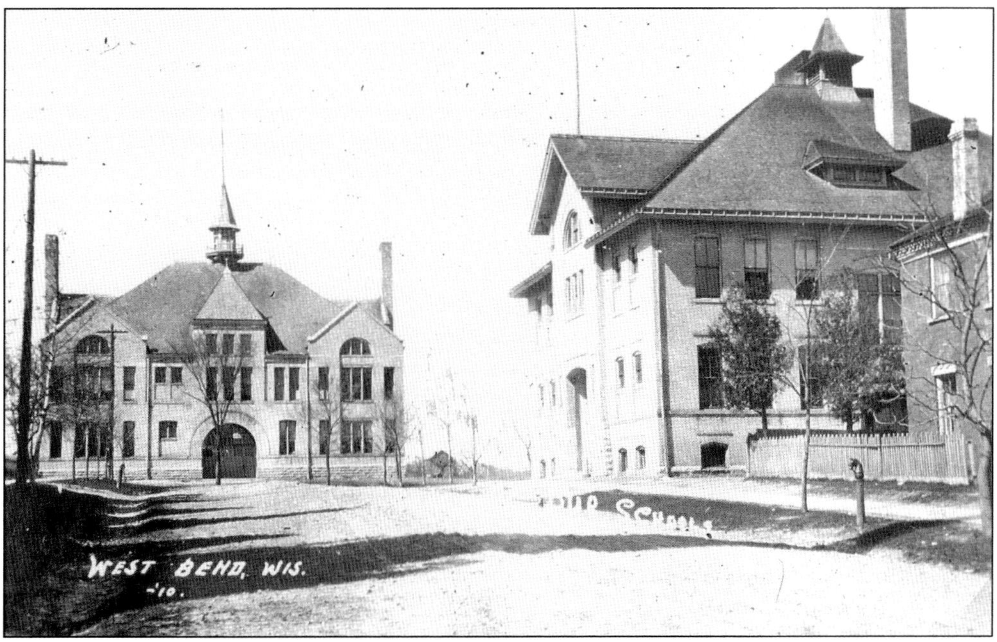

Constructed in 1889, the building in the distance is the old public elementary school that was used until McLane Elementary was built in 1939. The elementary school was sold to Holy Angels and used as a Catholic school until a new building was constructed in 1962. The building on the right, constructed in 1900, housed the high school. It houses private offices today.

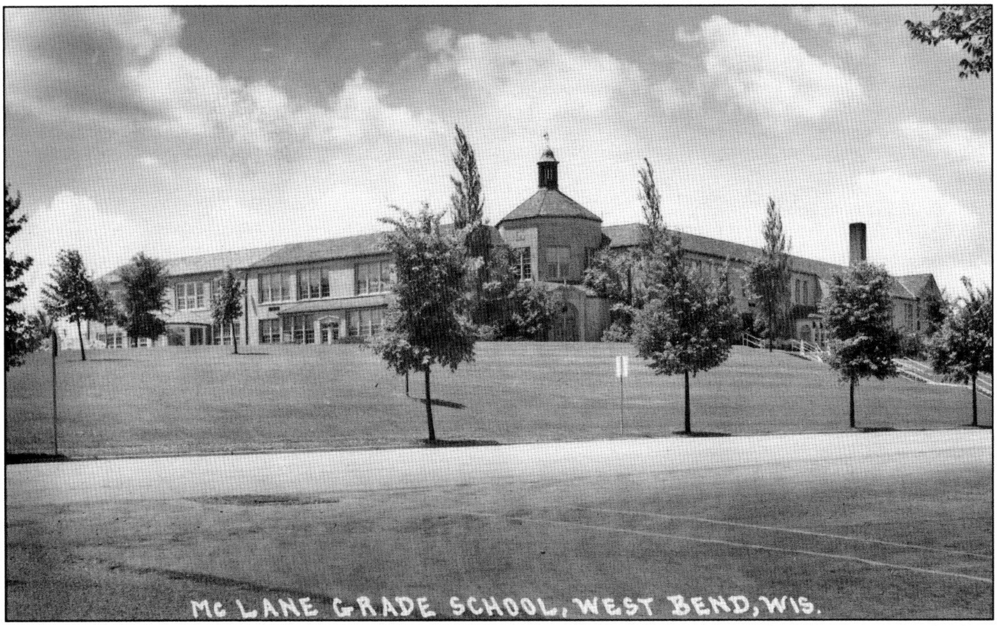

Located on Eighth Avenue and Chestnut Street, McLane Elementary School was named after long-serving superintendent of schools D.E. McLane. It was meant to ease the crowding at the old West Bend Grade School, which was sold and became Holy Angels Catholic School. McLane Elementary School opened in 1939.

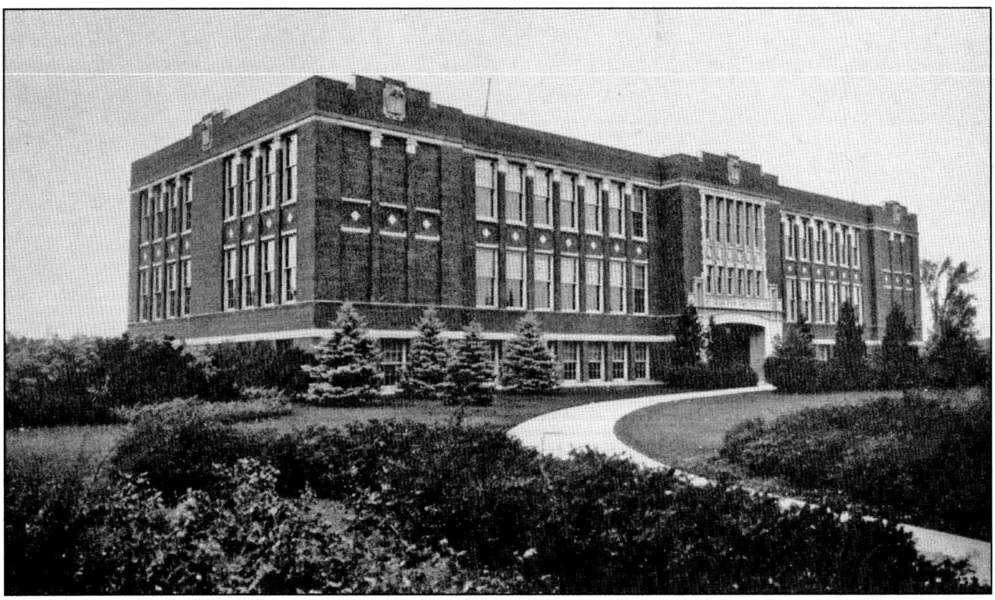

The West Bend High School seen here was built in 1927. Located on South Main Street and Decorah Road, it is the current location of Badger Middle School. Several additions to the building over the years alleviated crowding until the new East and West High Schools were constructed in 1971. This old portion of the school was torn down in 2011 to construct a modern addition.

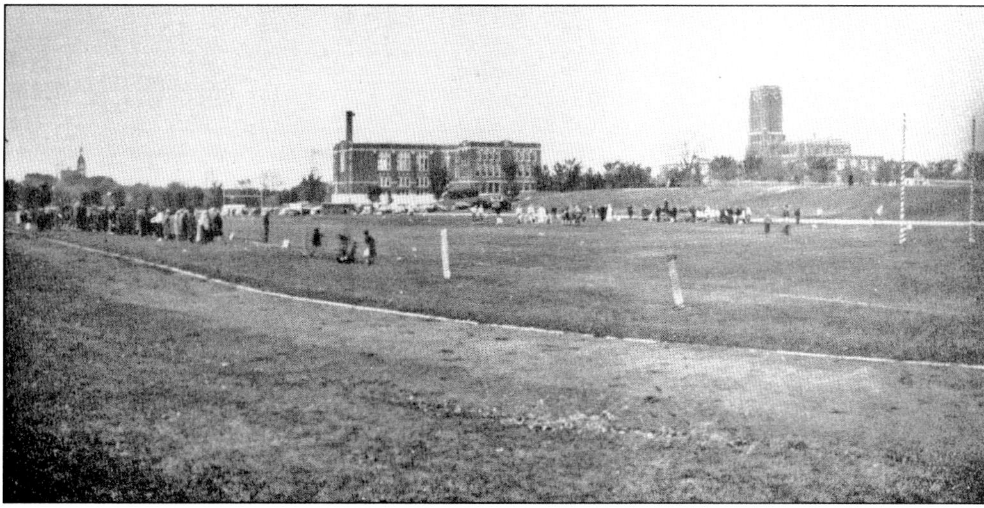

Bruhy Field was named in commemoration of Harvey Bruhy, an aviator who was killed in action during World War I. It was the West Bend High School athletic field until 1970, when the current high school was built. The school and Amity Leather Products Company can be seen in the background. Today, the field is mostly occupied by the newly remodeled Badger Middle School.

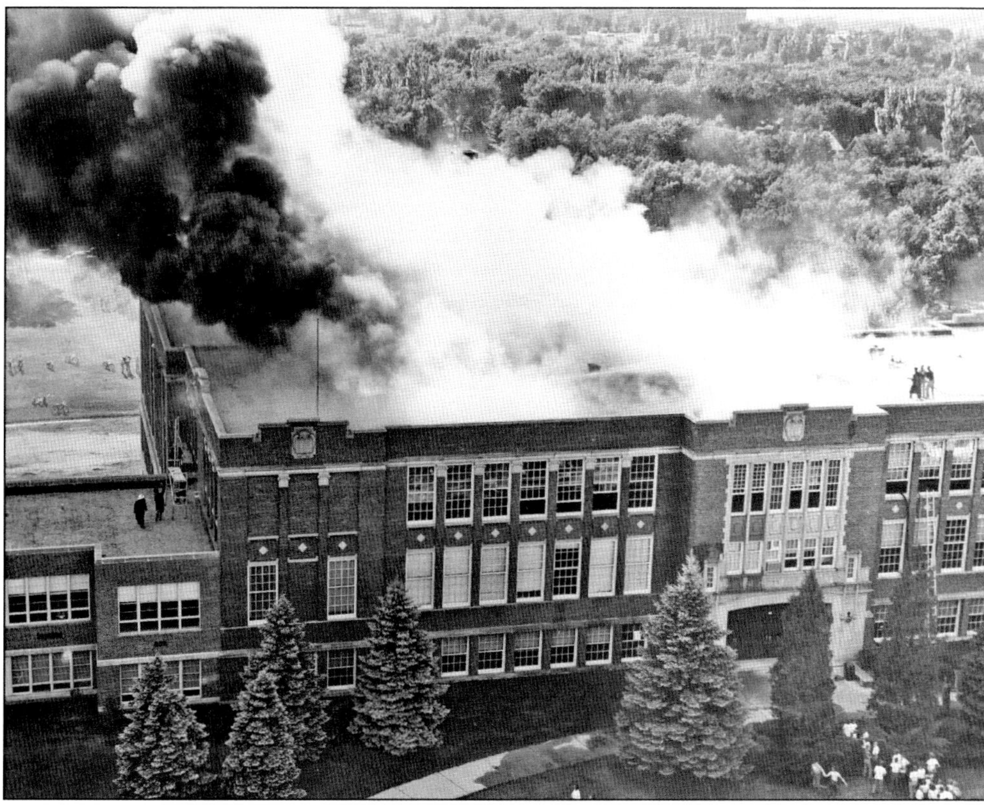

This photograph was taken on August 19, 1953, when a fire broke out at the old high school on Main Street. The damage to the building was estimated at $200,000. This portion of the school, which is now Badger Middle School, was demolished in 2011. The photograph was taken from across the street in the old Amity Leather Products Company tower. (Photograph by Bob Boltz.)

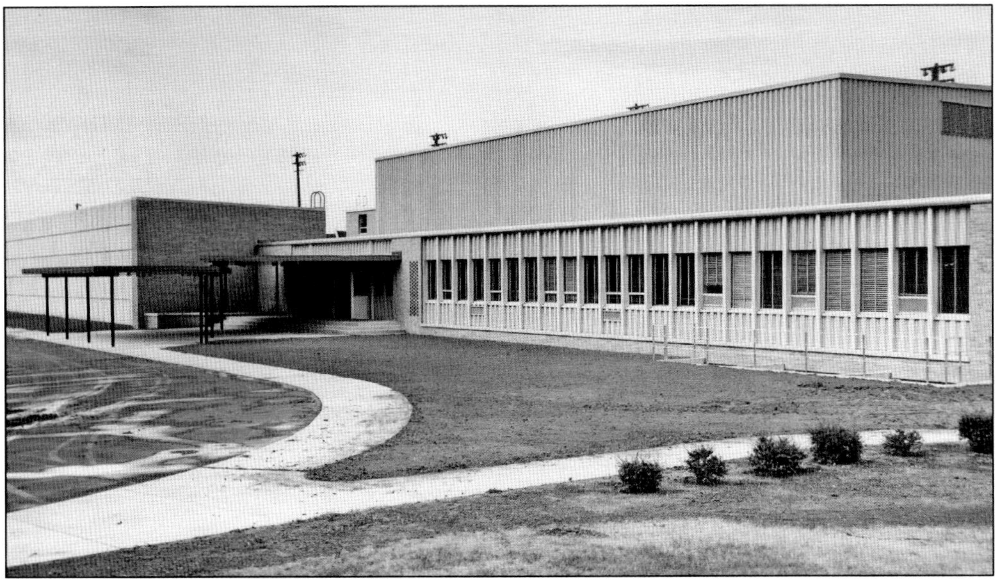

In 1958, the high school built a new addition. The expanded facilities allowed for more classroom space and extended offerings in vocational training, choir and band rooms, and a large multipurpose activity room, which was open to the public after school hours. This room provided pool tables, television, a jukebox, and other activities. The cost of the project was $1.4 million. (Photograph by Bob Boltz.)

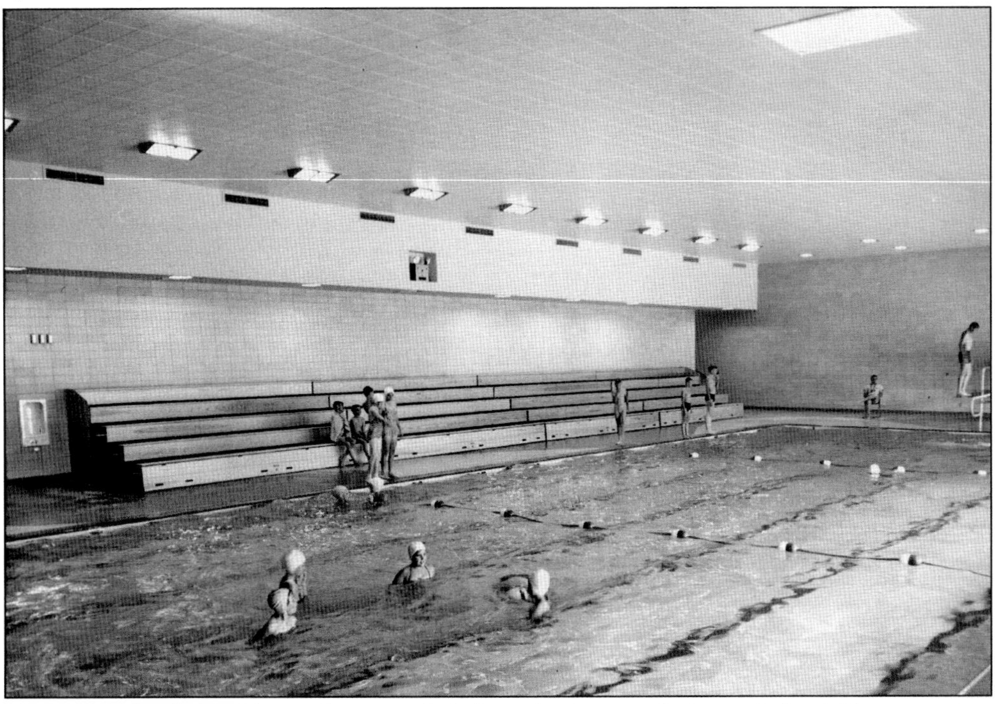

The 1958 high school addition also expanded physical education facilities. A dividable gymnasium and pool were added. In previous years, students had to use the McLane Elementary gym for some activities. The building was used as the high school until 1971, when the joint West Bend East and West High Schools were built. (Photograph by Bob Boltz.)

Six

WAR AND REMEMBRANCE

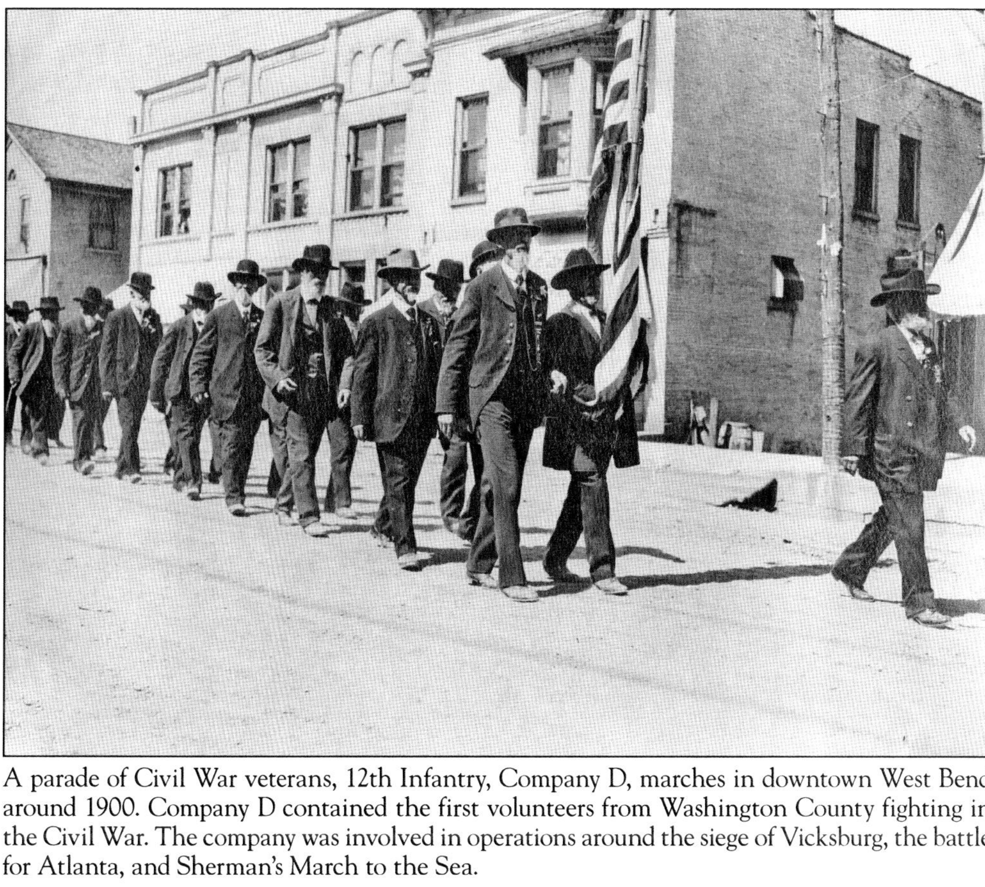

A parade of Civil War veterans, 12th Infantry, Company D, marches in downtown West Bend around 1900. Company D contained the first volunteers from Washington County fighting in the Civil War. The company was involved in operations around the siege of Vicksburg, the battle for Atlanta, and Sherman's March to the Sea.

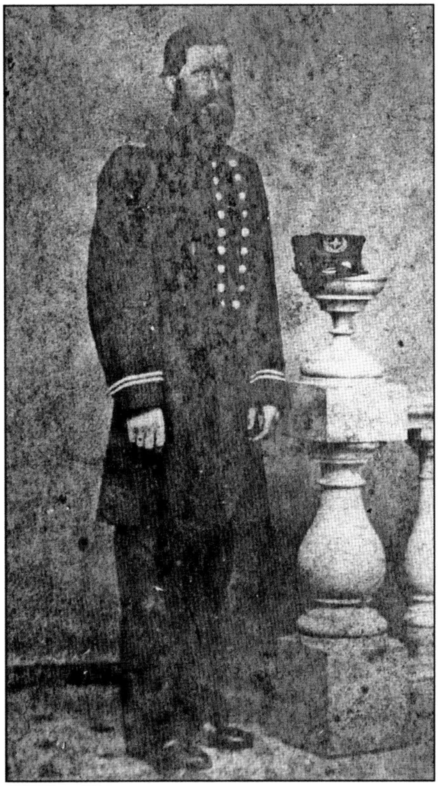

Charles Silberzahn was born in Germany and trained as a blacksmith before coming to America in 1850. He settled in St. Louis before joining the Union army and serving in the Civil War. He and his family eventually moved to West Bend and took over Lucas Foundry, changing the name to Silberzahn Manufacturing Company before selling it to John Gehl in 1902. Today, the company is known as Gehl Company.

This group of World War I veterans poses on the hill north of the Washington County Courthouse around 1925. The area behind the soldiers is now the Washington County Veterans' Memorial Plaza and has several monuments to the Washington County soldiers who served their country.

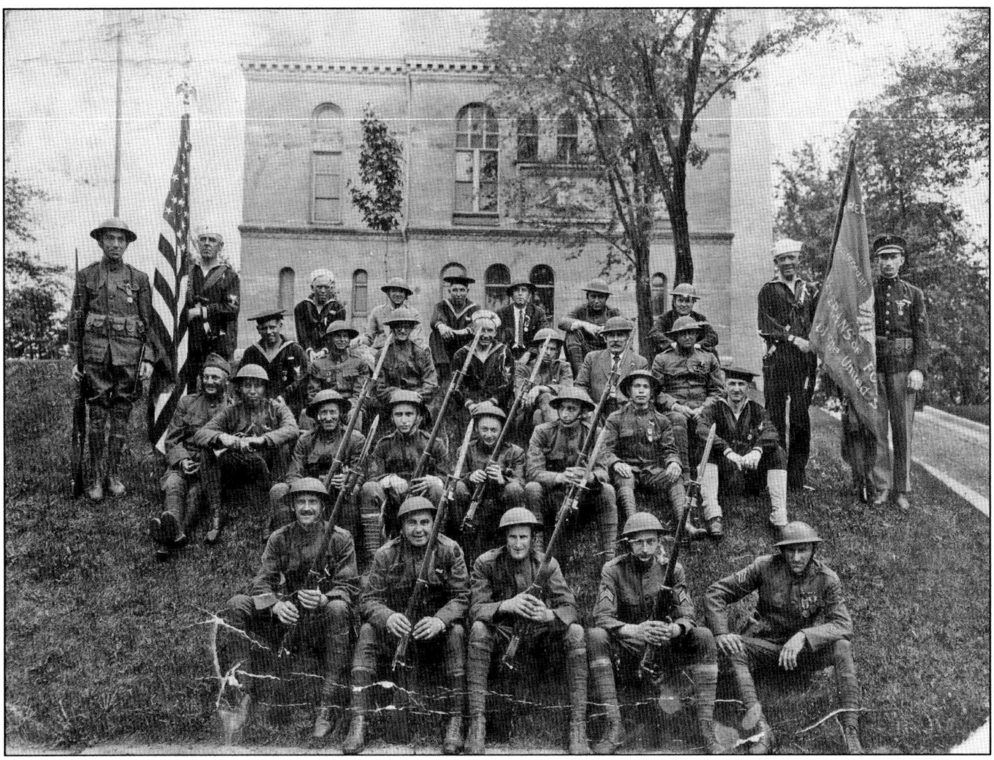

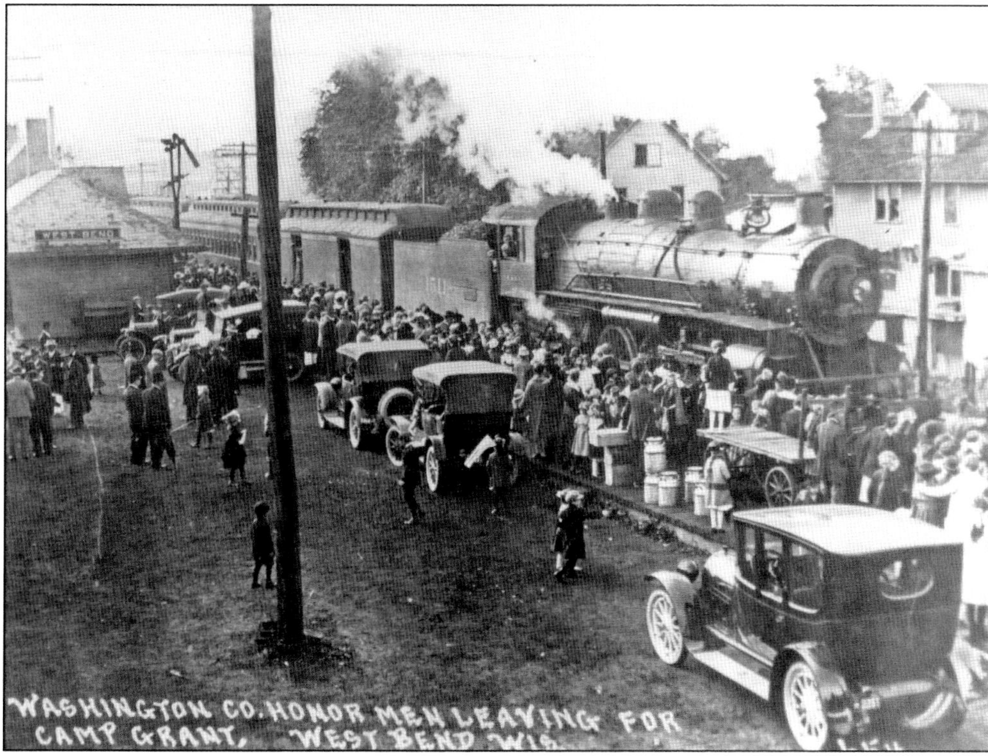

This photograph is of unidentified Washington County World War I soldiers leaving for training at Camp Grant in Rockford, Illinois, around 1917. It was taken outside the West Bend passenger rail depot. Camp Grant was one of the largest training facilities during World War I. Soldiers did basic training there before being assigned to their specific units and shipping out.

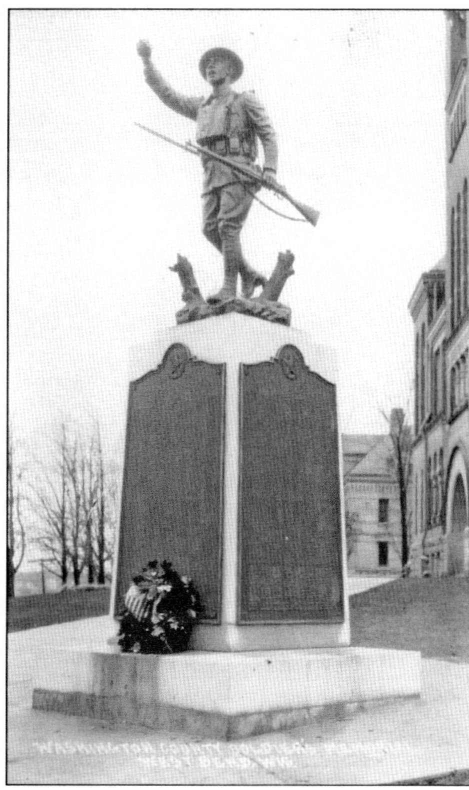

This monument, *The Spirit of the American Doughboy*, is dedicated to those who served in the armed forces of the United States. The monument is located at the corner of Fifth Avenue and Poplar Street, near the Old Courthouse Museum. Two other plaques, dedicated to those who died in World War II and the Korean Conflict, are mounted at the entrance to the Old Courthouse Museum.

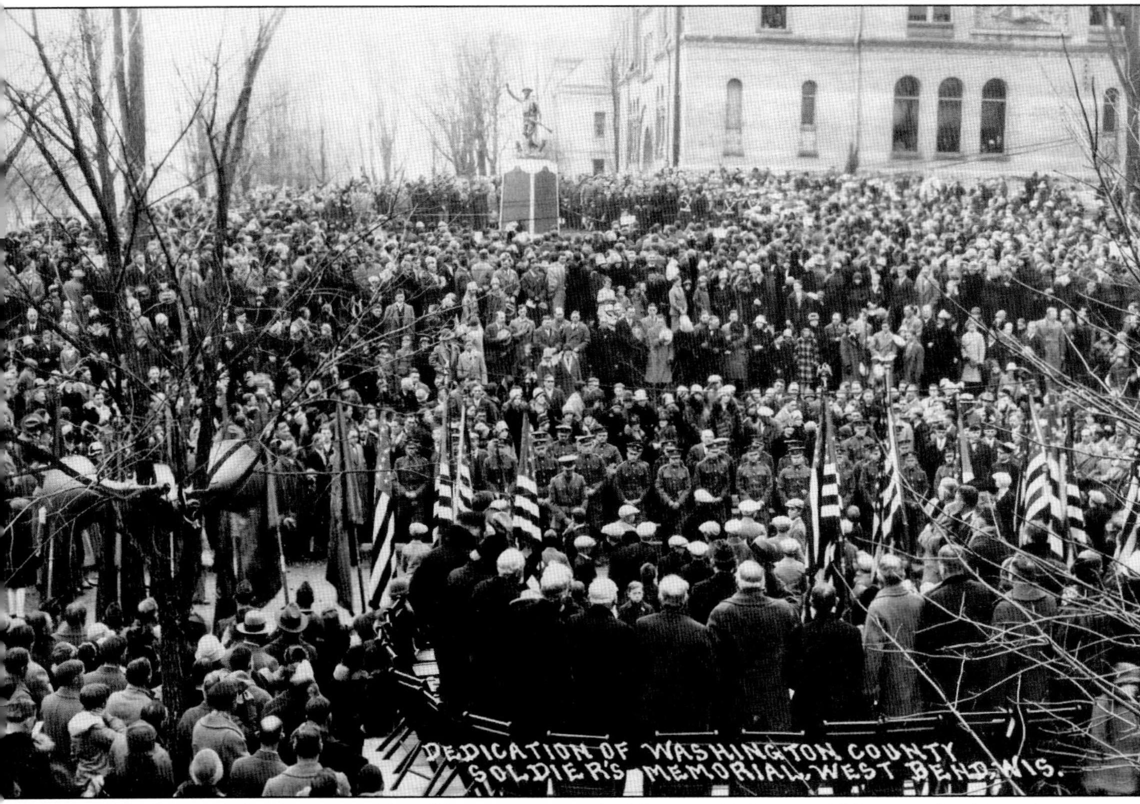

The Spirit of the American Doughboy statue on the Veterans' Memorial Plaza at the Courthouse Square was dedicated on November 13, 1927. Memorializing soldiers from the Civil War, Spanish-American War, and World War I, the work was one of many similar statues created around the country by sculptor E.M. Viquesney. Funds for the statue were in part provided by schoolchildren in a penny drive. Included in the dedication was a parade of soldiers, soldiers' wives, Boy Scouts and Girl Scouts, and nine bands. The parade stretched over a mile and a half long. It was estimated that over 10,000 people attended the dedication. A movie was taken of the event and shown later at the local Mermac Theater. In 1999, the statue went through extensive conservation work. Today, it still stands in the Veterans' Memorial Plaza near downtown West Bend, where it has been joined by two additional memorial statues.

During World War II, many of the city's manufacturers had contracts with the government to produce products for the military. Most of these contracts were fulfilled by female workers since many of the men had joined the army. Enger-Kress Pocketbook Company was no exception. The company switched from leather purses and wallets to military helmet straps, gun holsters, belts, and tents. (Photograph by Bob Boltz.)

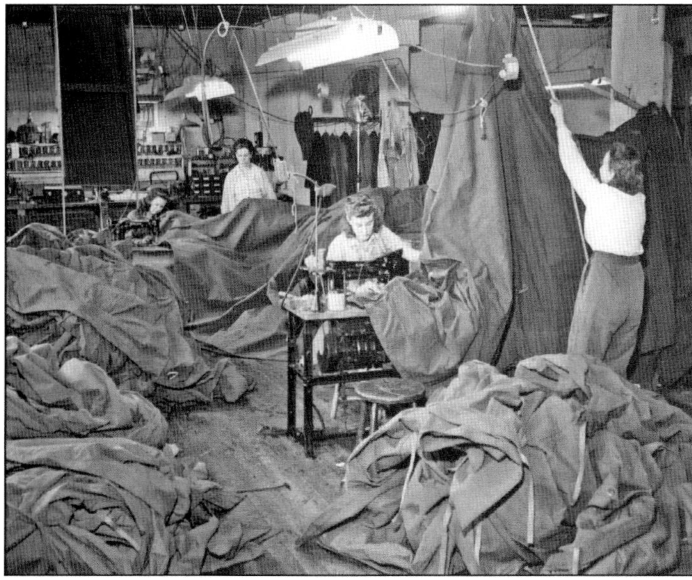

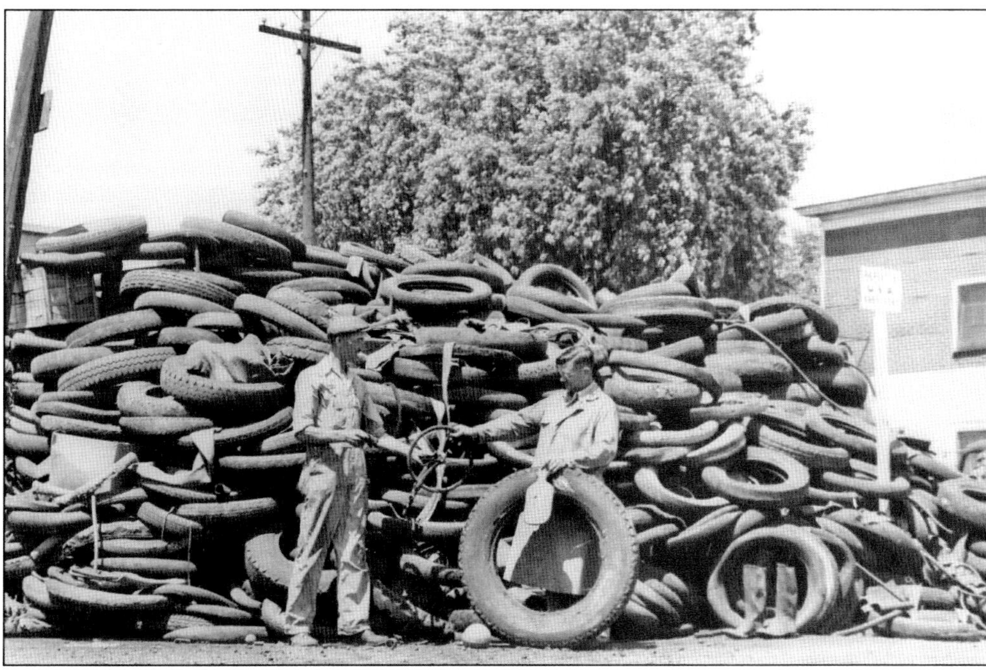

During World War II, the government promoted the collection of several types of scrap toward the war effort. One of these was scrap rubber. Here, two unidentified men collect old tires for the rubber drive. The recycled rubber was used in gas masks, boats, tires, and other military items. Rubber was in short supply because many of the natural supplies of rubber in Southeast Asia were cut off by Japan.

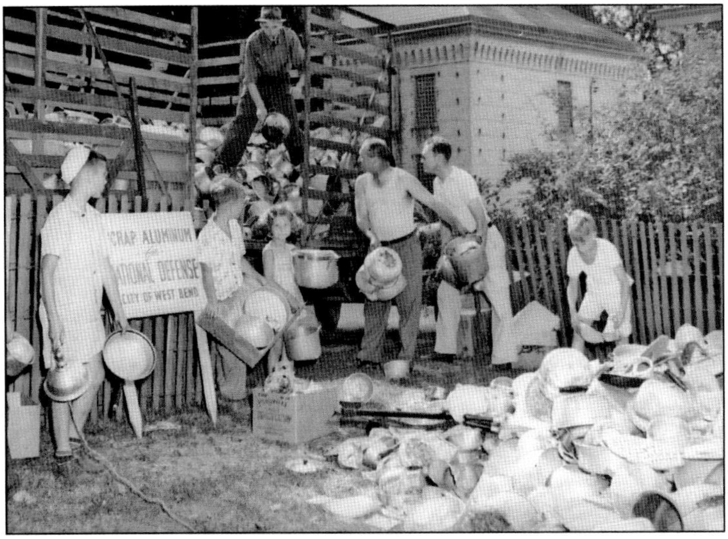

Along with most communities in the United States, West Bend participated in scrap drives to support the war effort during World War II. This collection site was located behind the Washington County Courthouse in July 1941. The chairman of the scrap drive, E.E. Skaliskey, is pictured in the center, loading scrap aluminum donated by citizens of West Bend.

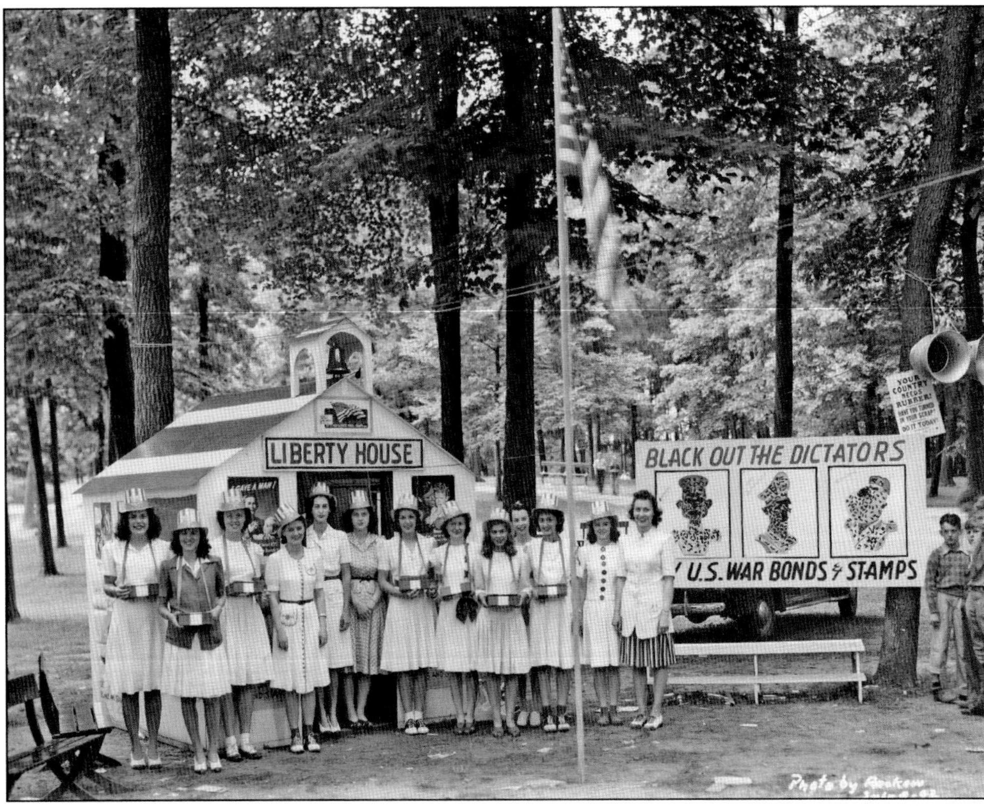

During World War II, the federal government sold war bonds to supplement the war effort. On July 4, 1942, these women helped by selling bond stamps during the annual festivities. The Liberty House was part of several war-effort events. The women are, from left to right, Marjorie Pick, Marguerite Weiss, Maribel Hanson, Gloria Krejci, Patricia O'Meara, unidentified, Betty Krieger, Violet Blecha, Vivian Geib, Joyce Wiskirchen, Shirley Geib, and two unidentified ladies.

Gasoline was not overlooked during the rationing efforts of World War II. In May 1942, gas was put on the rationed list in order to conserve it for use in the war effort. In this photograph, gas-ration stamps are being issued in the West Bend High School gym.

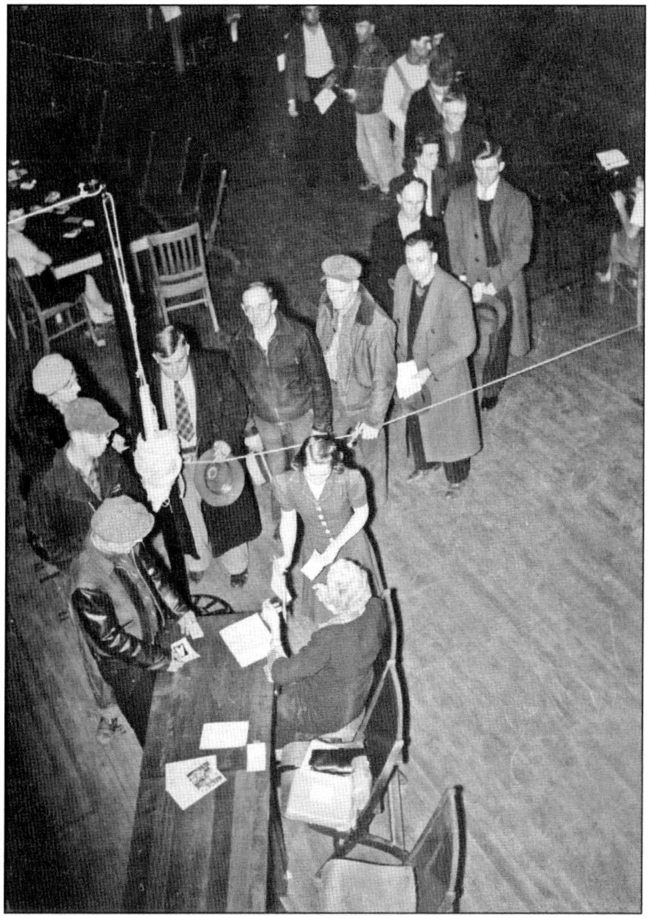

This Japanese midget submarine toured the United States during the 1940s. Here, the submarine is in downtown West Bend. Also known as two-person or "suicide" subs, these short-range machines were involved in the attack on Pearl Harbor in 1941. The captured submarine traveled to raise support and funds for the war effort.

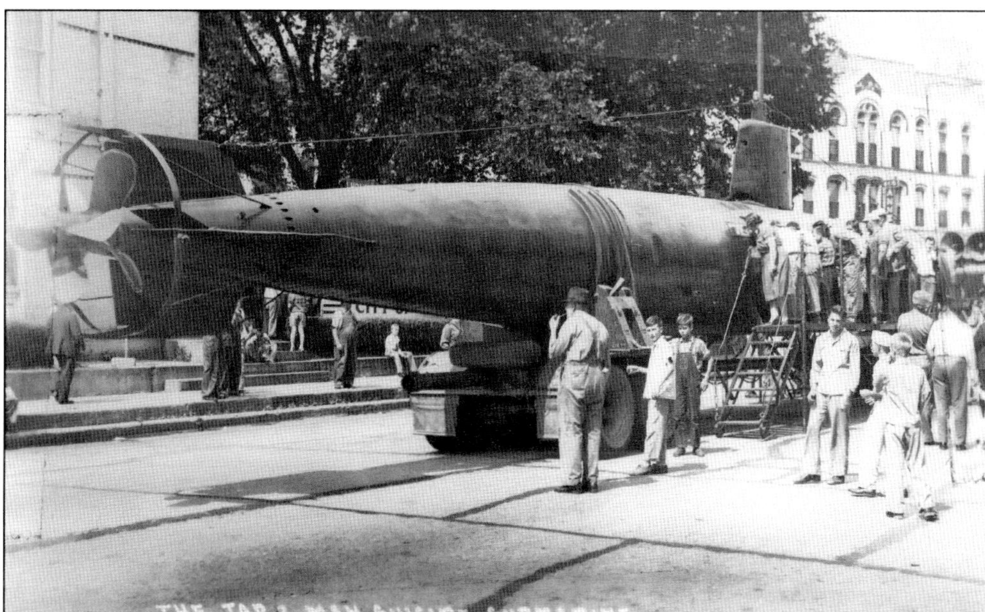

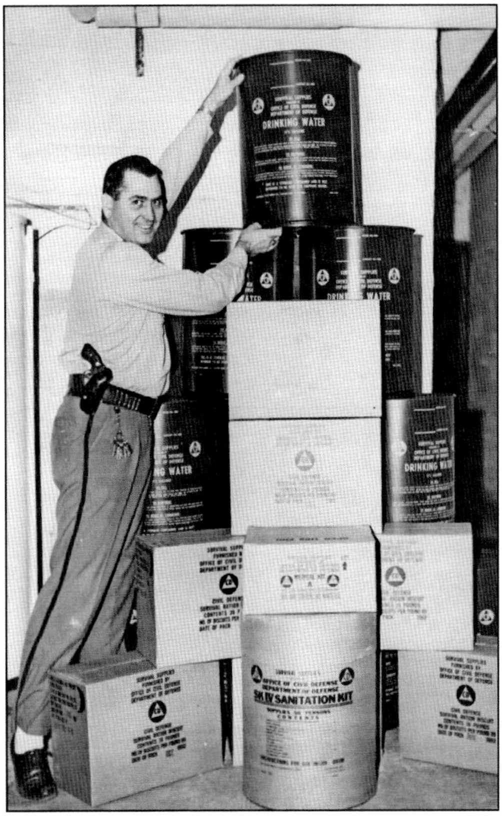

A local policeman stocks civil defense supplies in the 1950s. During the Cold War, government agencies, schools, and many individuals stockpiled long-lasting supplies in case of emergency. Drinking water, ration packets, and a chemical toilet are among the supplies here. Such items were often stored in the basements of public buildings used as shelters, such as schools.

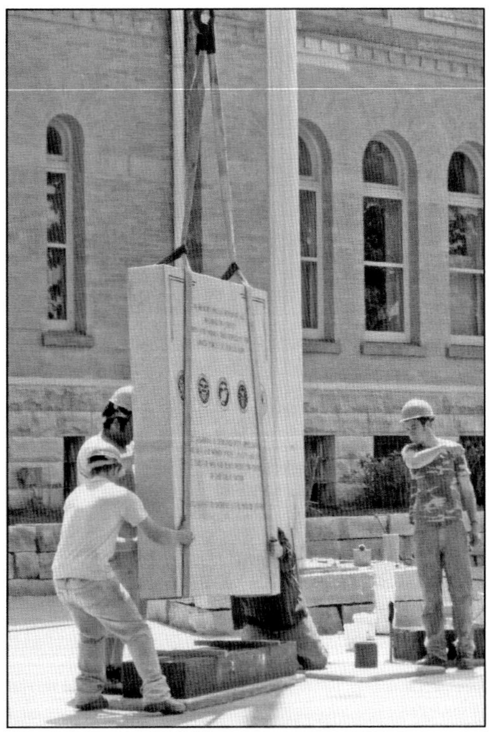

The Washington County Freedom Memorial was dedicated on May 31, 2008. Here, the final installation is taking place. Added to the Washington County Veterans Memorial Plaza, the memorial honors county soldiers killed in action since the Vietnam War. The project cost $150,000, most of which was raised through private donations. Two other monuments on the plaza honor veterans of previous conflicts.

Seven

Entertainment and Weather

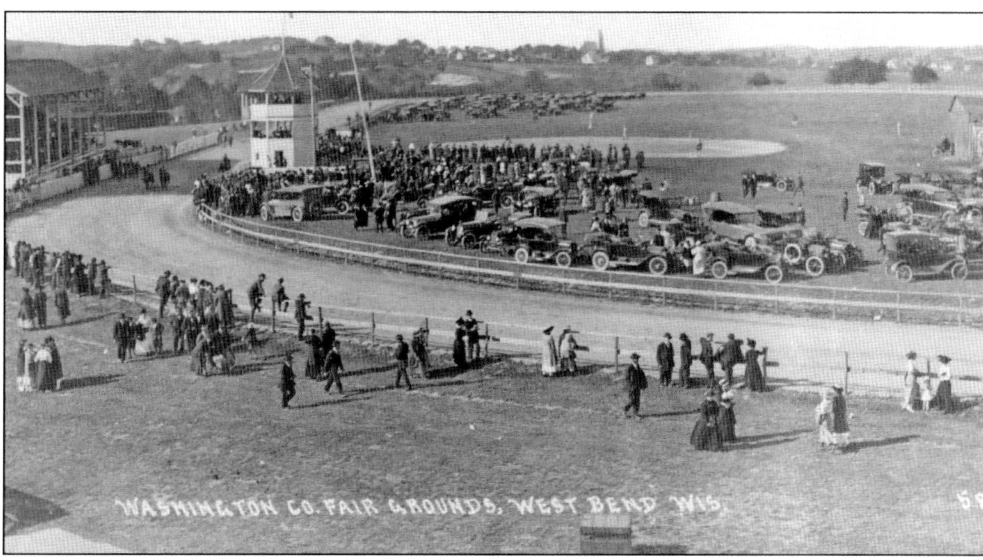

A day out at the fair was a highlight of the summer months. This photograph of the racetrack at the Washington County Fairgrounds around 1915 shows fairgoers waiting for the races and watching a baseball game taking place inside the racetrack. The fairgrounds were located on Pleasant Hill, where modern-day Fair Park Elementary School stands.

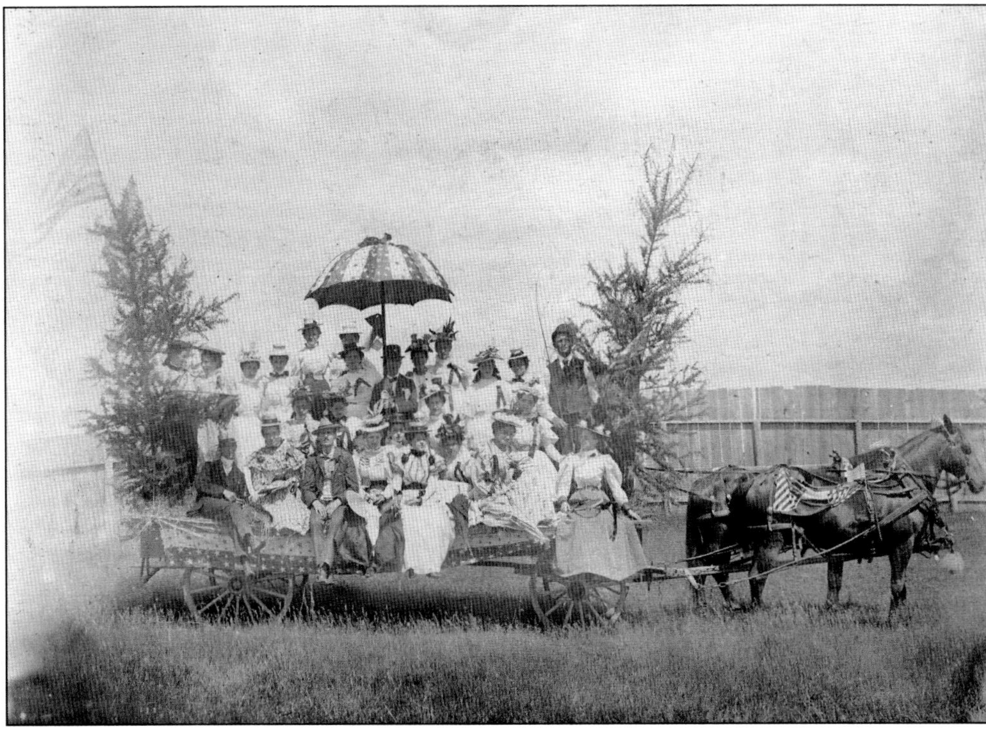

Decorated with a patriotic motif, these well-dressed women and gentlemen are likely at the Washington County Fairgrounds around 1890. At that time, the fair was held in West Bend near what is today Fair Park Elementary School.

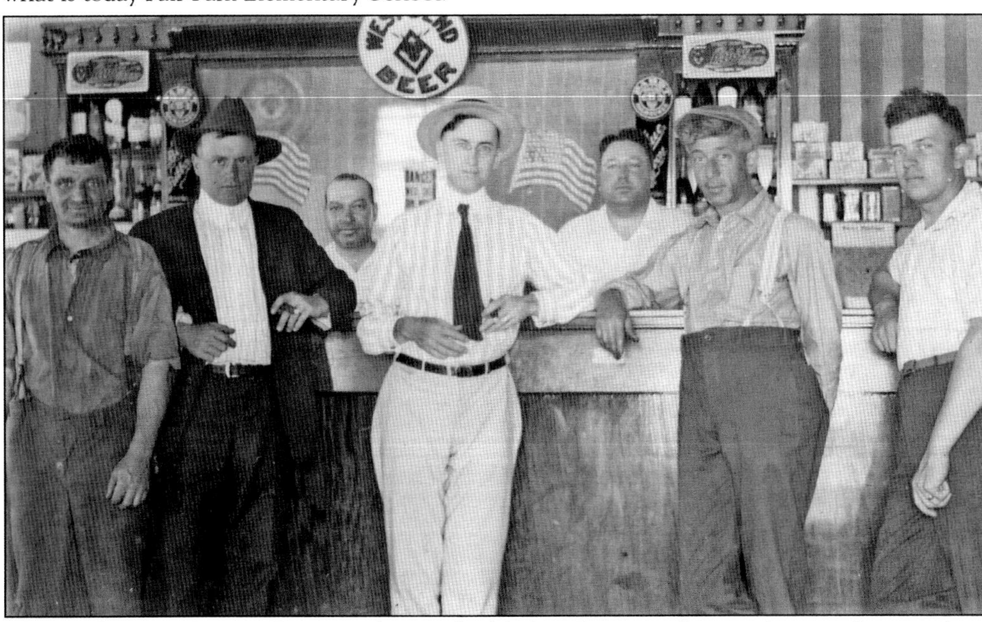

The Washington County Fair was always a highlight of summer. It served as a gathering place, an opportunity to take a break from the busy summer farming season and catch up with friends. It also provided education on the newest techniques and equipment. These men are taking a break in one of the beer tents.

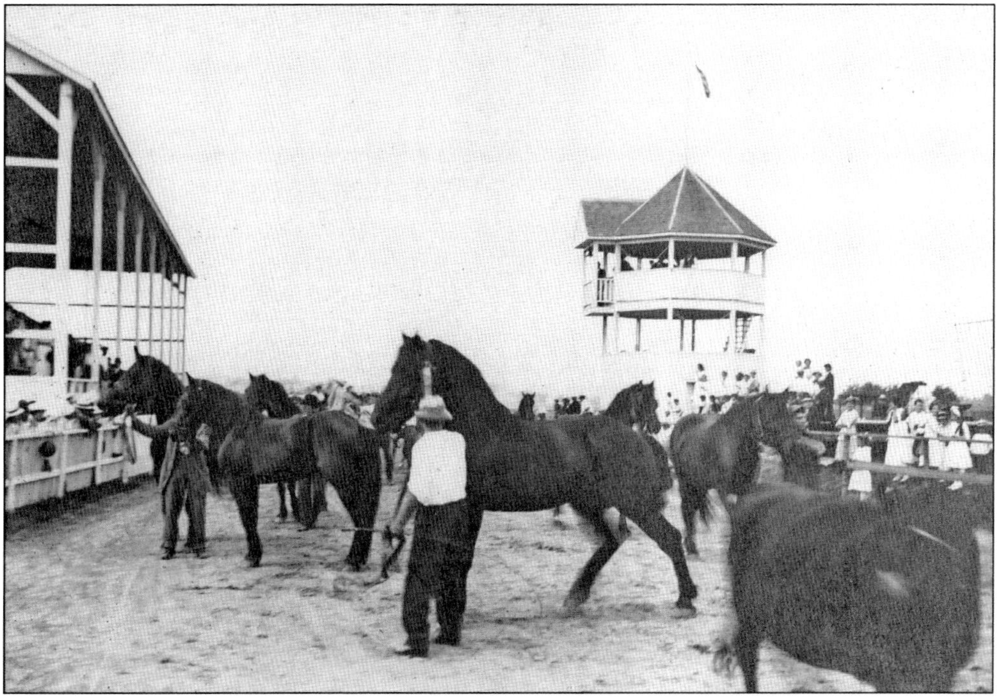

This image shows a horse show on the racetrack at the Washington County Fair around 1905. At the time, the fairgrounds were located on what was known as Pleasant Hill near today's Fair Park Elementary School. The first Washington County Fair was held in 1858 at the Courthouse Square in West Bend. The last county fair held in West Bend was in 1937; after that, it was held in Slinger.

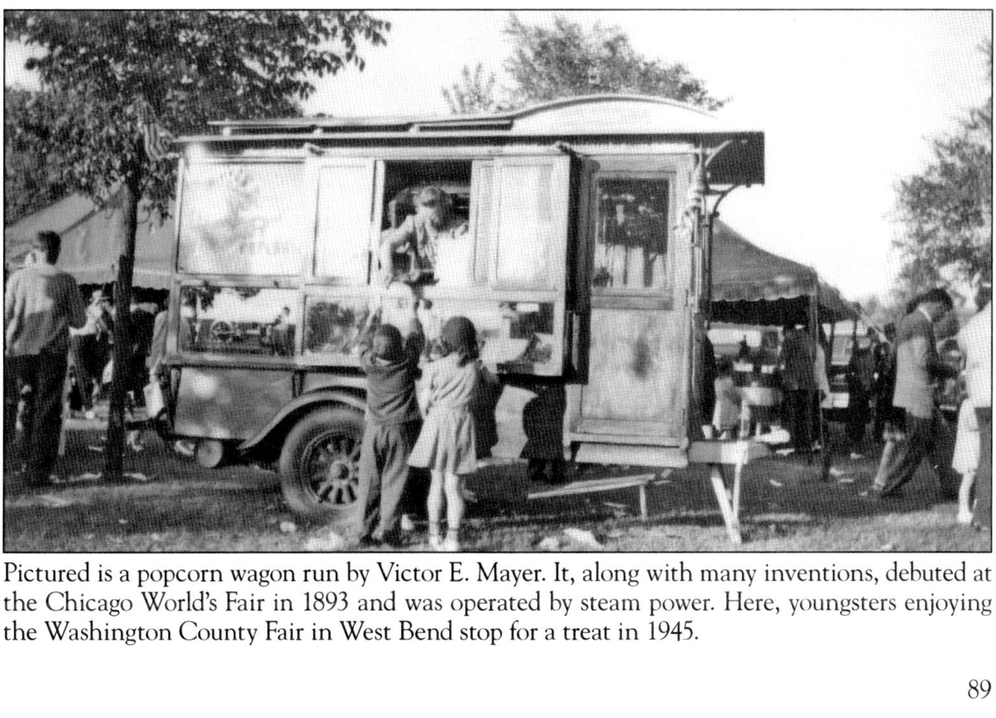

Pictured is a popcorn wagon run by Victor E. Mayer. It, along with many inventions, debuted at the Chicago World's Fair in 1893 and was operated by steam power. Here, youngsters enjoying the Washington County Fair in West Bend stop for a treat in 1945.

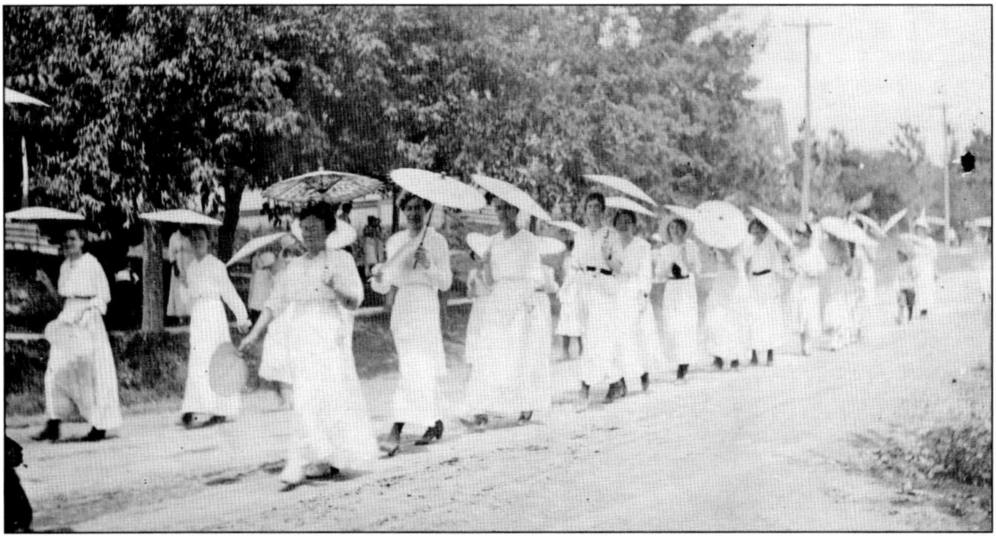

This parade of local ladies is, unfortunately, not well documented. Only two of the women are identified, sisters Agatha and Hedwig Weinert. Both were employed by Enger-Kress Pocketbook Company in the sewing department. Agatha later worked in the laundry department at St. Joseph Community Hospital. It is likely this parade took place during July 4th celebrations around 1910.

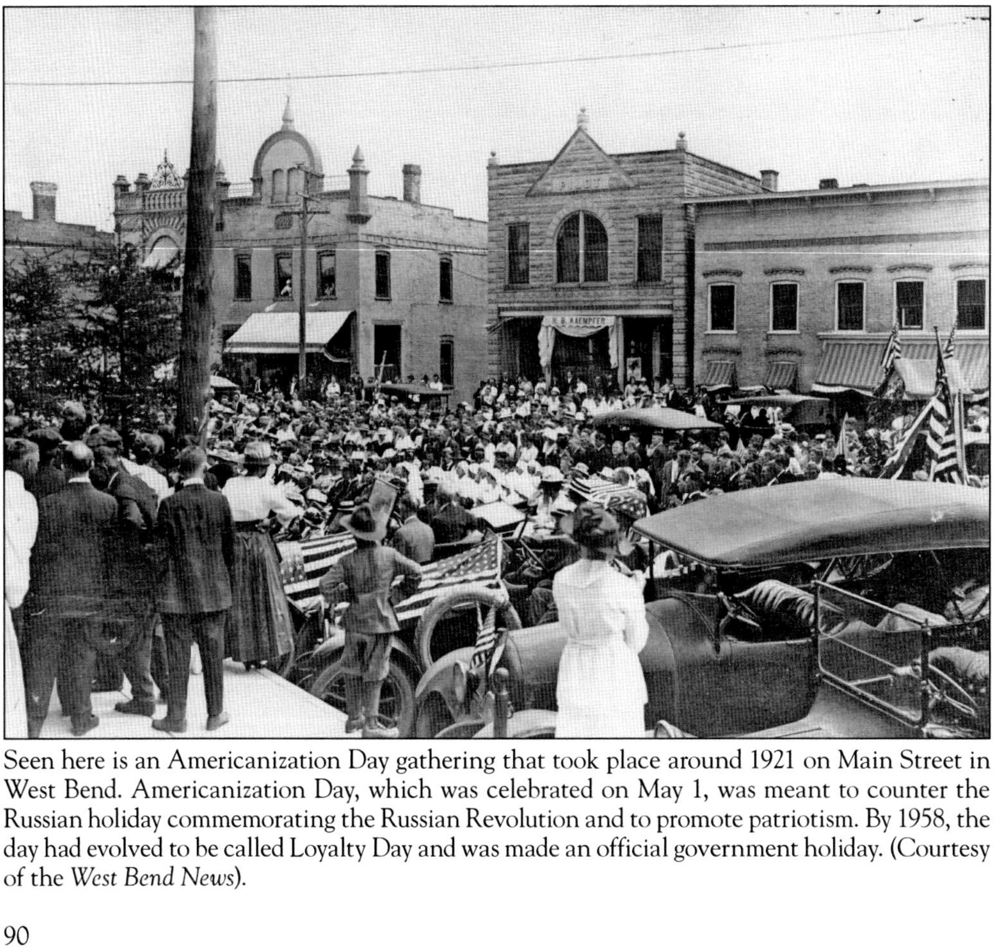

Seen here is an Americanization Day gathering that took place around 1921 on Main Street in West Bend. Americanization Day, which was celebrated on May 1, was meant to counter the Russian holiday commemorating the Russian Revolution and to promote patriotism. By 1958, the day had evolved to be called Loyalty Day and was made an official government holiday. (Courtesy of the *West Bend News*).

In July 1935, West Bend put on a golden-anniversary homecoming celebrating 50 years since its incorporation as a city. This photograph was taken downtown looking south down Main Street from the intersection of Mill Street. The anniversary program included a parade and the dedication of City Park, today known as Regner Park. (Courtesy of the *West Bend News*.)

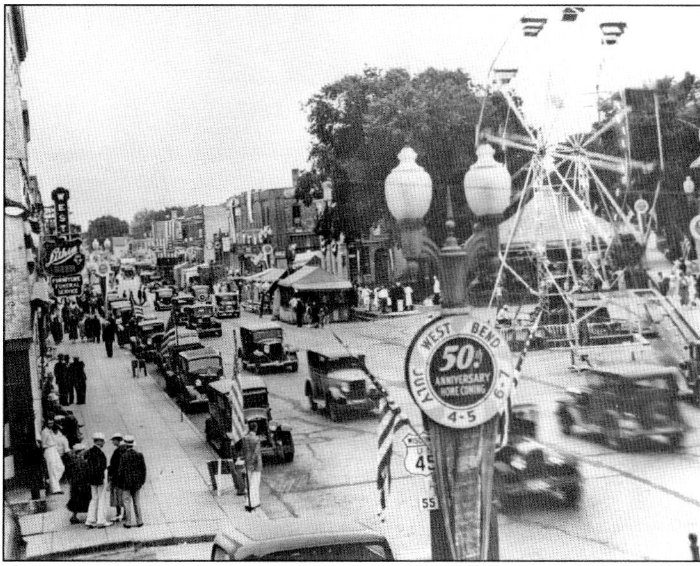

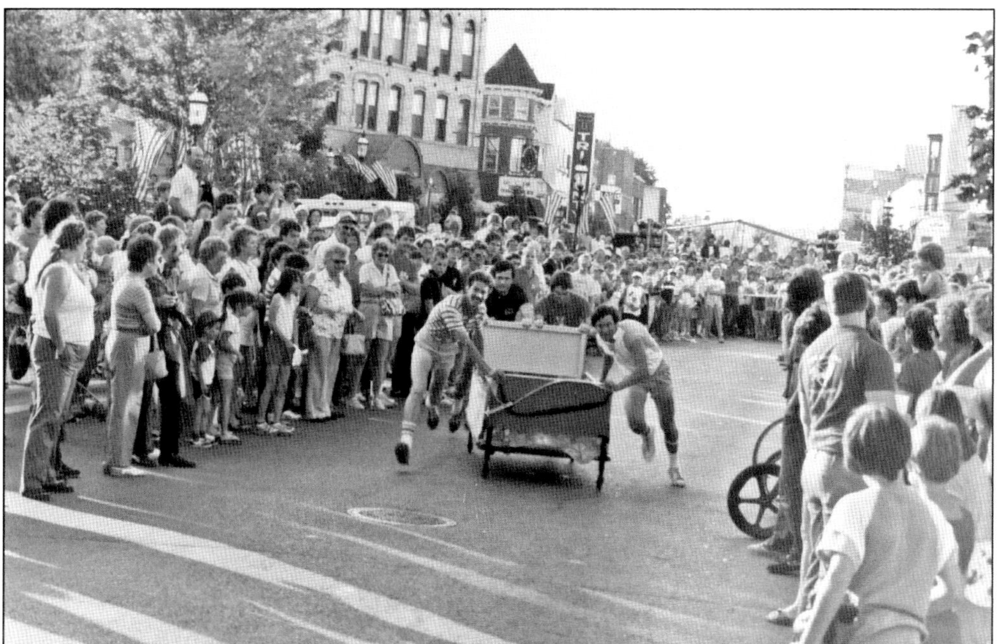

In 1985, West Bend celebrated 100 years since incorporation as a city. Citywide activities took place. Concerts by local bands, Roy Orbison, and Ricky Nelson were held at Regner Park. Downtown saw parades, music, and soapbox races. Activities also included free Jazzercise classes in the blocked-off street and guests dressing in historical costumes.

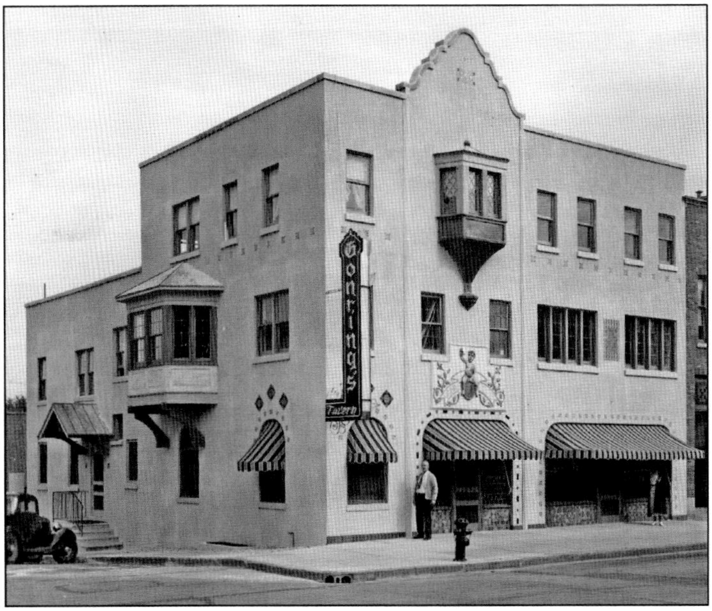

Michael J. Gonring Sr. is standing in front of his newly remodeled tavern building around 1937 on the corner of Main and Mill Streets in downtown West Bend. Gonring owned the American House and Tavern, which stood at the corner before the remodel. The new building was styled after northern German architecture and provided space for the tavern, a rental space for a store, and apartments above.

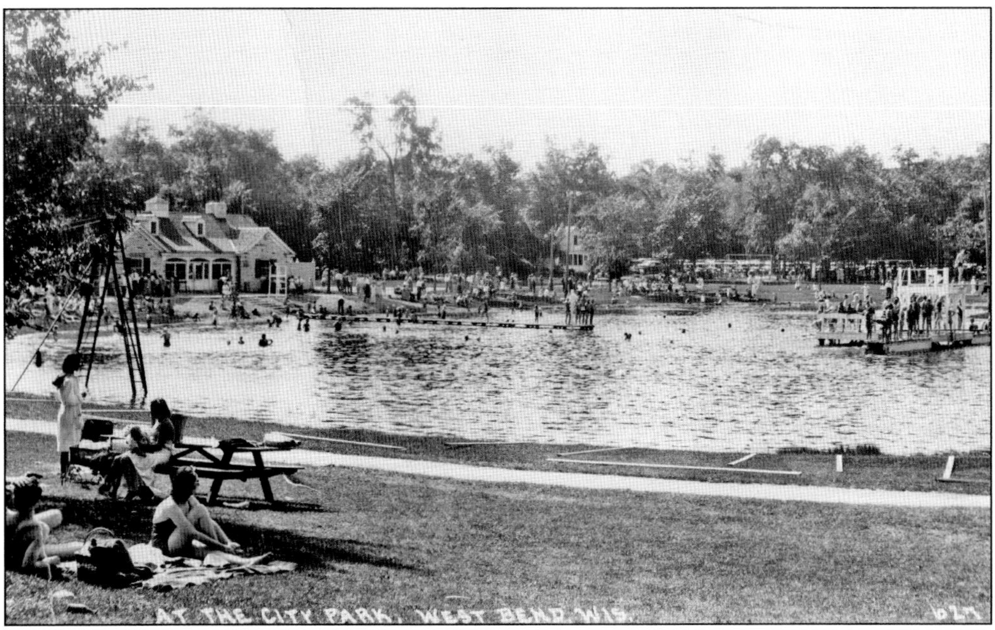

The lagoon at today's Regner Park is pictured around 1950. The lagoon was part of several projects funded in part by the New Deal program. The bathhouse was completed in 1935 and still stands in remodeled form. Today, along with the pond, there is a splash pad nearby for zero-depth water play.

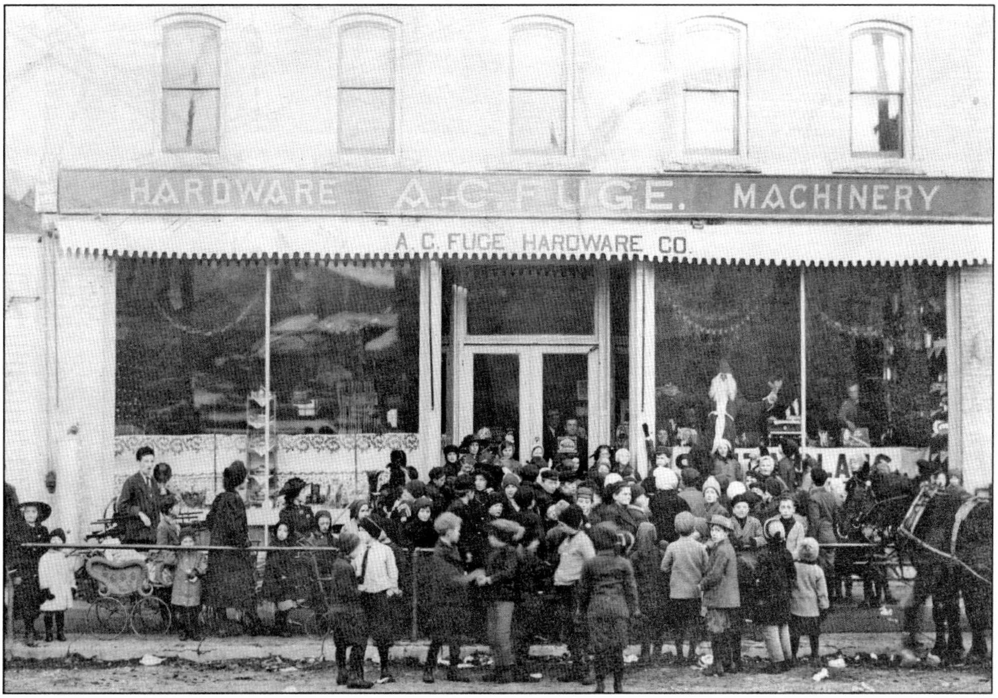

In December 1910, children from the area crowded the street outside Fuge Hardware Store on Main Street for a chance to visit with Santa Claus. This annual children's Christmas party was a tradition for many local families. Fuge Hardware was in operation at varying downtown locations from 1869 to 1931.

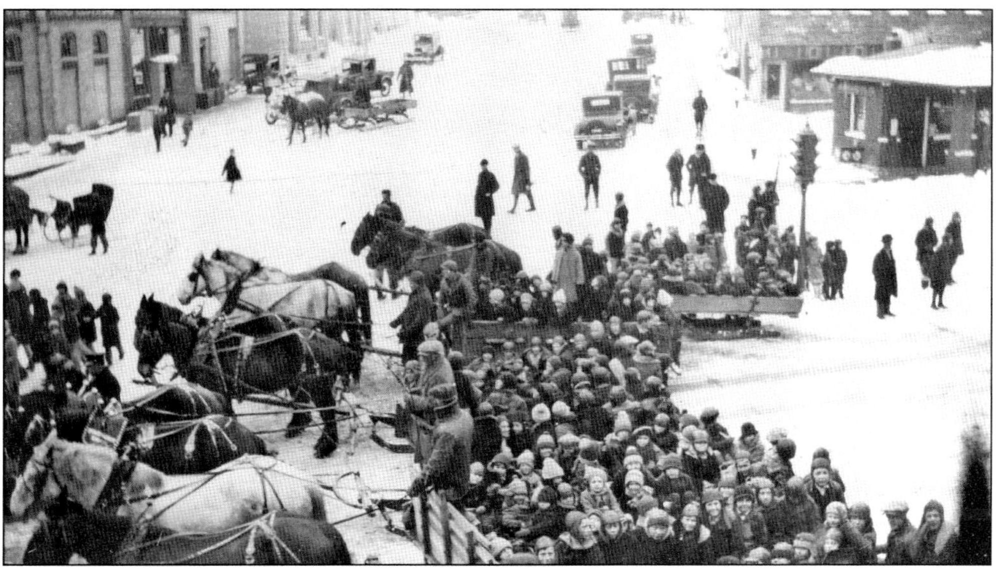

This photograph shows the children's sleigh ride parade on Main Street around 1912. Fuge Hardware Company held an annual children's Christmas party for local kids. Along with sleigh rides, children met Santa and were given sweet treats and nuts. The party also served to bring parents into the store to do their Christmas shopping.

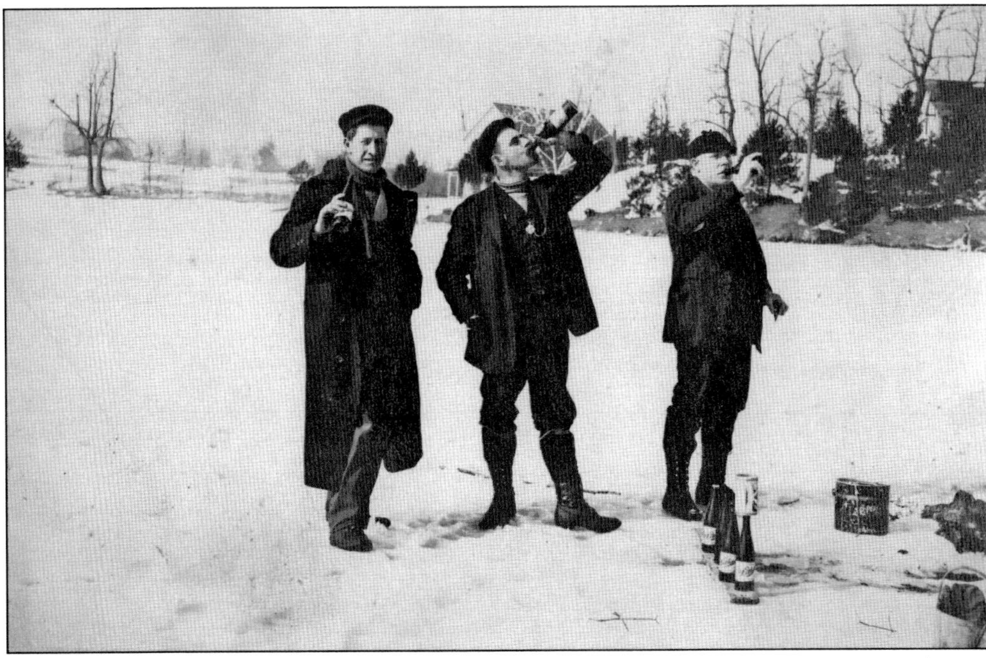

These men are ice fishing on the Milwaukee River around 1900. A common pastime and social occasion still today, ice fishing was often accompanied by alcoholic drinks. The fishermen here are drinking the West Bend–brewed Lithia beer. Jacob Kaempfer is the man on the right.

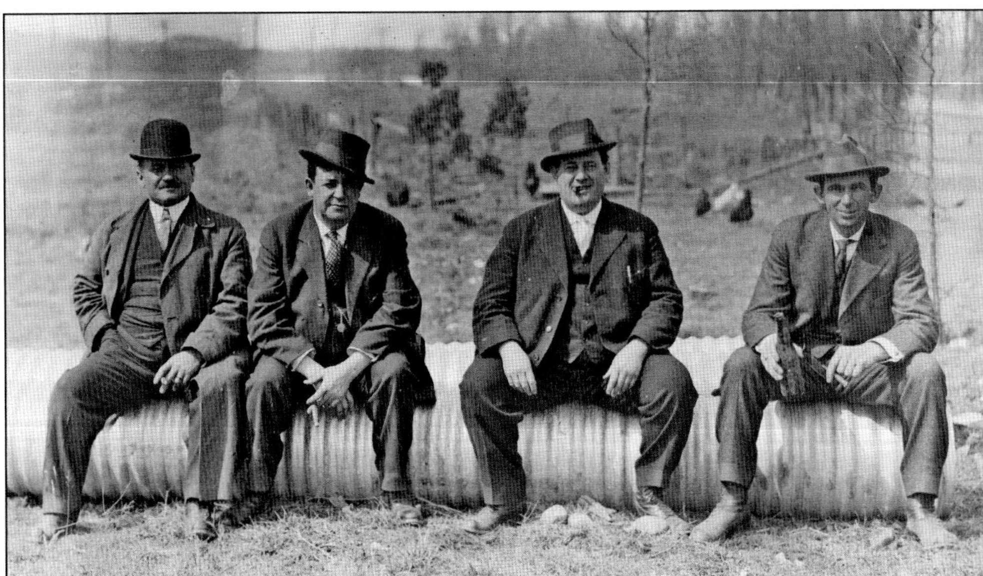

One common way to relax was to have a cigar and beer with friends. Here, Fred "Ackerman" Schultz (far right) and Joseph F. Huber (second from the left) unwind with two friends on an culvert pipe waiting to be installed around 1912. Huber was the owner of the local newspaper, the *West Bend News*. (Photograph by Herman Trakat.)

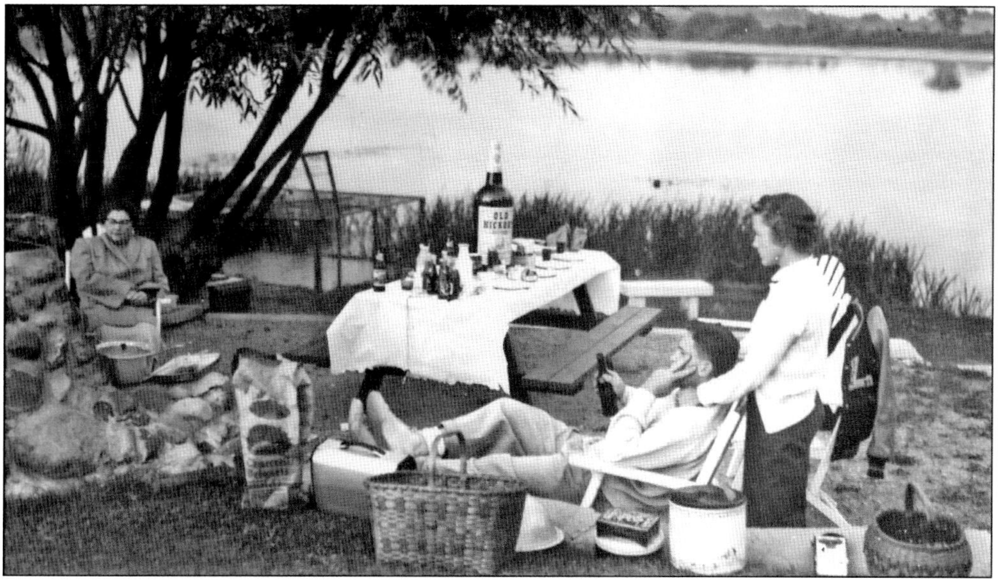

Picnics and outdoor parties were a great way to relax with friends. Here, the Weiss family is hosting a picnic in their backyard on Kuester Lane North around 1960. The woman wearing a coat on the left is Ethel Weiss Gill, the West Bend High School librarian.

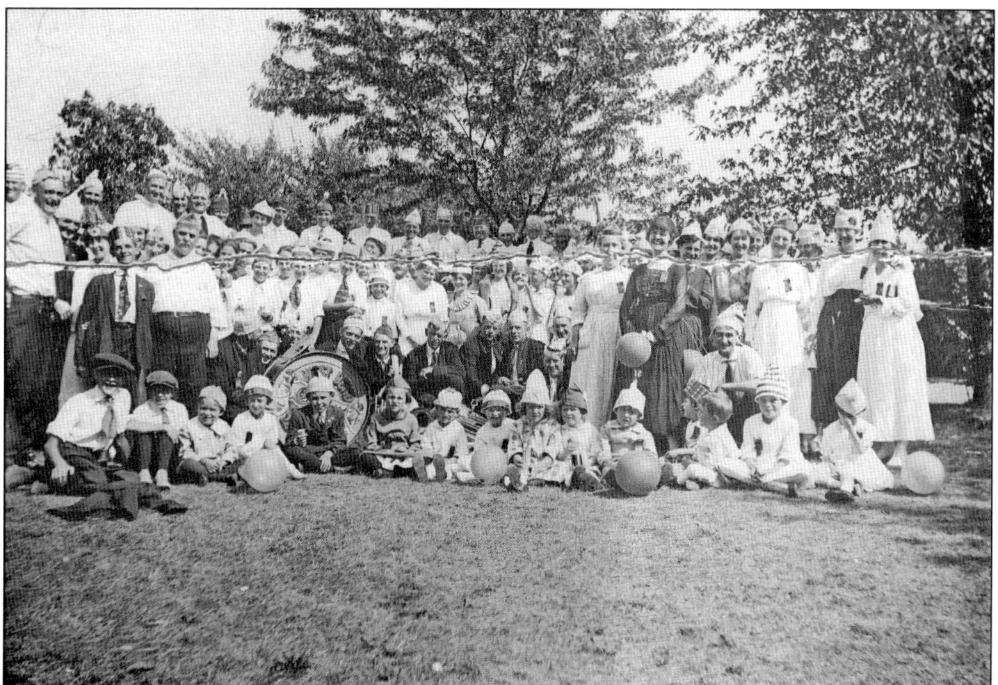

Many of the local manufacturers and businesses had an annual picnic for their employees. The event allowed workers and their families to socialize and showed the company's appreciation for a year of hard work. Here, Amity Leather Products Company employees and families have gathered for a day of food and fun around 1925.

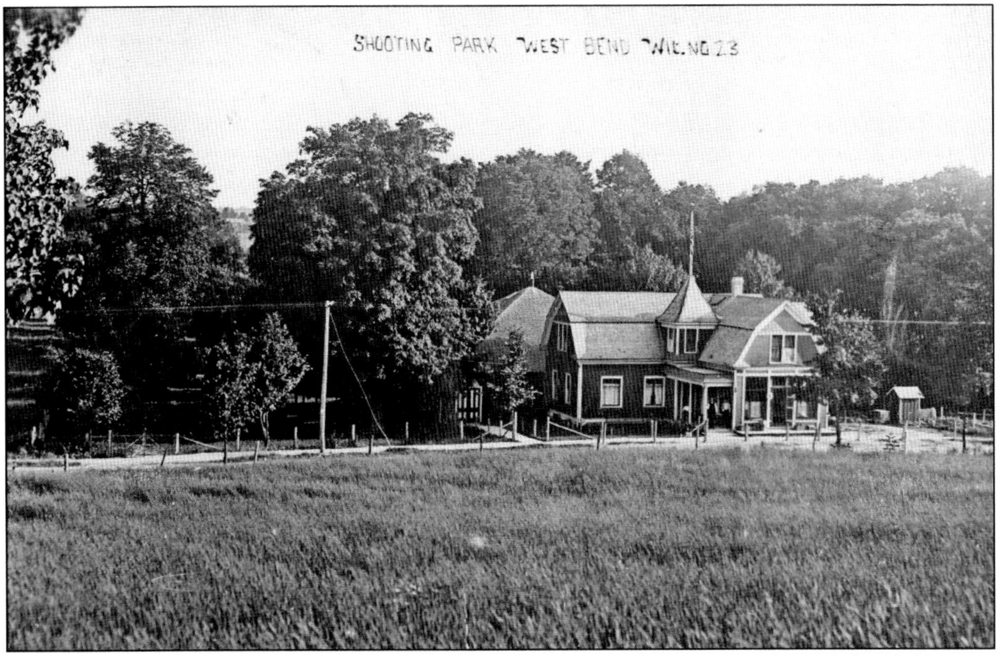

This photograph is of the clubhouse in Shooting Park. Opened in 1868 as a private park, the name derives from the German *schuetzenverein*, competitive sport shooting or marksmanship clubs set up in a manner similar to today's golf clubs. The site is now the location of the Kettle Moraine YMCA on Washington Street.

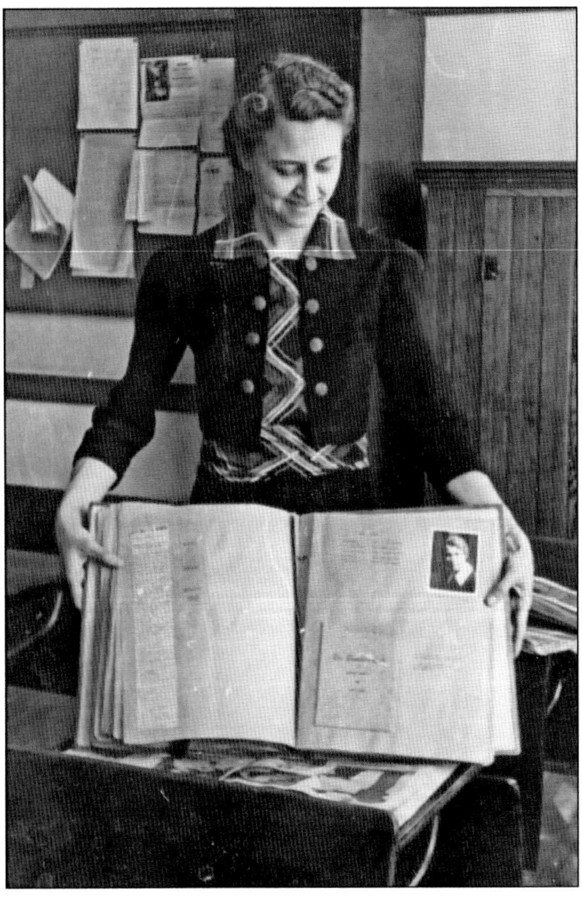

Here, teacher Ruth Nickel holds a West Bend Woman's Club scrapbook at the hobby show held at West Bend High School in 1940. The West Bend Women's Club was organized in September 1926. Along with starting the first public library in the city, the group put on the children's theater and supported many other community events and charities.

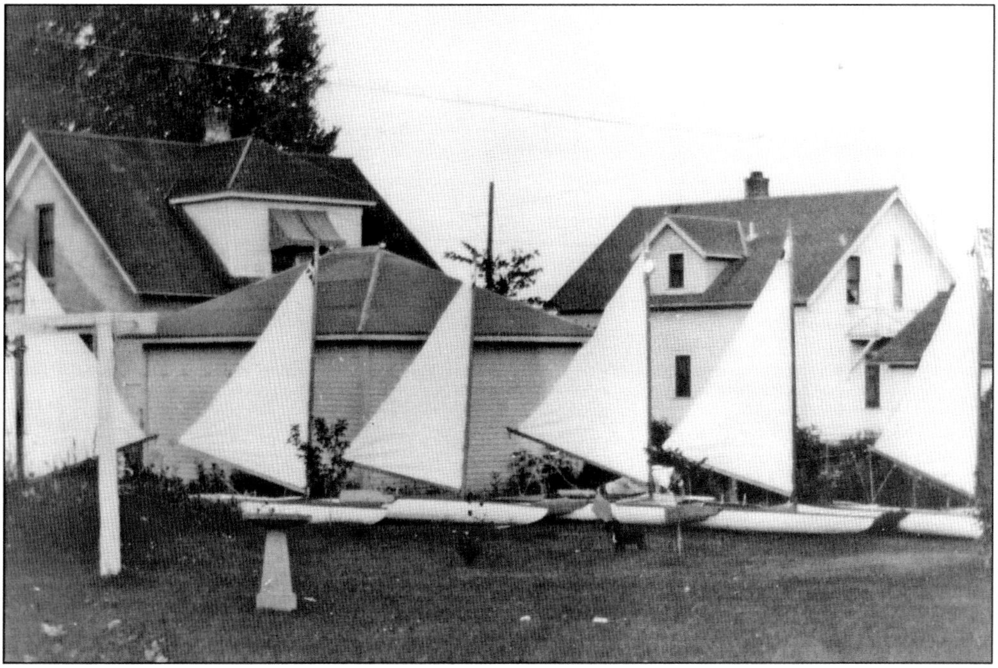

The Sea Scout organization was a club similar to the Boy Scouts but focused on water activities. The West Bend club was founded in 1939. In 1940, the Sea Scouts built their own one-man sailboats, seen here, in Albion Loebe's backyard. Along with learning to sail, the scouts participated in community service and learned new skills, such as first-aid and navigation.

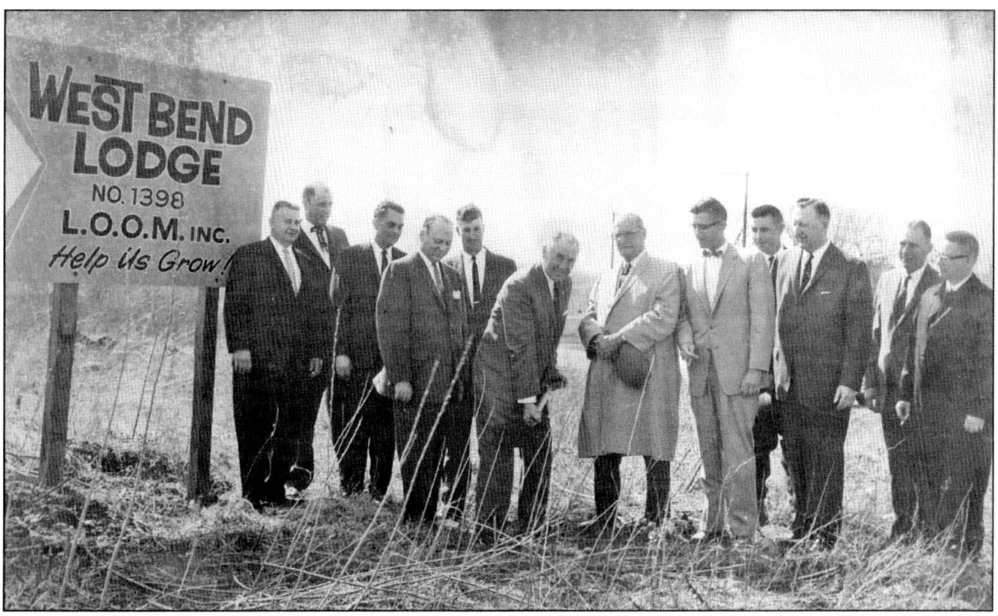

Ground-breaking for the Moose Lodge on Eighteenth Street and Chestnut Street occurred on April 29, 1963. It was also the 50th anniversary year for the local Loyal Order of the Moose. There were only 50 members in the lodge at the time of its founding in 1913. By 1953, the group had more than 700 members.

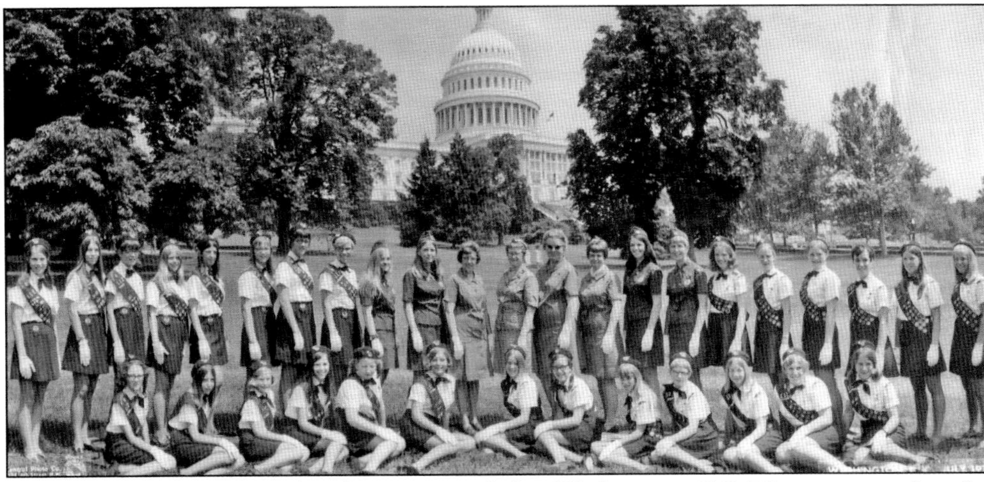

In July 1970, the West Bend Girl Scouts traveled to Washington, DC. The troop was founded in 1921 by 17 young women. For an unknown reason, the group disbanded in 1924 but was reorganized again in 1927. This time, there were enough interested girls for four troops. The Girl Scouts gathered to learn new skills and provide community service.

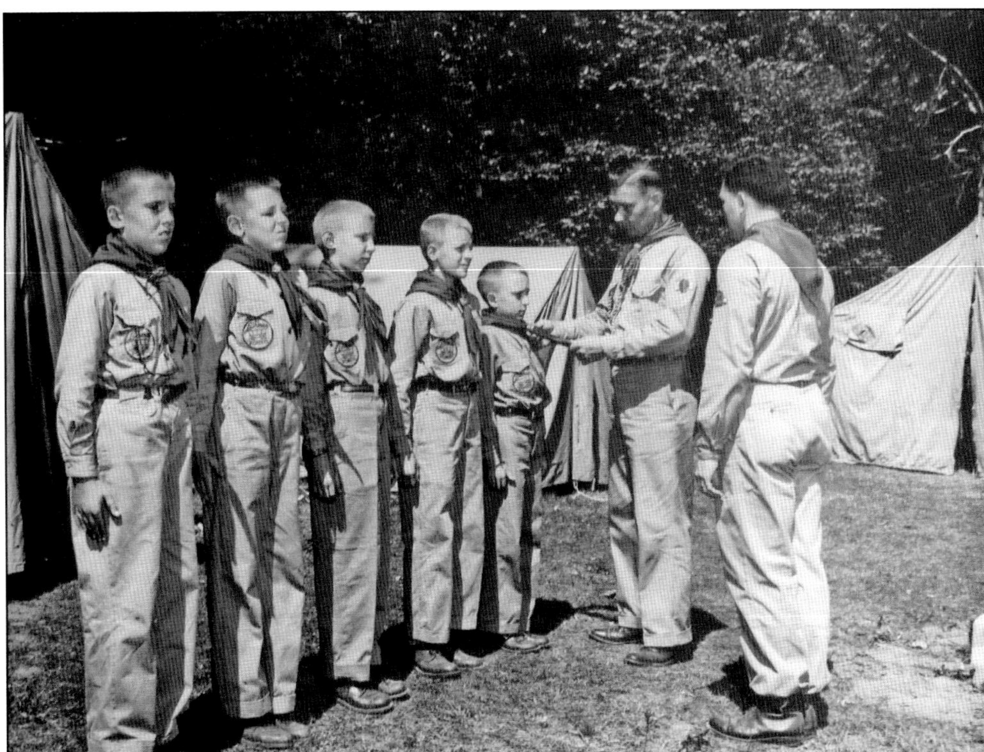

Leader John Gerner inspects his troop of Lutheran Pioneers of St. John's Evangelical Lutheran Church in 1954. The Pioneers were a group of young men from the church who met to learn basic camping skills. In 1963, the group changed its name to the Rangers and began a group for girls, the Rangerettes. (Photograph by Bob Boltz.)

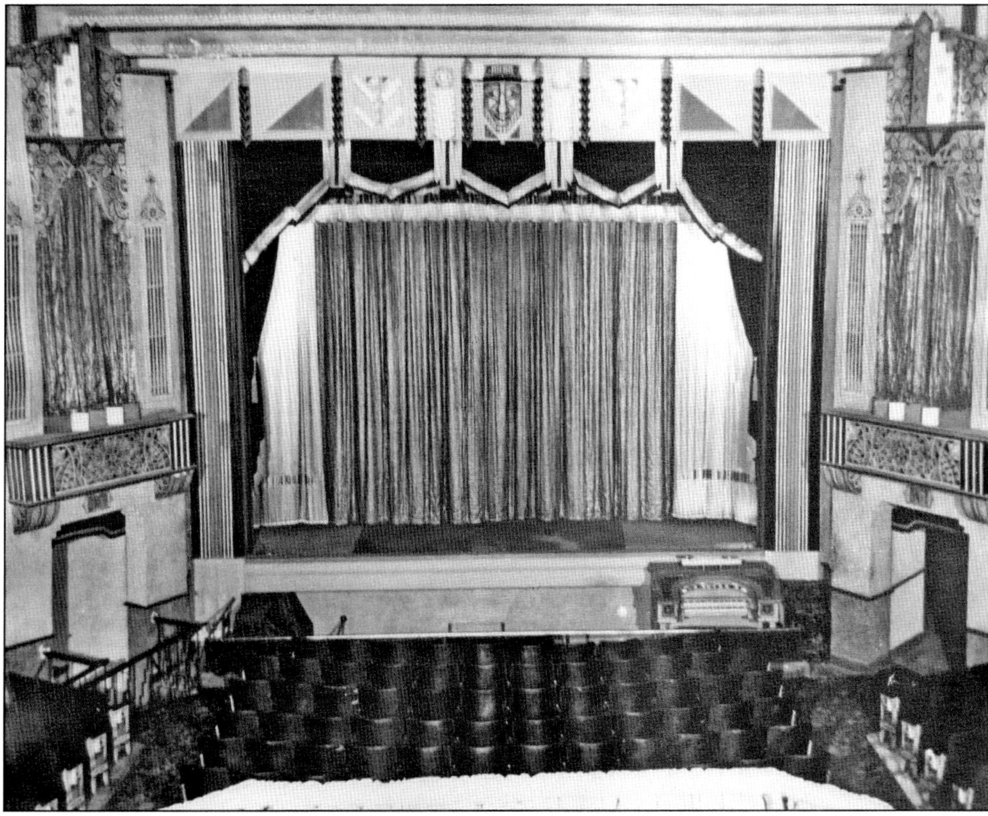

This photograph shows the interior of the West Bend Theater in 1951. The theater was located on Main Street, and the distinctive "West Bend" sign still hangs outside today. The building was constructed in 1929 as a single-room theater. Over the years, it was divided into three theaters. The business changed hands several times and finally closed in 2007.

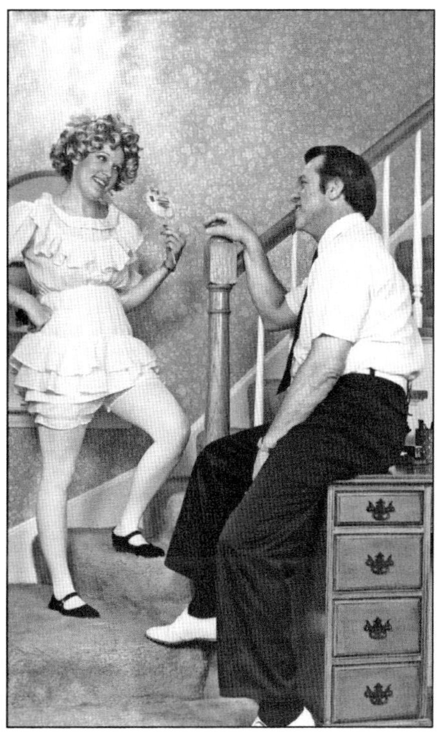

The Musical Masquers, one of West Bend's community theater groups (and the longest-running), began in 1962 with a production of *The Pajama Game*. In the early years, the majority of its performances were Broadway shows. In more recent years, the company began producing a comedy or drama along with an annual musical.

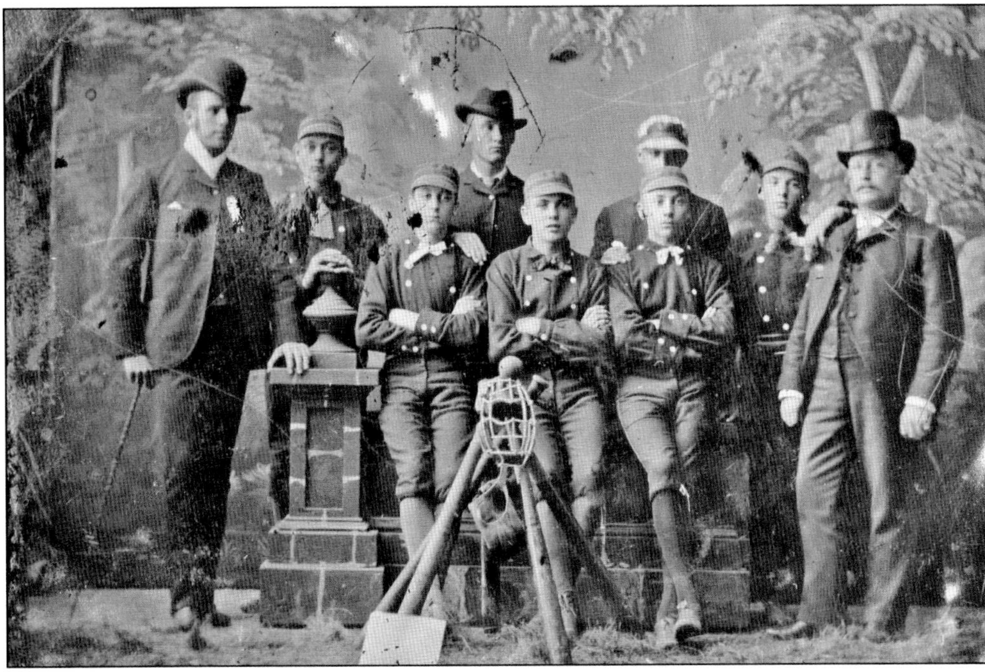

The local baseball team, the West Bend Blues, was captured on a tintype in 1887. Pictured from left to right are (first row) Albert Heipp, George Kuehlthau, and Math Fohn; (second row) manager Emil Koenen, George Weiss, manager Albert Glantz, Sam Weller, John Witteman, and manager Arthur Franckenberg.

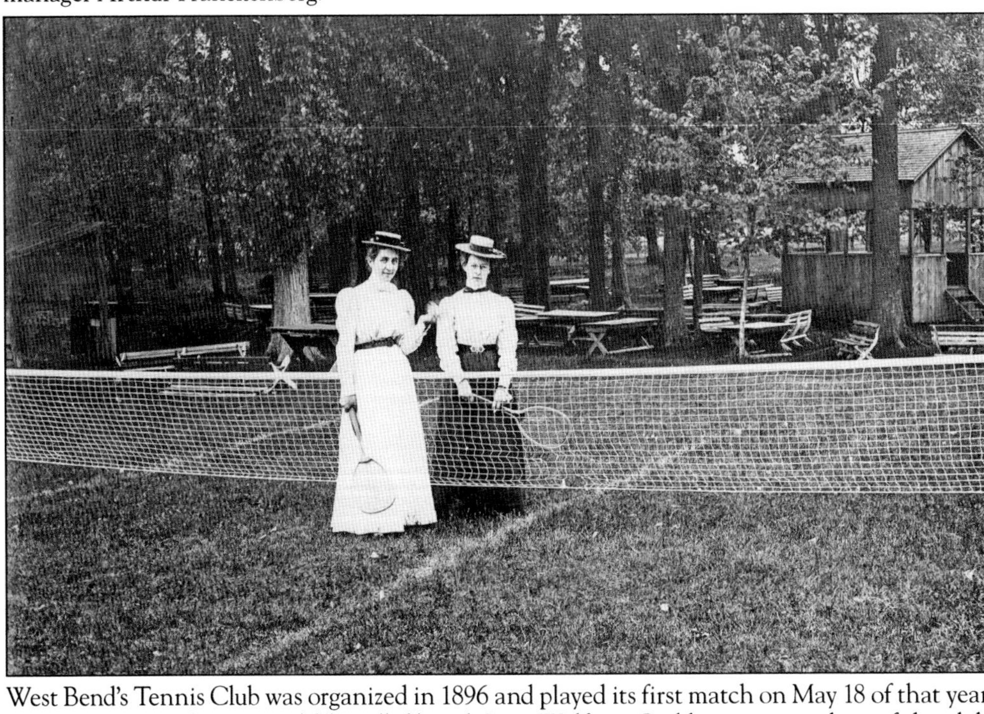

West Bend's Tennis Club was organized in 1896 and played its first match on May 18 of that year. These women, Lulu Rix Kuehlthau (left) and Cora Wolfrum Stubbs, were members of the club. This photograph was taken on a court at either Moser's Park or Shooting Park around 1899.

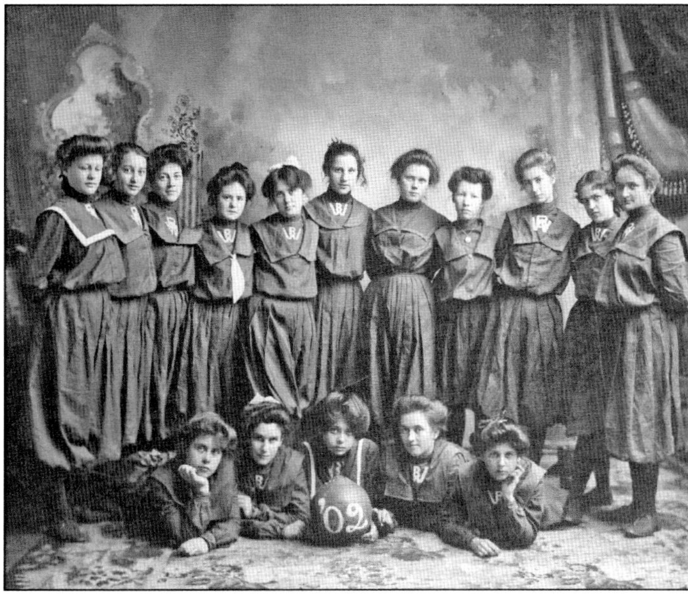

This photograph shows the earliest known West Bend High School girls' basketball team in 1902. Sebastian Albrecht was their coach. The players are from left to right (first row) Flora Wagner, Olive Flaherty, Minnie Weinand, Georgia Maxon, and Edna Klumb; (second row) Dorchen Pick, Florence Stork, Clarinda Sievers, Marion Mooers, Millie O'Meara, Katherine Thoma, Clara Law, Rachel Lynch, Madge McCormick, Irene Bennett, and Abbie Meyer.

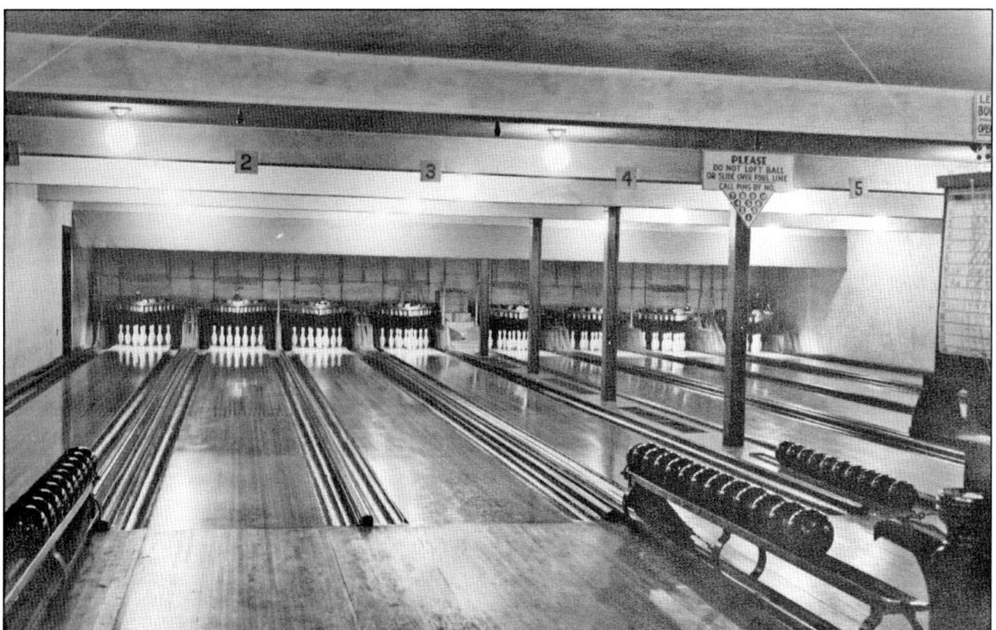

Gonring's Bowling Alley and Tavern was owned by Michael Gonring from 1932 to 1937. In 1937, Michael decided to go back to managing the American House Hotel and Tavern, which he also owned. The business was purchased by John Herdt, who resigned his position in the office of Enger-Kress Pocketbook Company to manage his new venture. (Photograph by Cliff Hutchenson.)

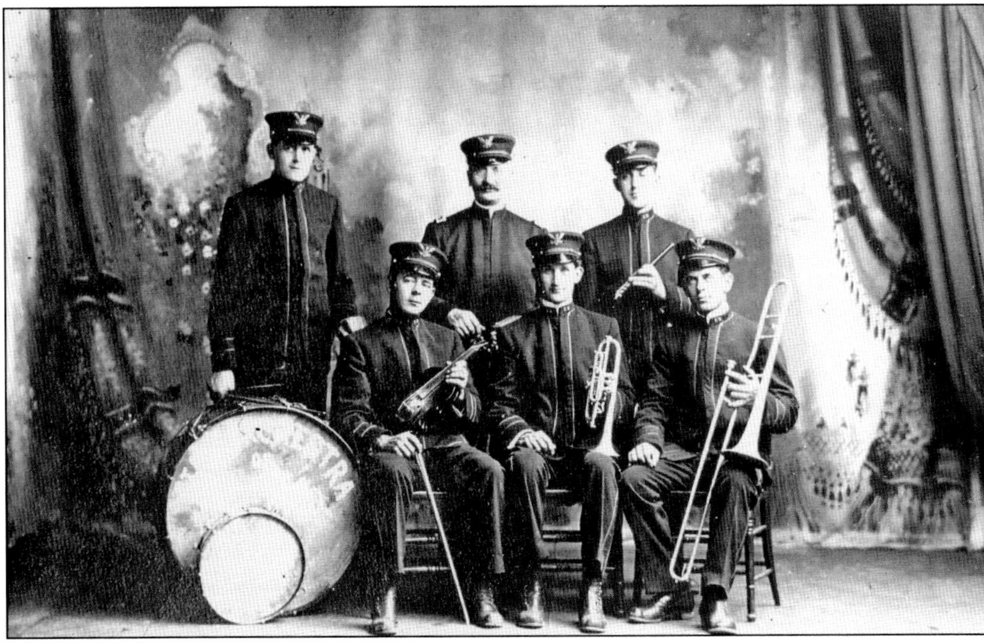

The Star Orchestra of West Bend played from the late 1800s to the start of World War I. Popular throughout the area, the band was managed by William F. Hron. The members seen here are, from left to right, (first row) Al Hron (violin), Bill Hackbarth (trumpet), and Bill Hron (trombone); (second row) Oscar Shalles (clarinet), an two unidentified musicians.

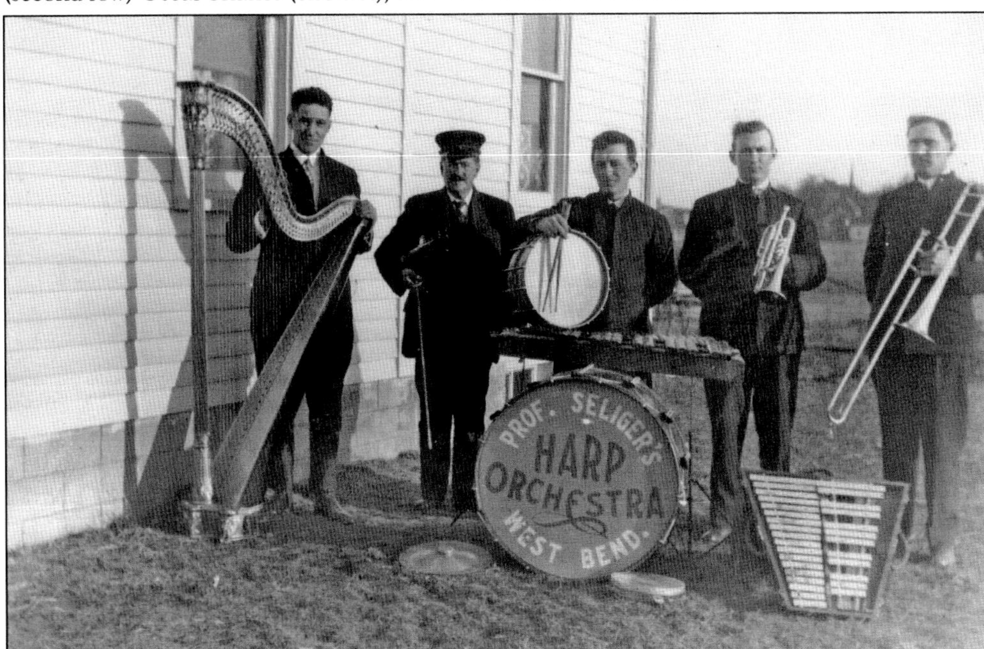

Several bands played around West Bend over the years; the members and names of many have been lost to history. Bands like Professor Seligan's Harp Orchestra, pictured here, played at local taverns, opera houses, and dances. The only person identified in this photograph is John Willkomm (second from the right).

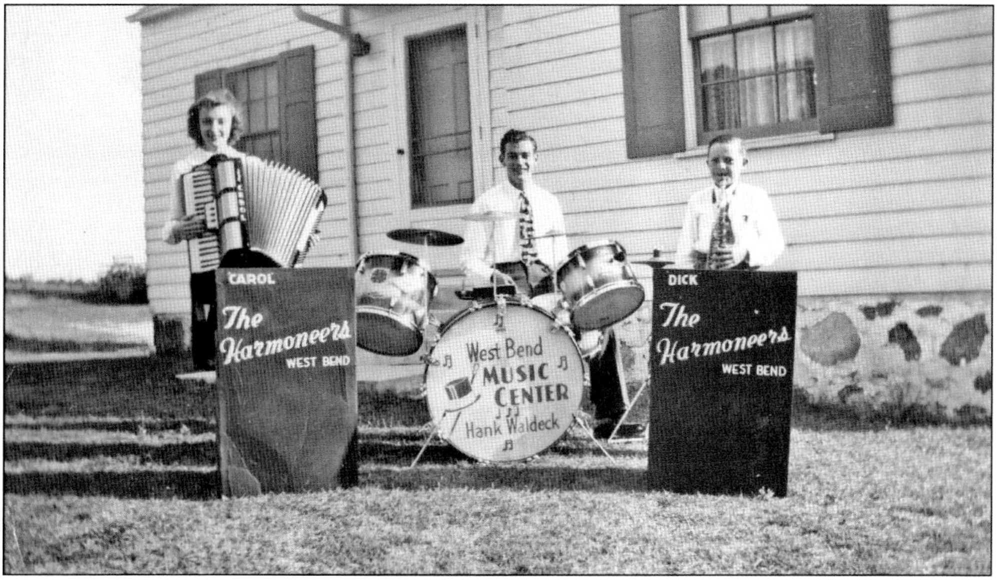

The Harmoneers were a group formed from the students at the West Bend Music Center. Drummer Hank Waldeck was a teacher at the school. The West Bend Music Center opened in 1947 in downtown West Bend and offered instruments for purchase or rent, as well as lessons on a variety of instruments. The last names of accordion player Carol and saxophone player Dick are unknown.

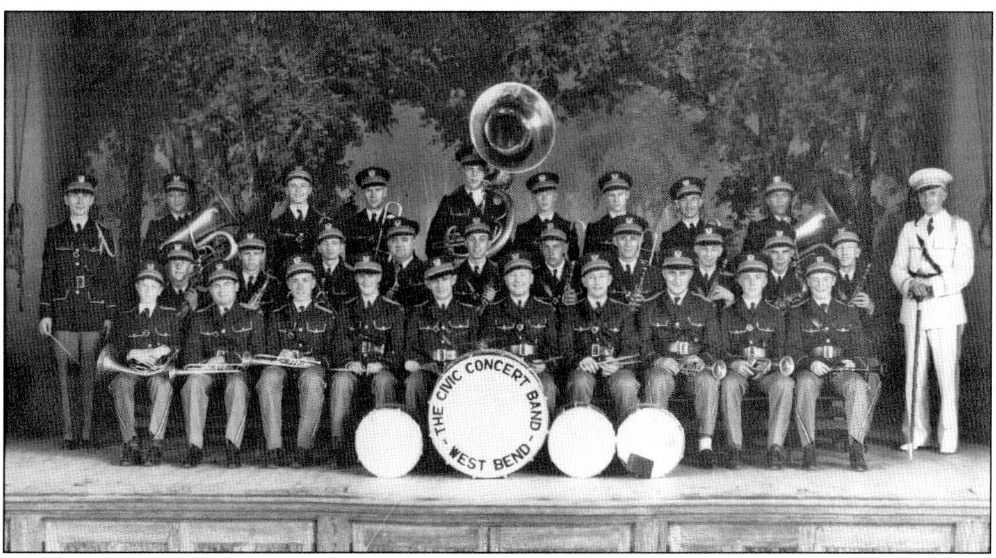

The West Bend Civic Concert Band played at various festivities and parades during the 1930s and 1940s and was directed by Leonard Oelhafen. The group dispersed when too many members entered the service during World War II. The band did not reform after the war. This photograph was taken around 1940.

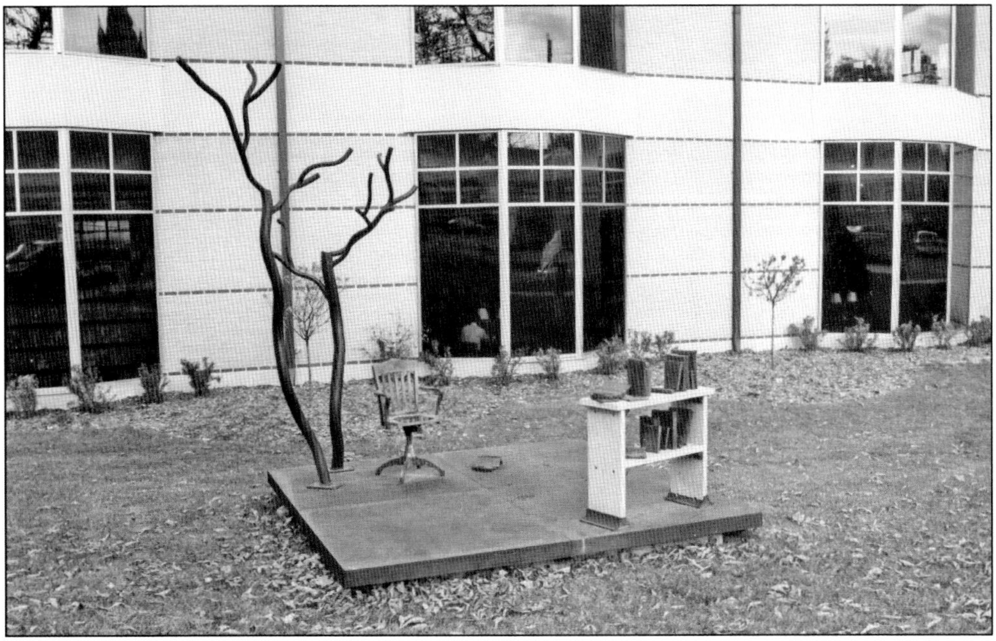

The West Bend Friends of Sculpture was founded in 1992 to continue a tradition of placing sculptures in public areas. The artwork represents the city's industrial and cultural connection to the Milwaukee River over the years. This sculpture, *For Edna St. Vincent Millay* by Roger Colombik, is located outside the West Bend Memorial Library on Poplar Street. (Courtesy of West Bend Friends of Sculpture.)

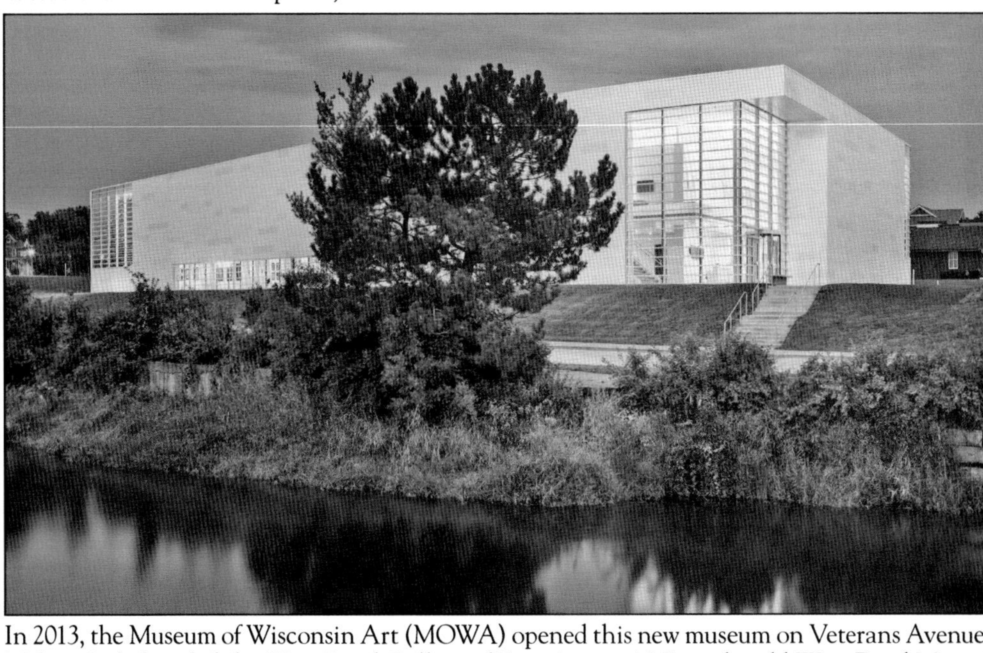

In 2013, the Museum of Wisconsin Art (MOWA) opened this new museum on Veterans Avenue. Melitta Pick founded the West Bend Gallery of Fine Arts in 1961 in the old West Bend Mutual Insurance Company on Seventh Avenue and Poplar Street. In 1993, the organization was renamed West Bend Art Museum. In 2007, it became MOWA. The museum holds more than 4,000 works of art and presents 12 to 14 exhibitions each year.

Pres. Franklin Delano Roosevelt's train stopped briefly near the West Bend depot on August 9, 1934. More than 3,000 people waited in the heat to see the president on his way through the city from Green Bay. His train stopped only long enough for him to wave and say hello before continuing on to Washington, DC.

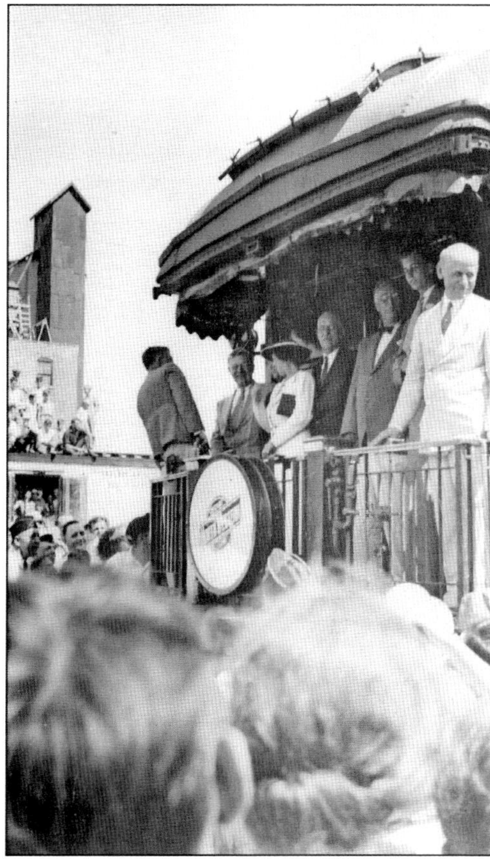

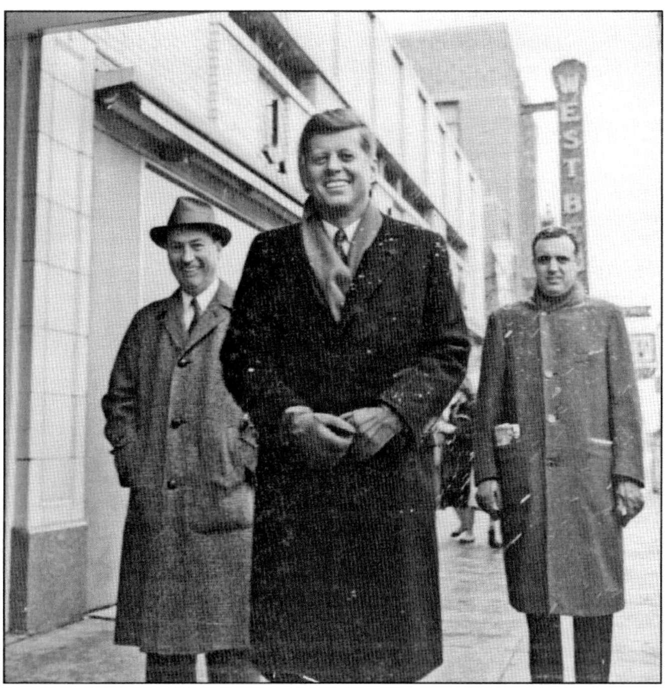

During his first presidential campaign, Sen. John F. Kennedy made a stop in West Bend. On February 18, 1960, he addressed the crowd at the VFW before lunching at the Mermac Hotel and meeting residents. This photograph was taken as the senator strolled downtown in front of the West Bend Theater. The man to the left of Kennedy is Thomas O'Meara Jr.

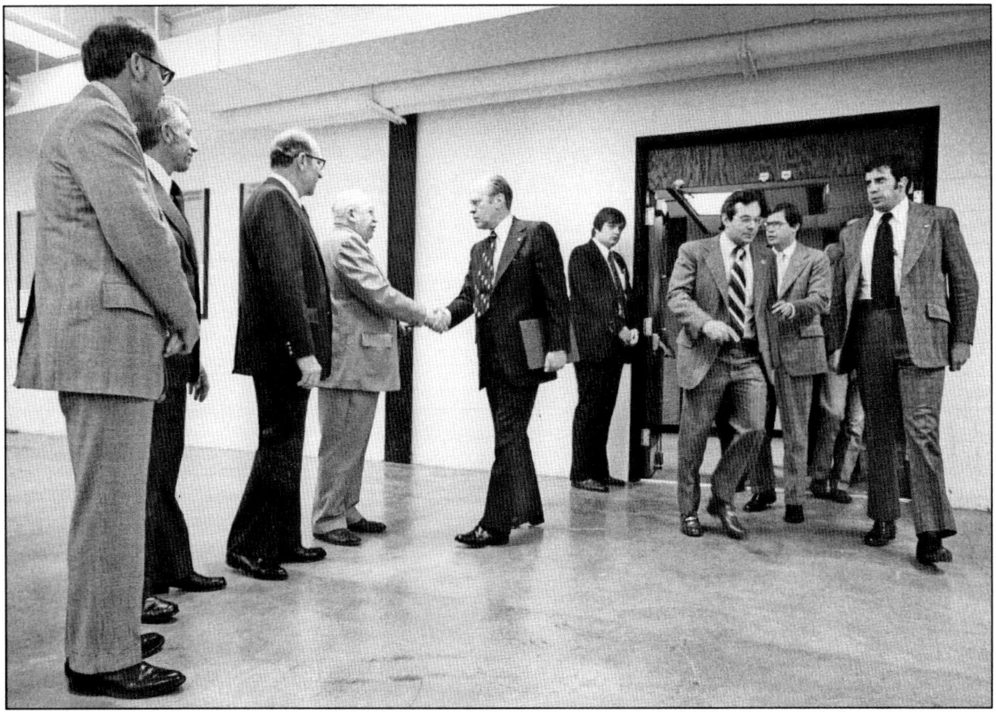

Pres. Gerald Ford visited West Bend on April 2, 1976. The president spoke at the high school field house to a crowd of over 5,000. Here, the president is arriving at the school and shaking hands with, from back to front, Ralph Schoenhaar (West Bend mayor), Rueben Schmahl (Washington County Board of Supervisors chairman), William Steinert (superintendent of schools), and John Sheehy (principal). (Photograph by William Stonecipher, *West Bend News*.)

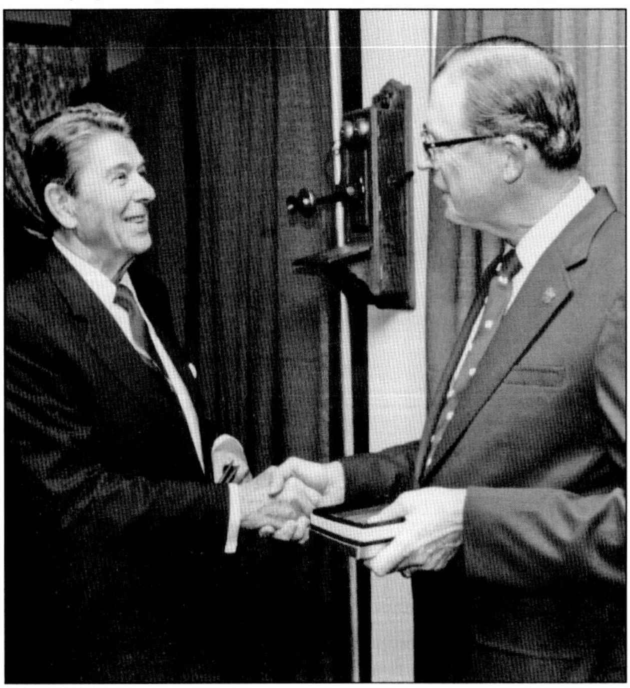

Robert Rolfs of Amity Leather Products Company presented Pres. Ronald Reagan a Jacarétinga skin (a small crocodilian from South America) wallet with an 18-karat gold signature plate during his West Bend stop on July 27, 1987. More than 25,000 people lined Main Street to welcome the president, who lunched with Noon Rotary members and spoke with local executives. This same type of wallet was given to Pres. Dwight Eisenhower in 1958 by the company's founder, Robert H. Rolfs.

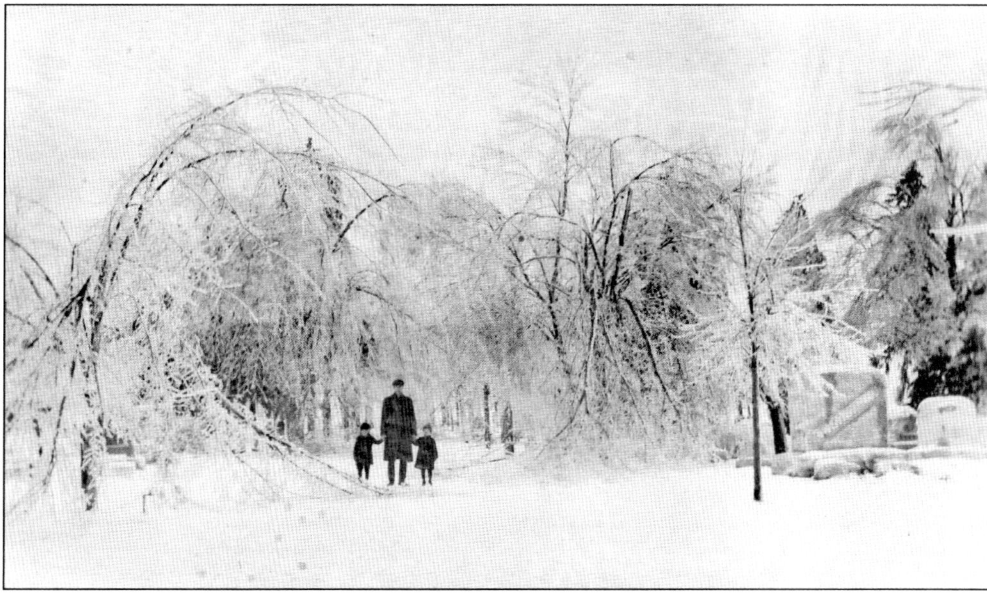

Local amateur photographer and Amity Company employee Stanley Suchy and his children explored Union Cemetery after the big April 15 ice storm in 1921. The storm dropped around 20 inches of snow in 20 hours. Wind did not help the situation, and roads and trains shut down. Within four days, there was no trace left of the storm.

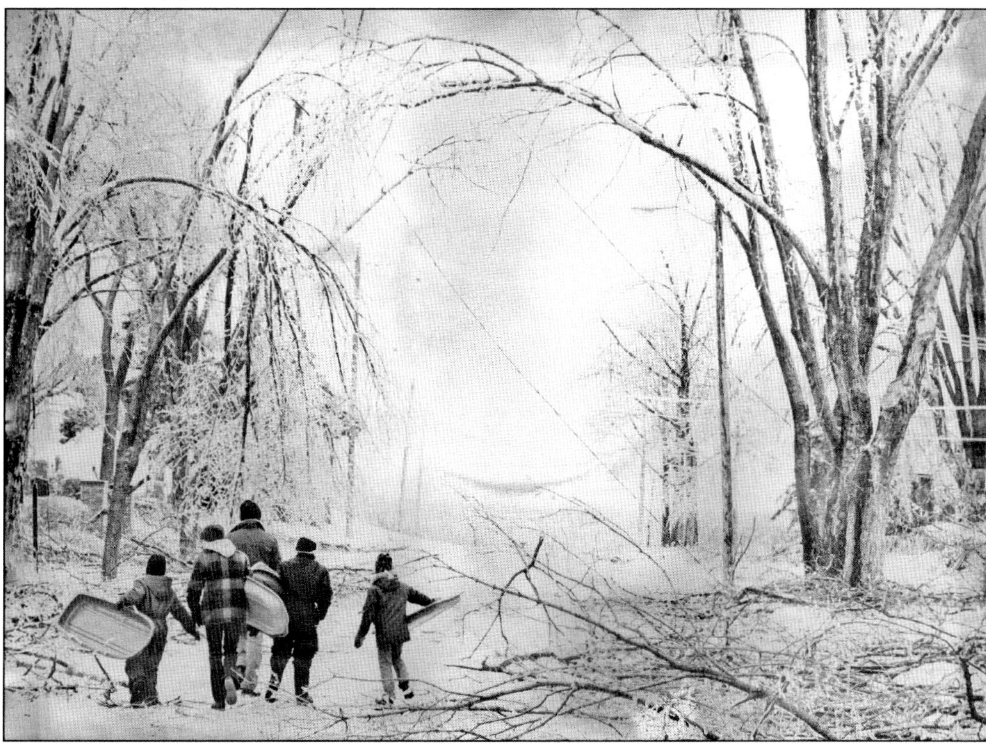

In March 1976, a three-day-long ice storm hit West Bend. Freezing rain, hail, and snow caused multiple power outages, downed limbs, travel hazards, and home and business damage. This photograph was taken in the aftermath of the storm. (Courtesy of the *West Bend News.*)

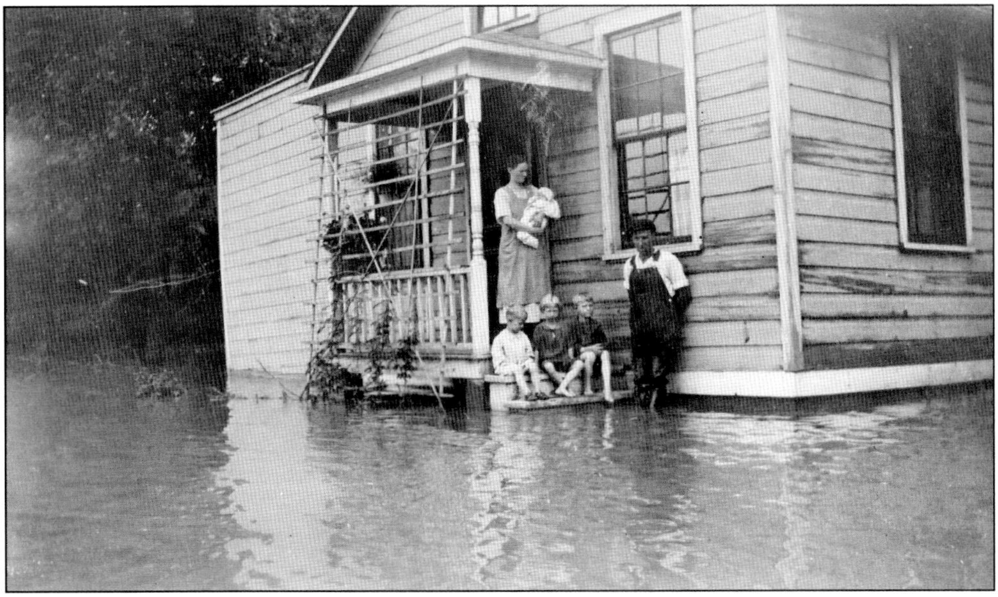

This photograph of the Degner home on Water Street on the east side of the Milwaukee River was taken during the flood of August 1924. Seated on the porch are, from left to right, Harold, Bernice, and Walter. Their father, Erwin, is standing in the floodwaters. Behind them is their mother, Matilda, holding baby Edith.

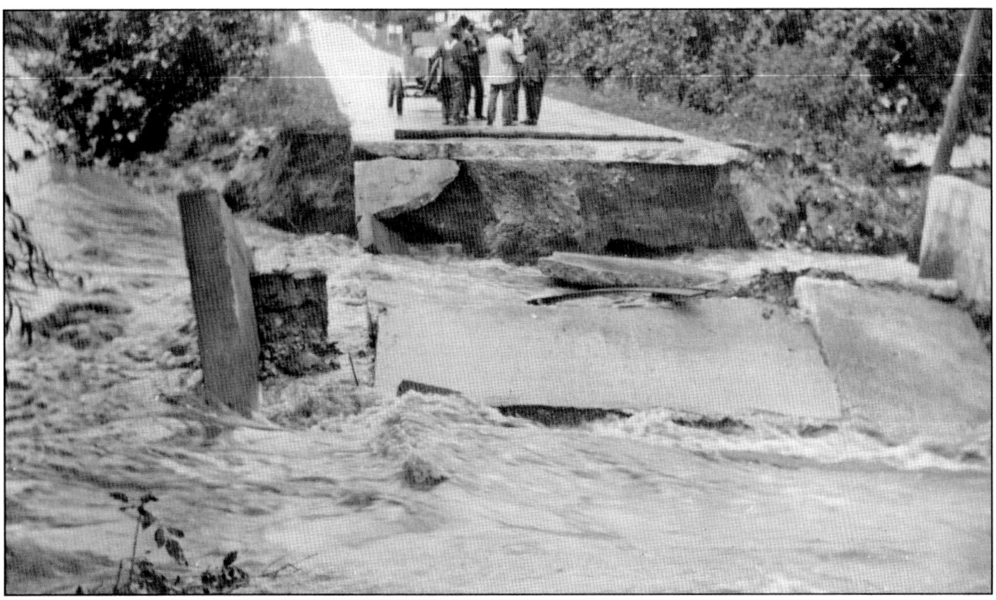

The new Silver Creek bridge on West Washington Street near Fifteenth Street was washed out in 1924 after torrential rains. It was located near today's Highway 33 and North Silverbrook Drive. The downpour destroyed 18 bridges in Washington County and flooded many houses and businesses in West Bend.

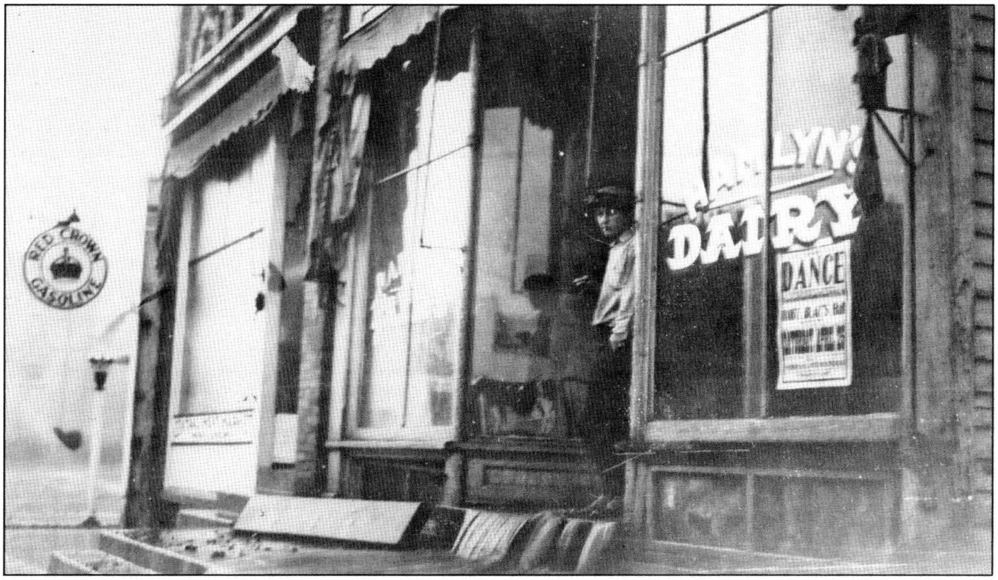

On April 22, 1925, one and a third inches of rain fell on West Bend in a half an hour. This photograph of the Consumers Milk and Ice Cream Company store on North Main Street shows the aftermath, with water running though the shop. The sloping backyard of the store allowed the overflowing Milwaukee River to run from the back door and out the front.

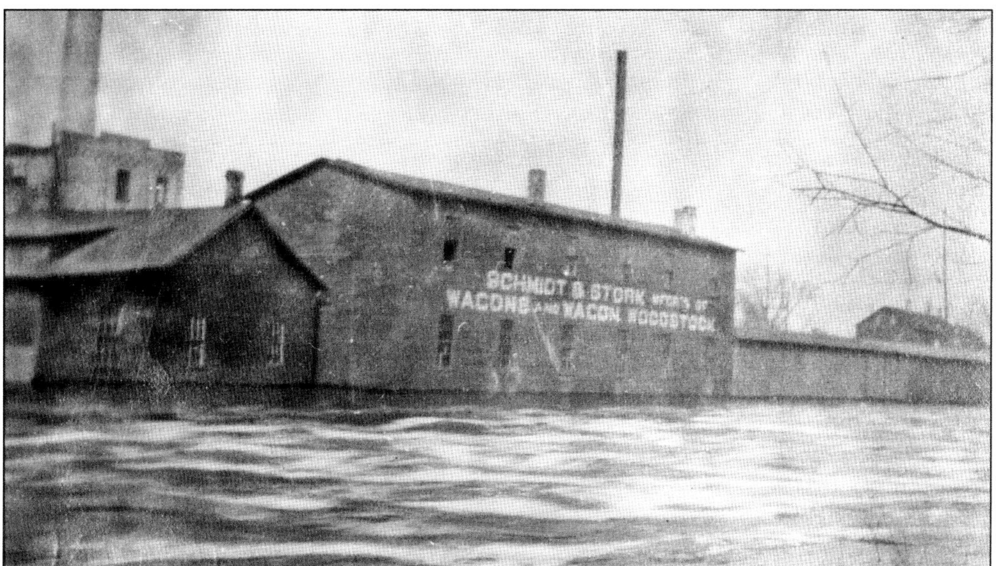

Businesses were not exempt from the 1924 flood damage. Schmidt and Stork Wagon Factory, located on what was then Division Street (now known as Washington Street) on the west bank of the Milwaukee River, was flooded. The yard of the factory was inundated to a depth of five feet. The factory closed for several days in order to dry out.

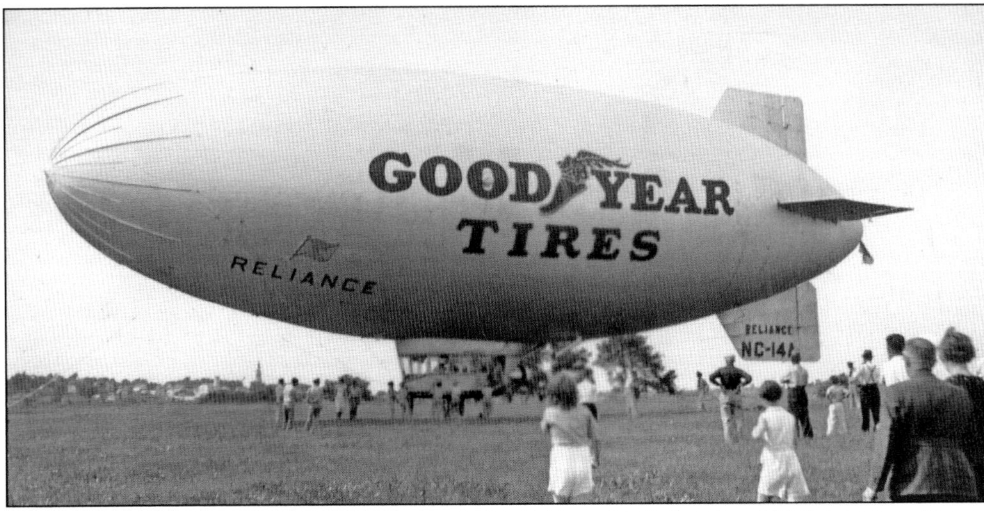

On July 5, 1935, the 141-foot-long Goodyear airship *Reliance* landed at the old Washington County Fairgrounds, located where Fair Park Elementary School stands today. Visitors could purchase rides for $3 per person. The blimp could accommodate up to six passengers and had a maximum speed of 60 miles per hour.

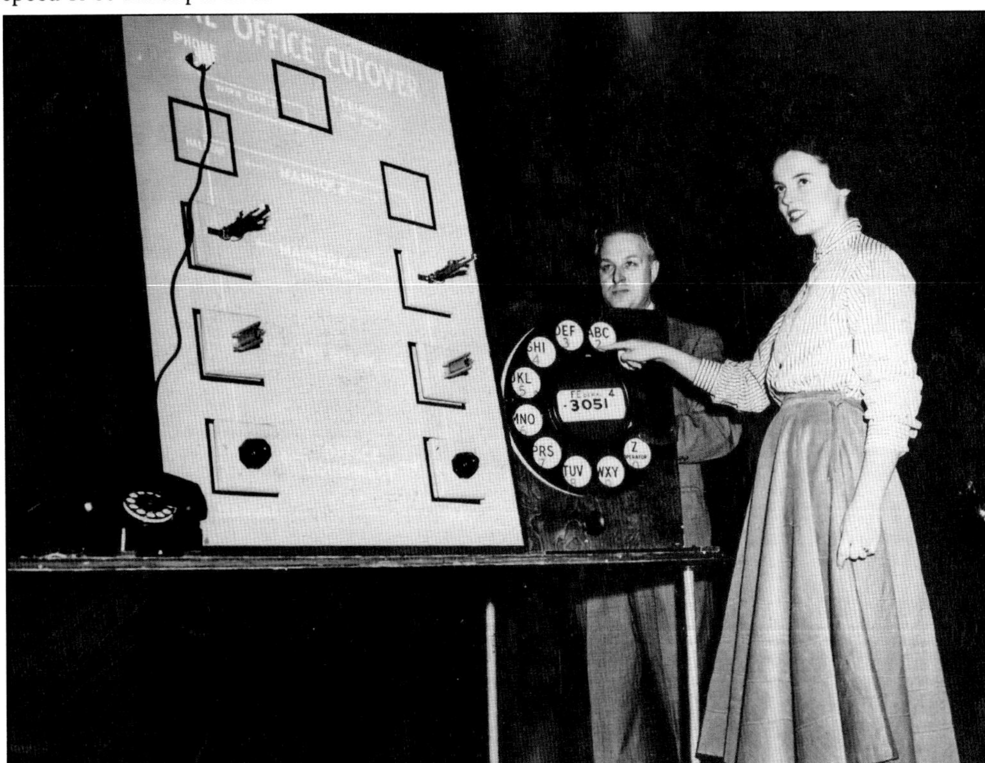

In 1878, West Bend installed its first telephone between the grain elevator and the Frankenberg and Karsten General Store. Early phones were operated by picking up the receiver and asking the operator to connect the caller. In the 1950s, an automatic switch system, rotary dial, and dial tone were introduced. Public instructional skits, like the one seen here, were common. This photograph was taken in 1959 at the West Bend High School.

Eight

Barton

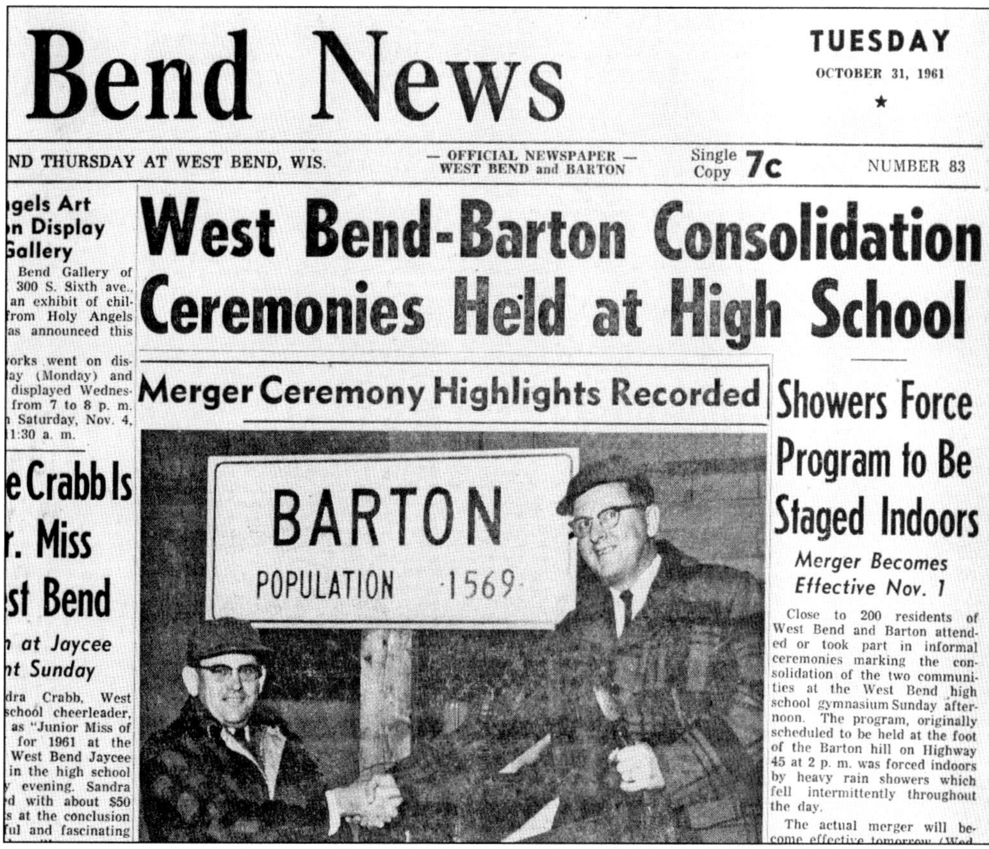

Bend News

TUESDAY
OCTOBER 31, 1961
★

ND THURSDAY AT WEST BEND, WIS. — OFFICIAL NEWSPAPER — WEST BEND and BARTON Single Copy 7c NUMBER 83

West Bend-Barton Consolidation Ceremonies Held at High School

Merger Ceremony Highlights Recorded

Showers Force Program to Be Staged Indoors

Merger Becomes Effective Nov. 1

Close to 200 residents of West Bend and Barton attended or took part in informal ceremonies marking the consolidation of the two communities at the West Bend high school gymnasium Sunday afternoon. The program, originally scheduled to be held at the foot of the Barton hill on Highway 45 at 2 p. m. was forced indoors by heavy rain showers which fell intermittently throughout the day.

The actual merger will become effective tomorrow (Wed...

gels Art
n Display
Gallery

Bend Gallery of
300 S. Sixth ave.,
an exhibit of chil-
from Holy Angels
as announced this

orks went on dis-
ay (Monday) and
displayed Wednes-
from 7 to 8 p. m.
Saturday, Nov. 4,
1:30 a. m.

e Crabb Is
r. Miss
st Bend

at Jaycee
t Sunday

dra Crabb, West
school cheerleader,
as "Junior Miss of
for 1961 at the
West Bend Jaycee
in the high school
evening. Sandra
d with about $50
s at the conclusion
ul and fascinating

On November 1, 1961, the village of Barton was merged with the city of West Bend. The merger allowed Barton to participate in municipal works and school systems already in place in the larger West Bend. Even so, to this day, locals refer to the northern portion of West Bend as Barton. This chapter highlights some of Barton's rich history.

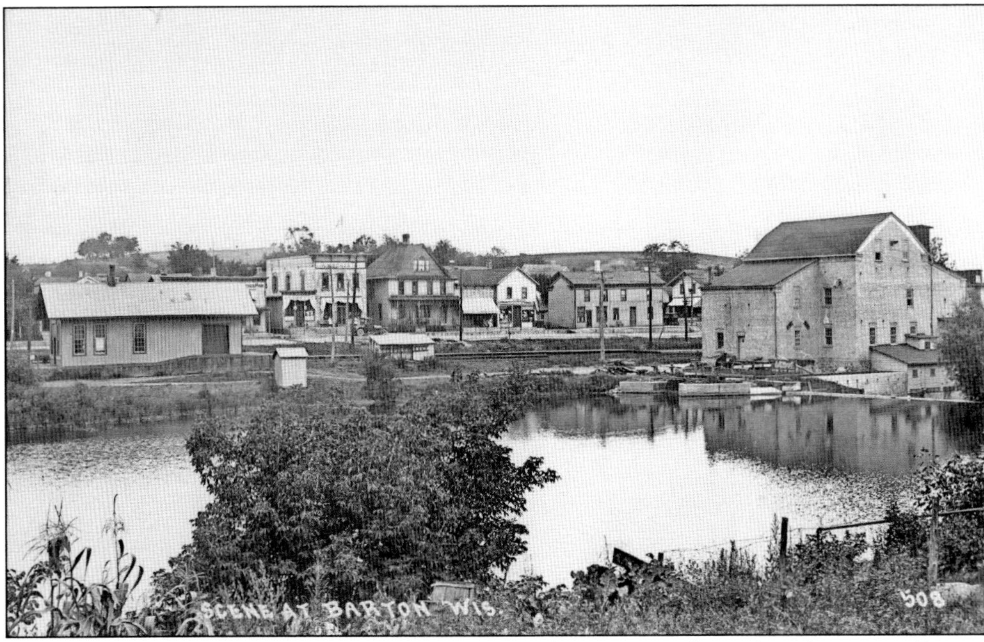

This photograph looks southwest across the Milwaukee River Mill Pond to downtown Barton. In the foreground across the river is the Barton Roller Mill. On the left is the Chicago & North Western Railroad depot, with its coal and oil house and outhouse in the foreground. The image was taken around 1920.

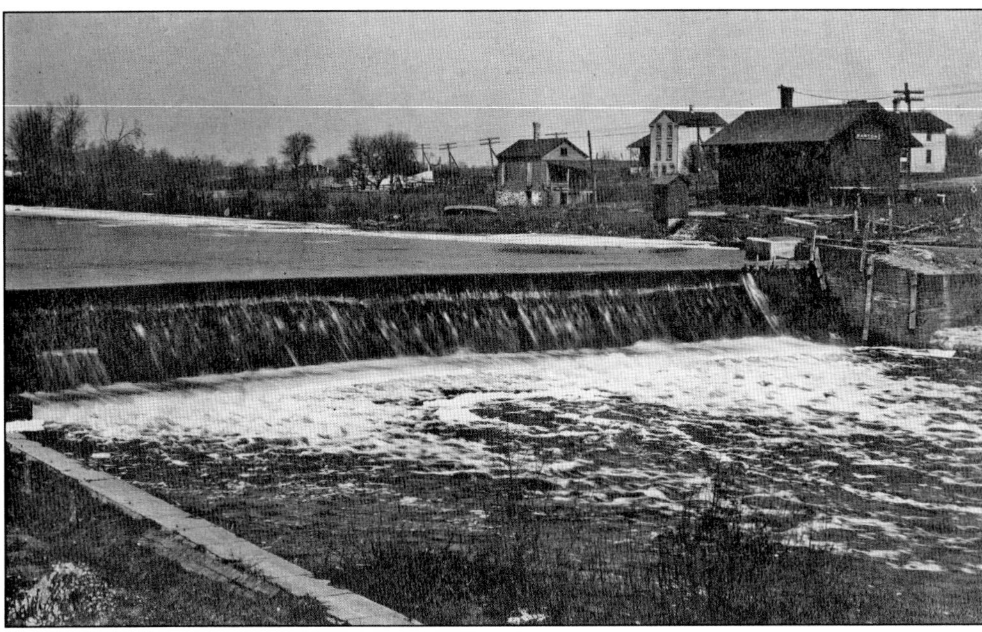

Here is the Barton dam around 1920. On the right is the Chicago & North Western Railroad depot. The Barton dam was essential to many of the early and long-running businesses in Barton and was at the heart of the community. Over the years, it was damaged by floods on several occasions but always rebuilt. (Photograph by Herman Trakat.)

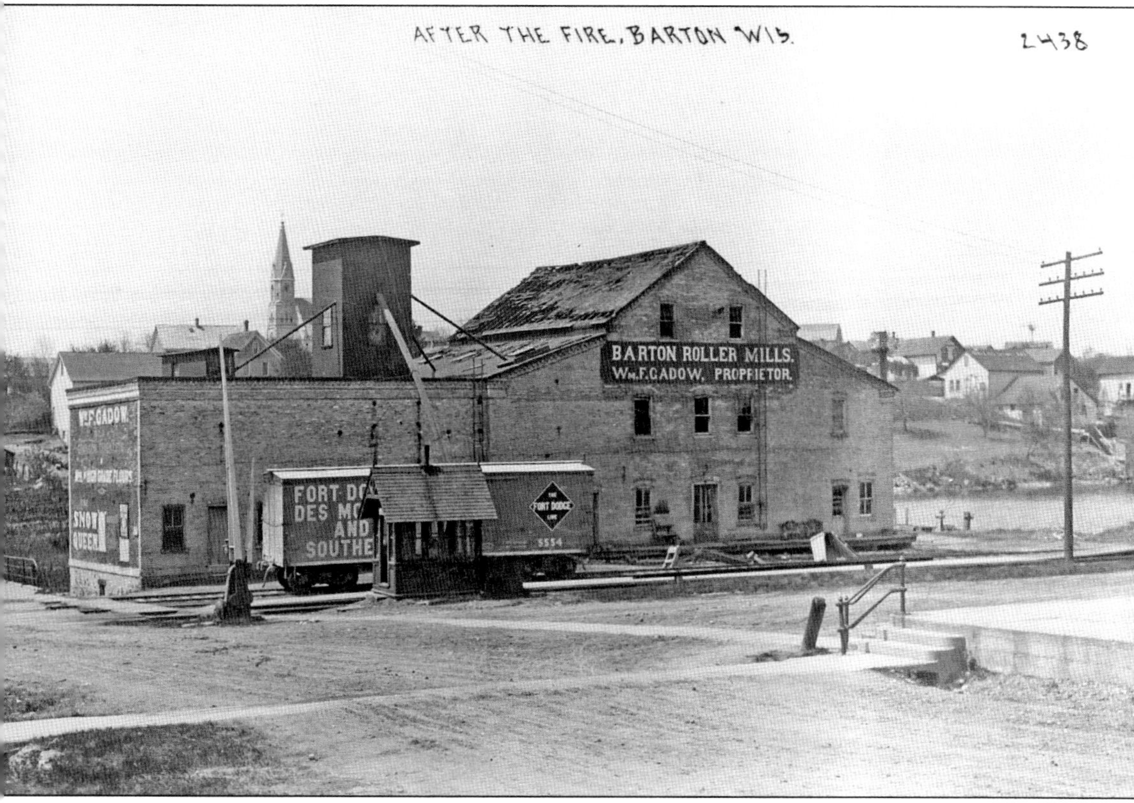

Barton was founded on the premise of a mill. The original mill was built by Barton Salisbury in 1845 and was on the opposite side of the Milwaukee River from its present home. Originally a sawmill, it was converted to flour production after Salisbury's death by new owner William Caldwell. Several mills inhabited the site over the years. The current building, seen here, was built by John Price around 1863. The mill changed hands, and Charles Suckow, owner of nearby Young America's flour mill, operated it until he sold to William Gadow in 1905. The mill continued to use waterpower (one of the last in Wisconsin) as its main power source until it closed in 1964. In the early 1990s, Len Dricken, wife Rhea Gadow Dricken, and their children, Kay and Michael, began renovation efforts to retain the historical context of the mill while modernizing it to include small shops. Today, the Barton Roller Mill houses business offices.

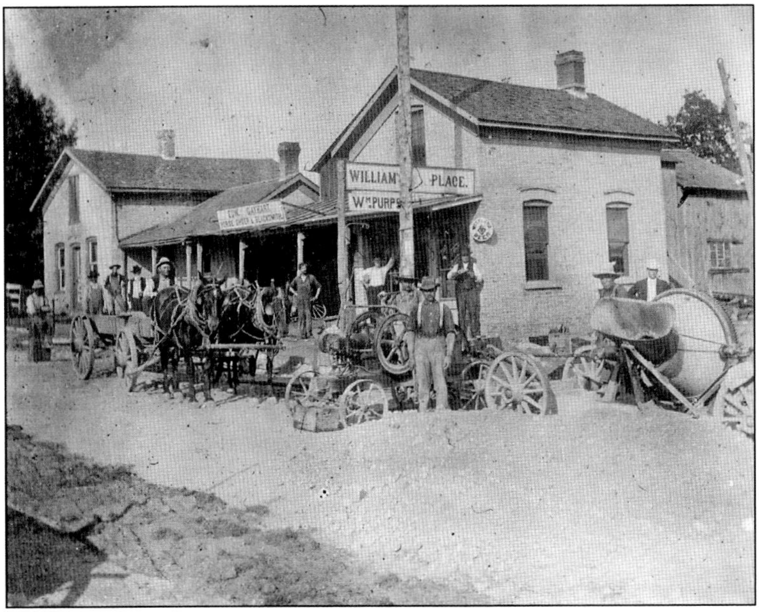

Ed Gayhardt owned this Barton-based blacksmith shop and saloon around 1900. Gayhardt owned the property until 1914, when his former apprentice, Joseph VanBeek, returned to town and purchased it. Joseph later operated the first automobile dealership and garage in Barton. The last blacksmith shop in Barton closed in the 1930s.

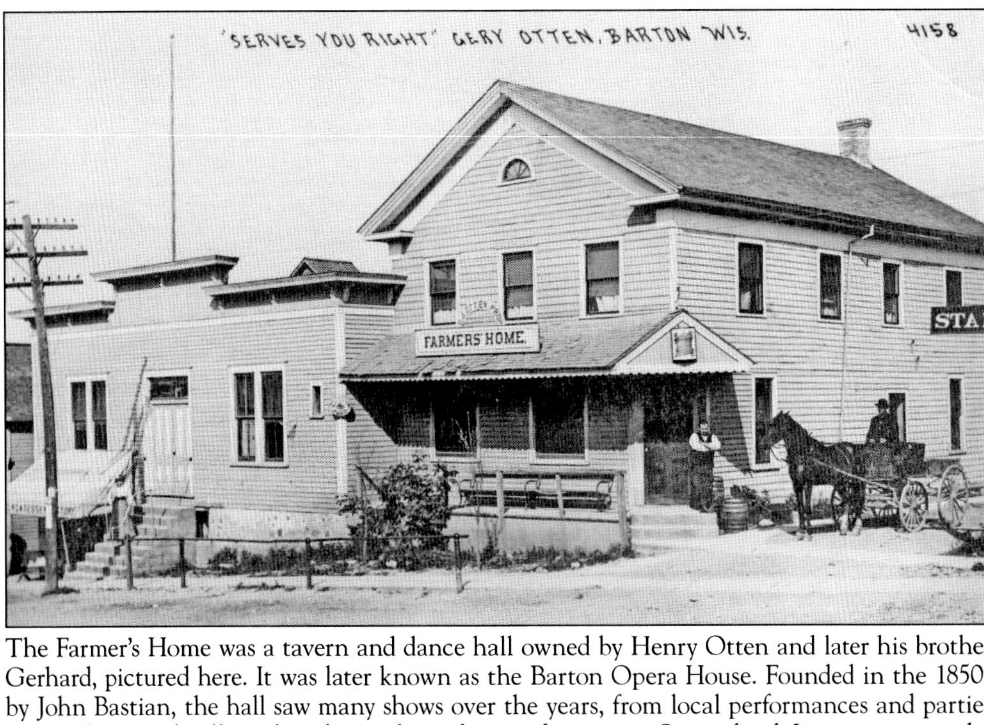

The Farmer's Home was a tavern and dance hall owned by Henry Otten and later his brother Gerhard, pictured here. It was later known as the Barton Opera House. Founded in the 1850s by John Bastian, the hall saw many shows over the years, from local performances and parties to traveling vaudeville and medicine shows from as far away as Switzerland. In recent years, the building has seen a wide variety of tenants.

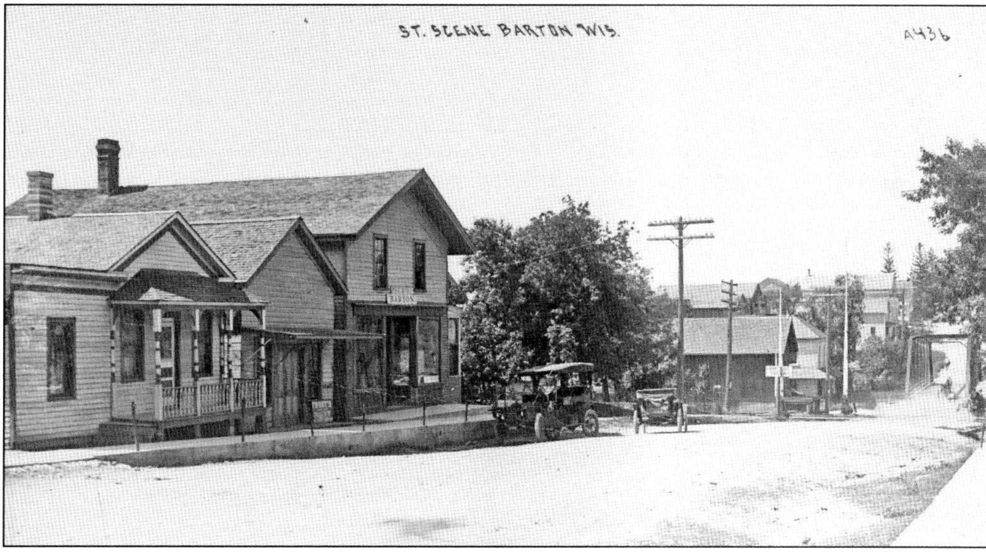

On the left of this photograph is the Otten General Store. There was a general store on this site continually since 1859. First owned by Peter Fraser, the business had several proprietors over the years until it was purchased by Henry Otten in 1914; the Otten family continued to run it until 1998. This photograph was taken around the time Otten took over.

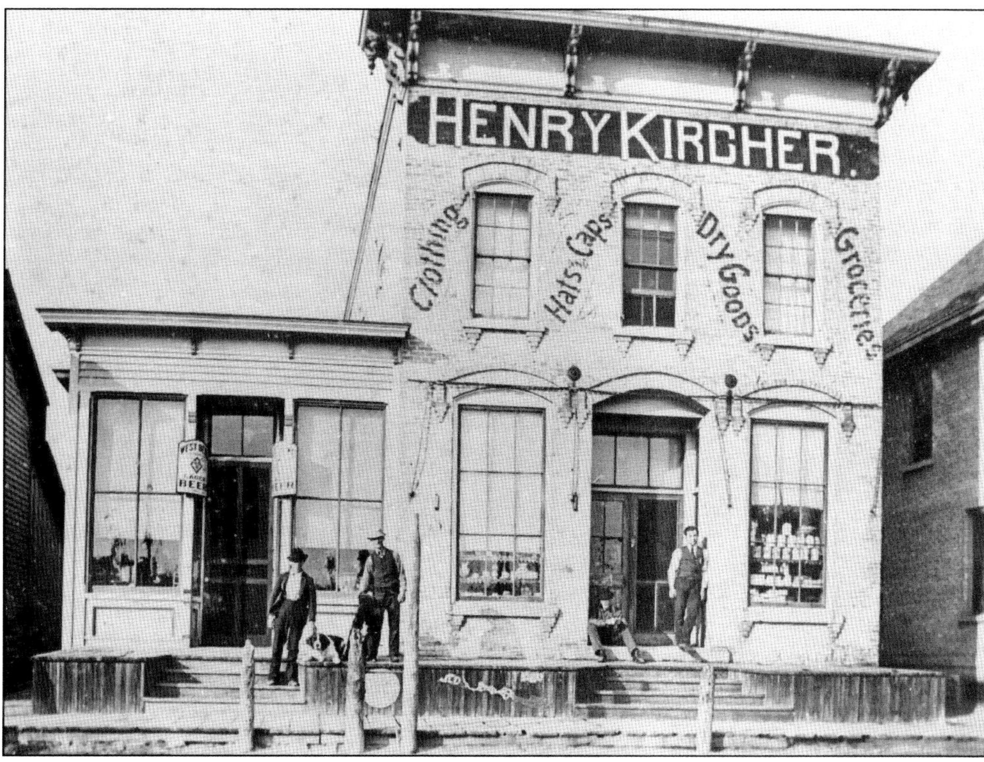

Henry Kircher owned the store and saloon located on Commerce Street. This photograph was taken around 1890 after the addition of the saloon, the small building on the left. Henry was a trained tailor and owned several businesses over the years, including this general store with tailor services, the adjacent saloon, and a dance hall.

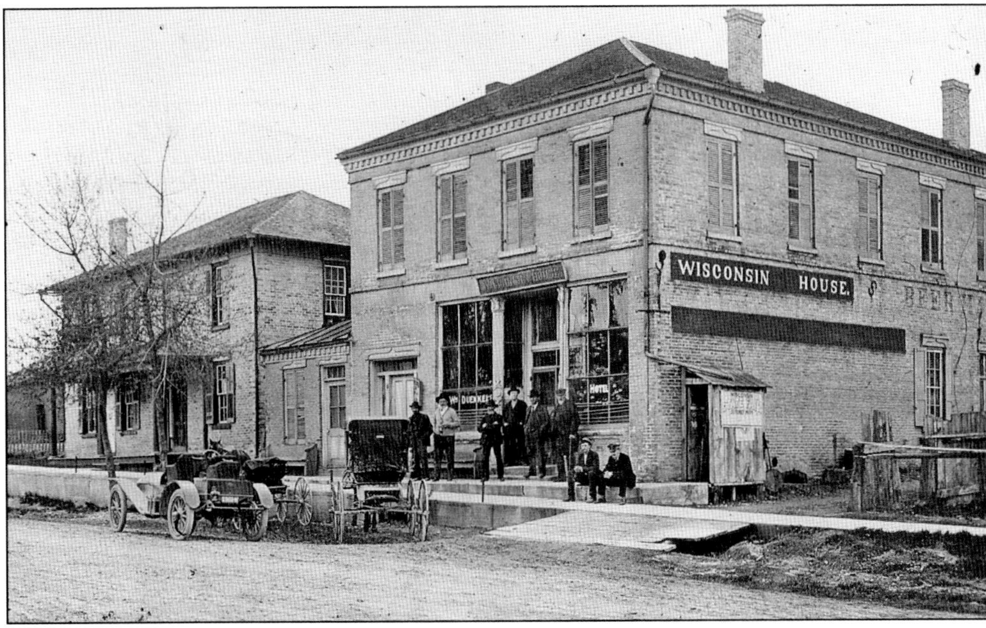

The Wisconsin House was a hotel owned and operated by William Duenkel. Opened in 1895, it had 10 bedrooms, two parlors, a dining room that held 20 people, and a dance hall. In 1914, William's son Grover took over the business. The only person identified in this photograph from around 1900 is Dr. Sylvester Driessel (far right). On the left, the car is identified as Dr. Driessel's first car.

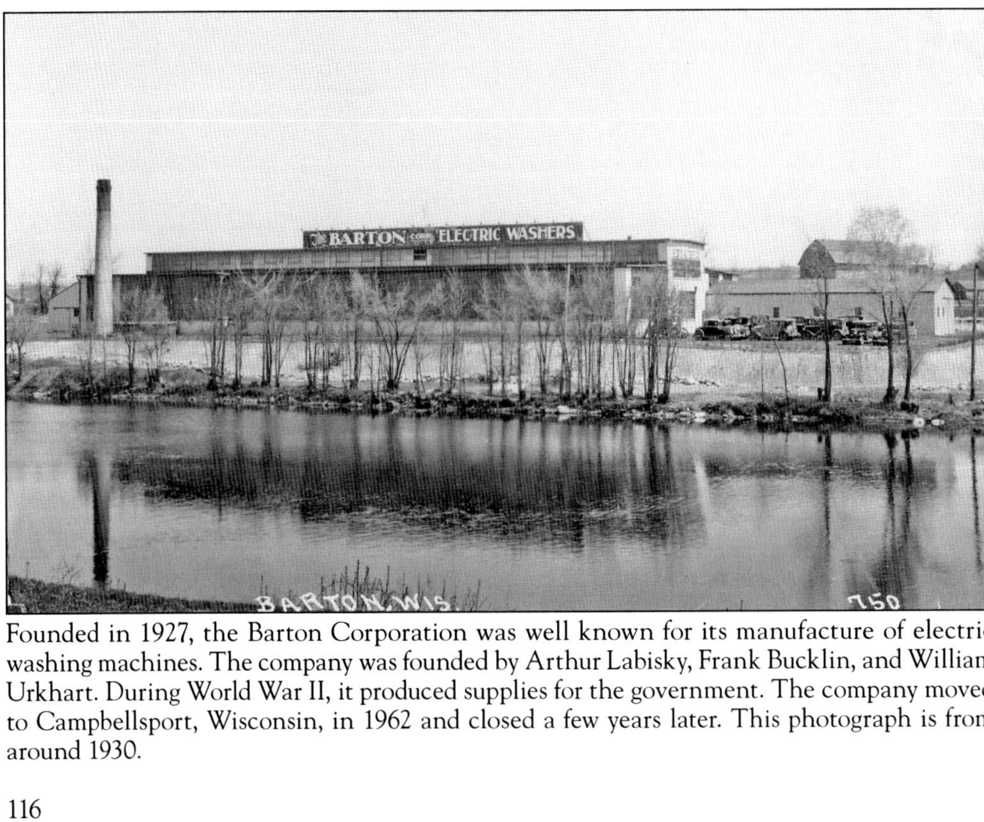

Founded in 1927, the Barton Corporation was well known for its manufacture of electric washing machines. The company was founded by Arthur Labisky, Frank Bucklin, and William Urkhart. During World War II, it produced supplies for the government. The company moved to Campbellsport, Wisconsin, in 1962 and closed a few years later. This photograph is from around 1930.

St. Mary Immaculate Conception Church was founded in 1854 and was attended by, among other missionary priests, Fr. Casper Rehrl, founder of the Sisters of St. Agnes convent. The original church was on the corner of Barton Avenue and River Drive. The second church, seen here, was constructed in 1857.

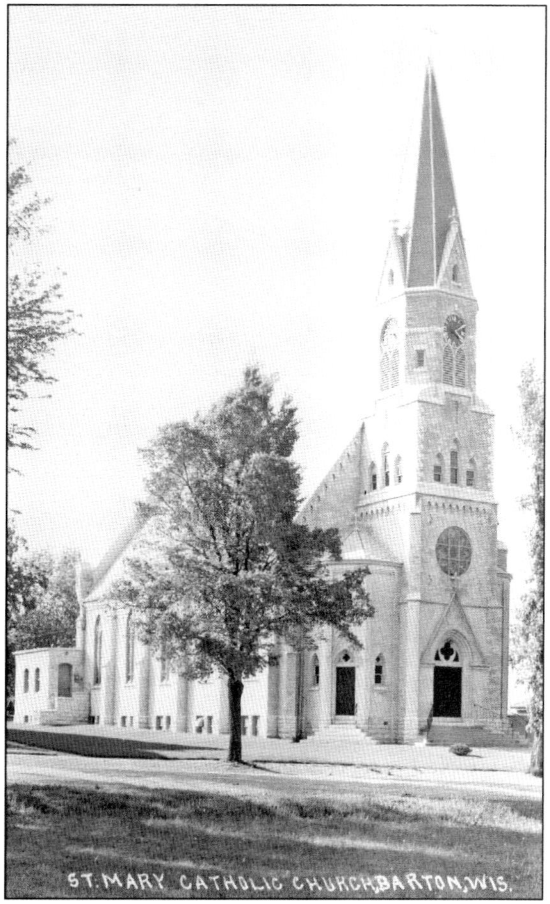

The first Catholic school in Barton also served non-Catholic children. Fr. Casper Rehrl established the school in 1856. As local needs grew, St. Mary Immaculate Conception Church opened a school. It was built in 1876. In this photograph, the school is to the right of the church, and the parsonage is to the left. The school is located on Roosevelt Drive and Monroe Street.

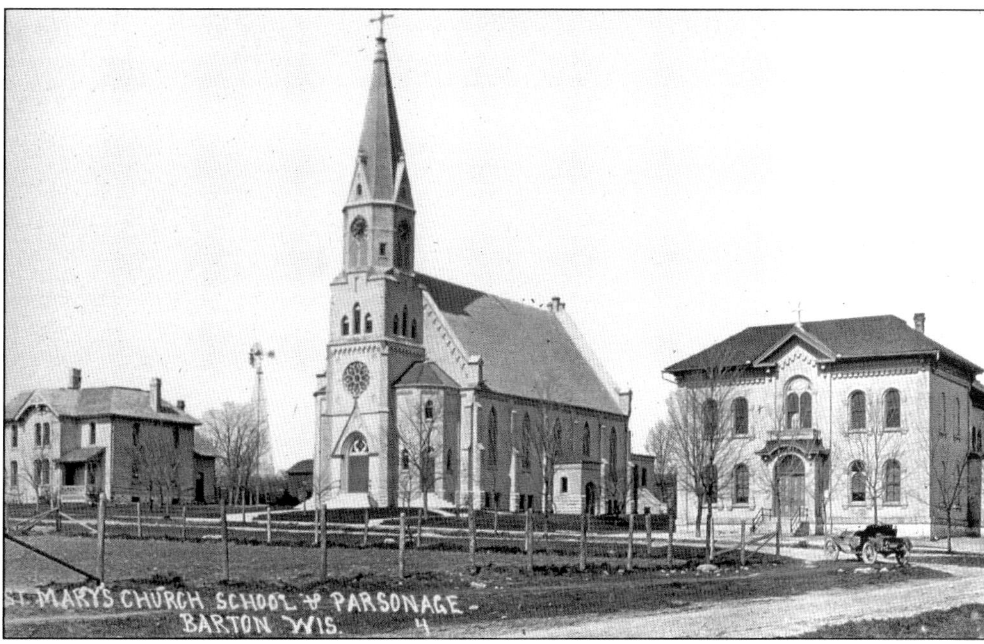

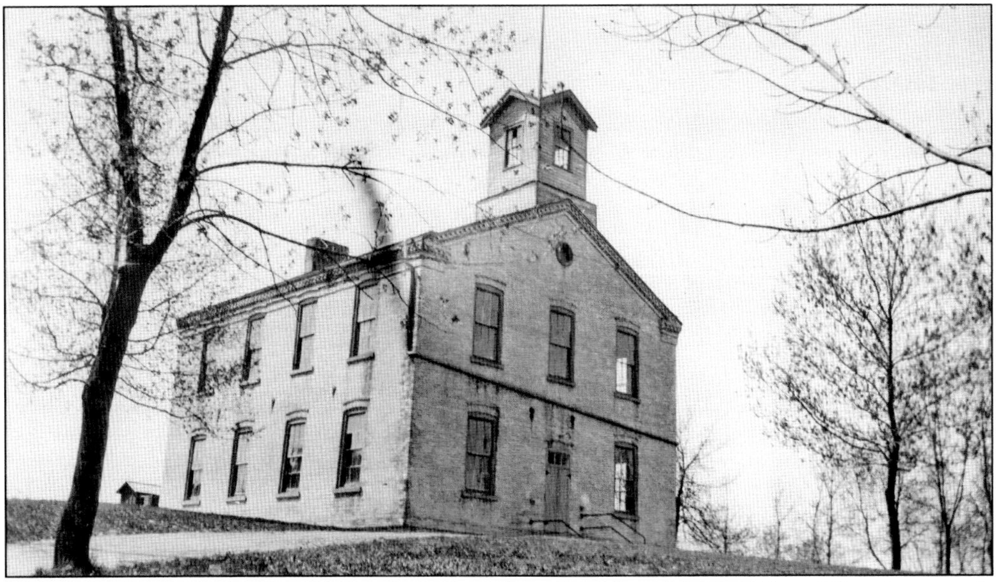

Barton Elementary School was located on River Drive North and School Place. This photograph shows the first building on the property. Erected around 1868, the structure was torn down in 1923 because it was overcrowded and structurally unsound. The new school building cost $30,000 to build and was located on the same site. Barton Elementary School closed in the spring of 2014 when the West Bend Public Schools were restructured.

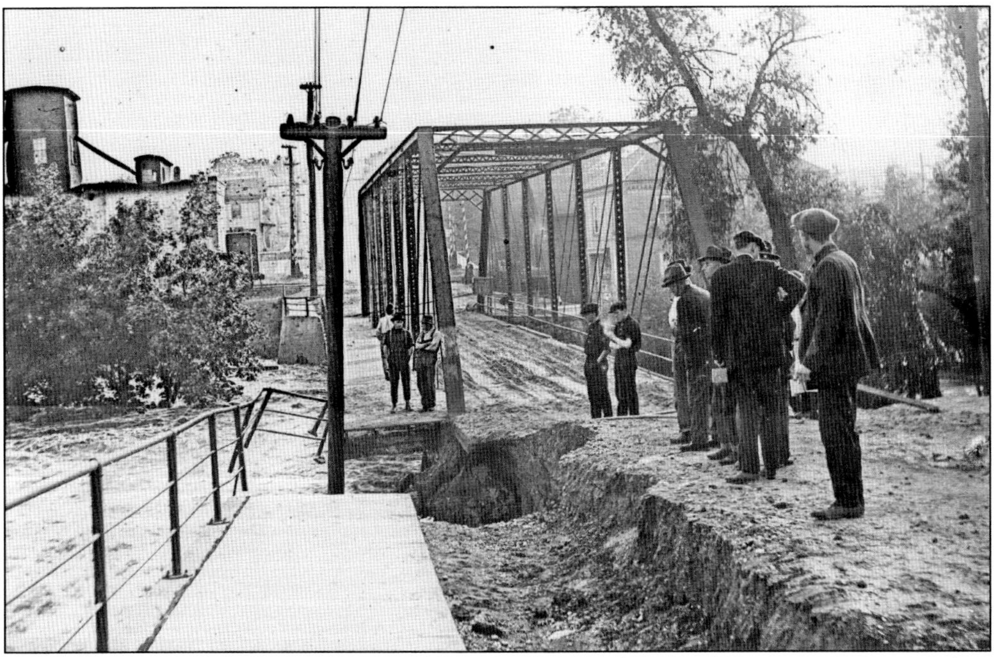

On April 22, 1924, a devastating flood hit the area when, during a very wet spring, more than an inch of rain fell in a half an hour. This iron bridge was located on Main Street in Barton and crossed the Milwaukee River. The photograph shows the damage to the roadside caused by the heavy, fast-moving rain.

Nine

PRESERVATION

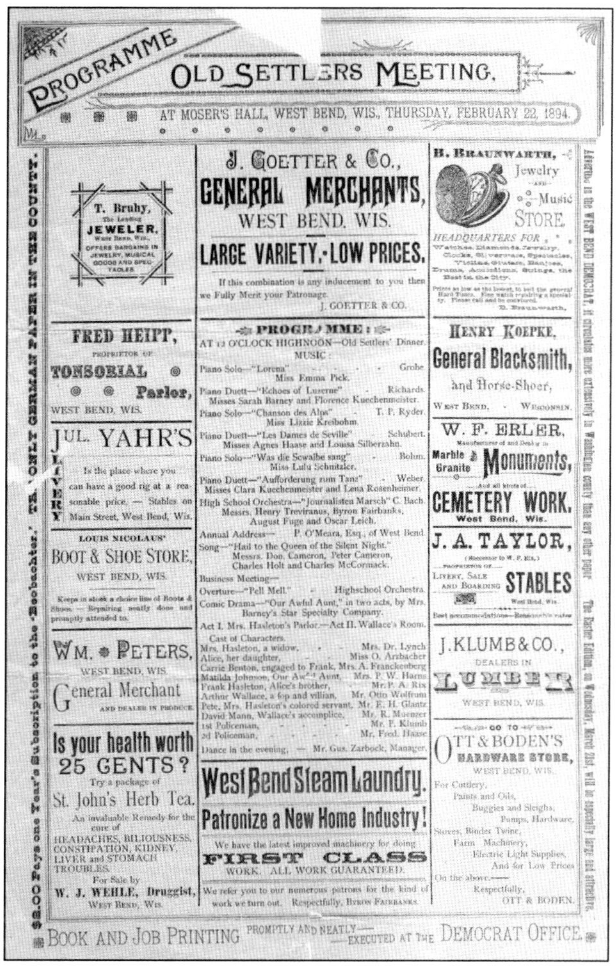

PROGRAMME

OLD SETTLERS MEETING,

AT MOSER'S HALL, WEST BEND, WIS., THURSDAY, FEBRUARY 22, 1894.

$2.00 Pays one Year's Subscription to the "Beobachter," The Only German Paper in the County.

T. Bruhy, The Leading JEWELER, West Bend, Wis., OFFERS BARGAINS IN JEWELRY, MUSICAL GOODS AND SPECTACLES.

J. GOETTER & CO., GENERAL MERCHANTS, WEST BEND, WIS.

LARGE VARIETY,-LOW PRICES.

If this combination is any inducement to you then we Fully Merit your Patronage.
J. GOETTER & CO.

B. BRAUNWARTH, Jewelry and Music STORE.

HEADQUARTERS FOR Watches, Diamonds, Jewelry, Clocks, Silverware, Spectacles, Violins, Guitars, Banjoes, Drums, Accordions, Strings, the Best in the City.

Prices as low as the lowest, to suit the general Hard Times. Fine watch repairing a specialty. Please call and be convinced.
B. Braunwarth.

FRED HEIPP, PROPRIETOR OF TONSORIAL Parlor, WEST BEND, WIS.

PROGRAMME:

AT 12 O'CLOCK HIGHNOON—Old Settlers' Dinner.

MUSIC:

Piano Solo—"Lorena" - Grobe
Miss Emma Pick.

Piano Duett—"Echoes of Luzerne" - Richards.
Misses Sarah Barney and Florence Kuechenmeister.

Piano Solo—"Chanson des Alps" - T. P. Ryder.
Miss Lizzie Kreibohm.

Piano Duett—"Les Dames de Seville" - Schubert.
Misses Agnes Haase and Louisa Silberzahn.

Piano Solo—"Was die Scwalbe sang" - Bohm.
Miss Lulu Schnitzler.

Piano Duett—"Aufforderung zum Tanz" - Weber.
Misses Clara Kuechenmeister and Lena Rosenheimer.

High School Orchestra—"Journalisten Marsch" C. Bach.
Messrs. Henry Treviranus, Byron Fairbanks, August Fuge and Oscar Leich.

Annual Address— P. O'Meara, Esq., of West Bend.

Song—"Hail to the Queen of the Silent Night."
Messrs. Don. Cameron, Peter Cameron, Charles Holt and Charles McCormack.

Business Meeting—

Overture—"Pell Mell." - Highschool Orchestra.

Comic Drama—"Our Awful Aunt," in two acts, by Mrs. Barney's Star Specialty Company.

Act I. Mrs. Hasleton's Parlor.—Act II. Wallace's Room.

Cast of Characters.

Mrs. Hasleton, a widow, - Mrs. Dr. Lynch
Alice, her daughter, - Miss O. Arzbacher
Carrie Benton, engaged to Frank, Mrs. A. Franckenberg
Matilda Johnson, Our Awful Aunt, Mrs. P. W. Harns
Frank Hasleton, Alice's brother, - Mr. P. A. Rix
Arthur Wallace, a fop and villian, Mr. Otto Wolfrum
Pete, Mrs. Hasleton's colored servant, Mr. E. H. Glantz
David Mann, Wallace's accomplice, Mr. R. Muenzer
1st Policeman, - Mr. F. Klumb
2d Policeman, - Mr. Fred. Haase

Dance in the evening, — Mr. Gus. Zarbock, Manager.

HENRY KOEPKE, General Blacksmith, and Horse-Shoer, WEST BEND, - WISCONSIN.

JUL. YAHR'S LIVERY Is the place where you can have a good rig at a reasonable price. — Stables on Main Street, West Bend, Wis.

W. F. ERLER, Manufacturer of and Dealer in Marble & Granite Monuments, And all kinds of CEMETERY WORK. West Bend, Wis.

LOUIS NICOLAUS' BOOT & SHOE STORE, WEST BEND, WIS.

Keeps in stock a choice line of Boots & Shoes. — Repairing neatly done and promptly attended to.

J. A. TAYLOR, (Successor to W. F. Rix,) PROPRIETOR OF LIVERY, SALE AND BOARDING STABLES West Bend, Wis.

Best accommodations—Reasonable rates

WM. PETERS, WEST BEND, WIS. General Merchant AND DEALER IN PRODUCE.

J. KLUMB & CO., DEALERS IN LUMBER WEST BEND, WIS.

Is your health worth 25 GENTS? Try a package of St. John's Herb Tea. An invaluable Remedy for the cure of HEADACHES, BILIOUSNESS, CONSTIPATION, KIDNEY, LIVER and STOMACH TROUBLES.
For Sale by W. J. WEHLE, Druggist, West Bend, Wis.

West Bend Steam Laundry. Patronize a New Home Industry!

We have the latest improved machinery for doing FIRST CLASS WORK. ALL WORK GUARANTEED.

We refer you to our numerous patrons for the kind of work we turn out. Respectfully, Byron Fairbanks.

GO TO OTT & BODEN'S HARDWARE STORE, WEST BEND, WIS.

For Cuttlery, Paints and Oils, Buggies and Sleighs, Pumps, Hardware, Stoves, Binder Twine, Farm Machinery, Electric Light Supplies, And for Low Prices On the above.—
Respectfully, OTT & BODEN.

Advertise in the WEST BEND DEMOCRAT, it circulates more extensively in Washington county than any other paper. The Easter Edition, on Wednesday, March 21st, will be especially large and attractive.

BOOK AND JOB PRINTING PROMPTLY AND NEATLY— —EXECUTED AT THE DEMOCRAT OFFICE.

The Old Settlers' Club was founded in 1874 by the original settlers to Washington County. Every year, the group held a meeting with a history program on February 22 at the Washington House in West Bend. The club also set up the first displays of artifacts at the county courthouse, the future home of the Old Courthouse Museum. These objects were the beginning of the Washington County Historical Society collections.

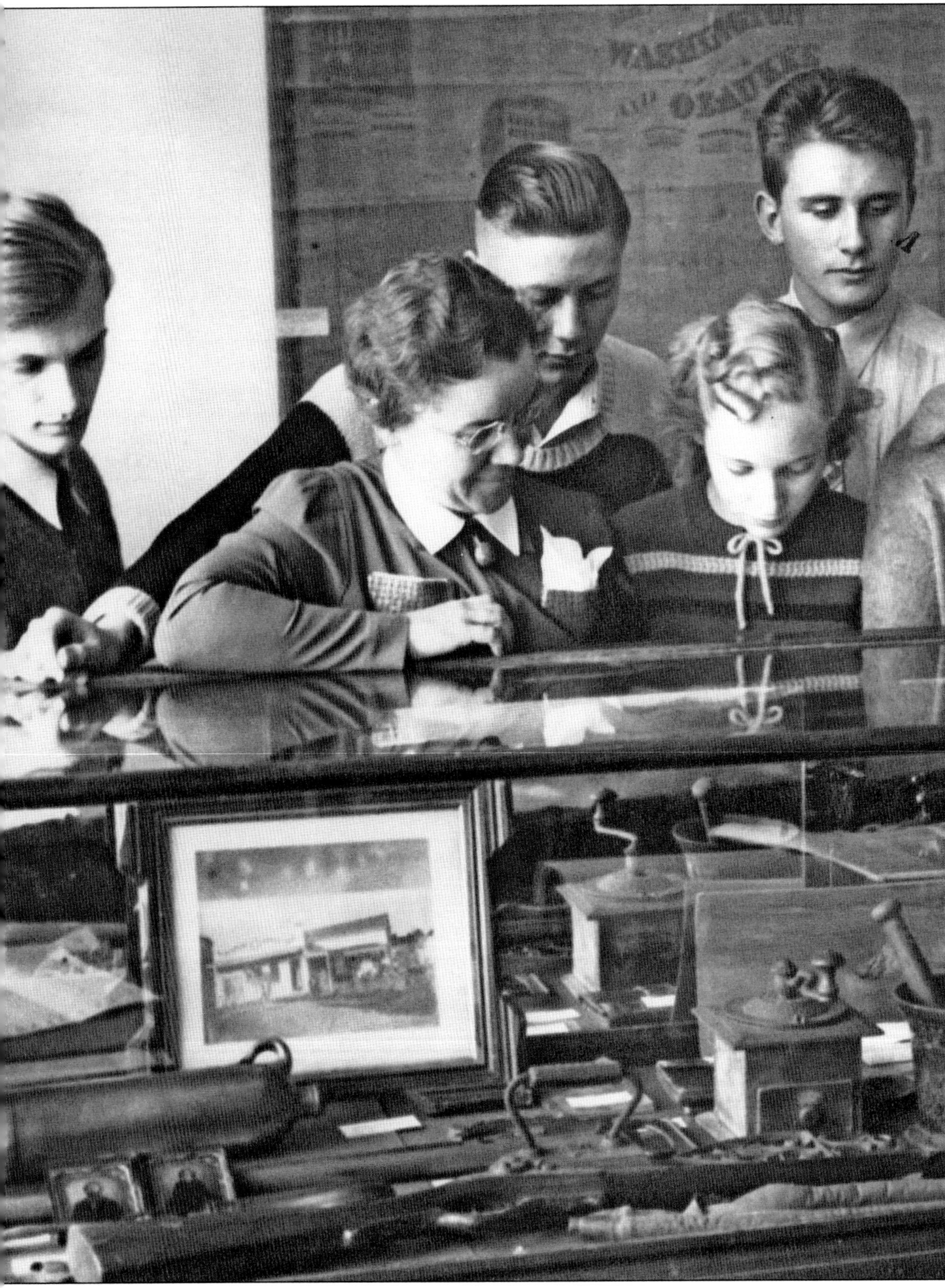

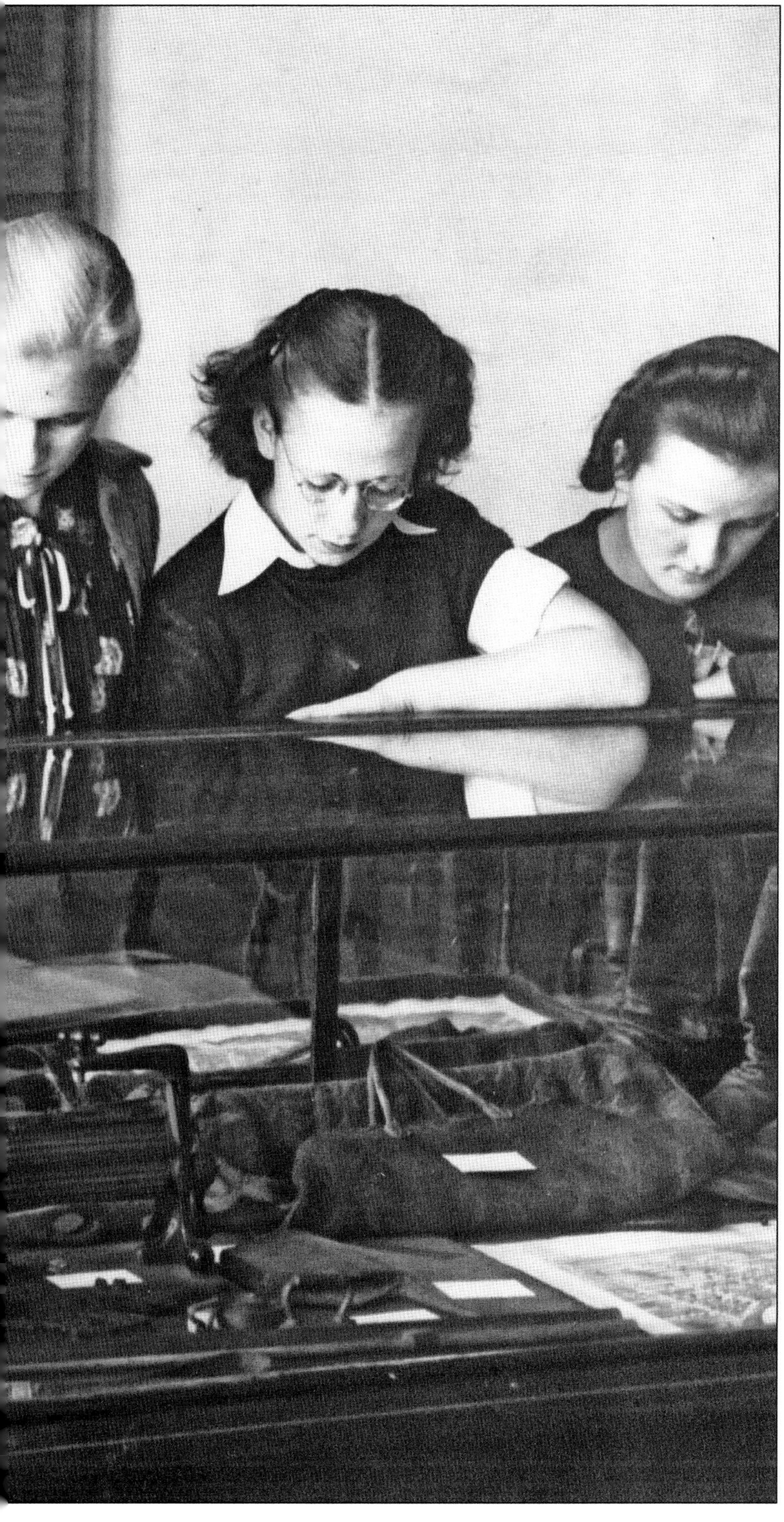

The first museum in West Bend, which would become the Washington County Historical Society, was begun by high school history teacher Edith Heidner and was on exhibit in the West Bend High School Library. The first public exhibit was on November 12, 1938, the date of this photograph. It remained in the high school until 1962, at which time renovations to the school pushed the museum out. It moved to the Old Sheriff's Residence and Jail and merged with the Old Settler's Club to become the Washington County Historical Society. Pictured are, from left to right, Paul Klingbiel, Edith Heidner, Ralph Hansen, Dolores Schneider, Eugene Hirschboeck, Cara Wegner, Florence Braasch, and Dolores Van Beek.

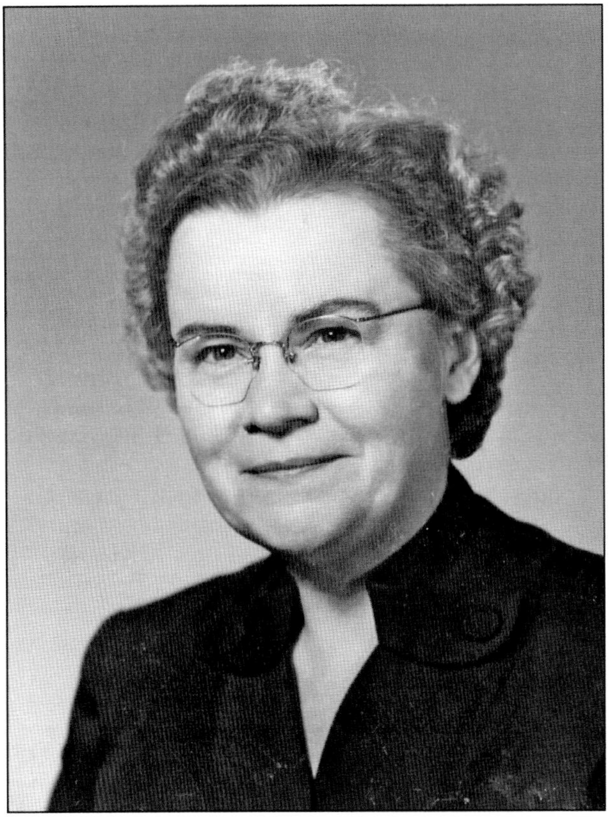

Edith Heidner was born in 1891. She earned her teaching degree from Milwaukee Downer College before teaching high school history in West Bend. As part of her work, Edith started the West Bend Museum in the school library. This collection merged with the Old Settlers' Club to become the current Washington County Historical Society. During her life, Edith was honored with awards for teaching, preservation, and community service. She died in 1981.

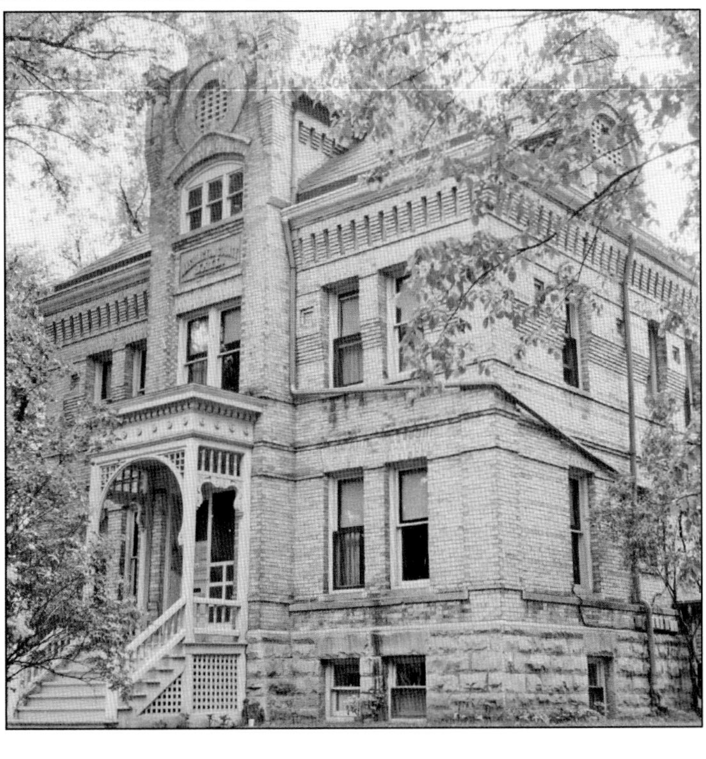

The Old Washington County Jail was built in 1886 to replace a wooden structure that had been located on the same site. The building was constructed to be "escape proof." The front of the building was a residence for the Washington County sheriff and his family, and the back portion included eight cells on two floors.

The Congregation of the Sisters of St. Agnes was founded in Barton in 1858 by Fr. Casper Rehrl. This photograph shows the convent, which also served as one of the first schools in the region. In 1870, the sisters broke from Father Rehrl and moved to Fond du Lac, where they remain today. Today, the convent serves as a residence and is owned by the Washington County Historical Society.

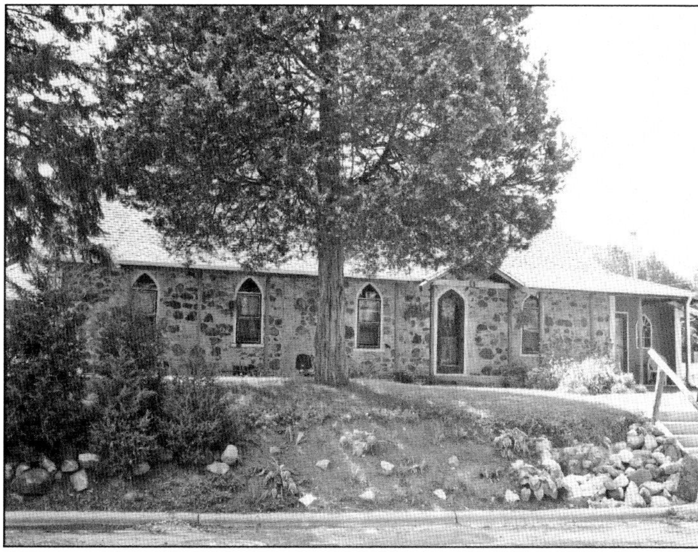

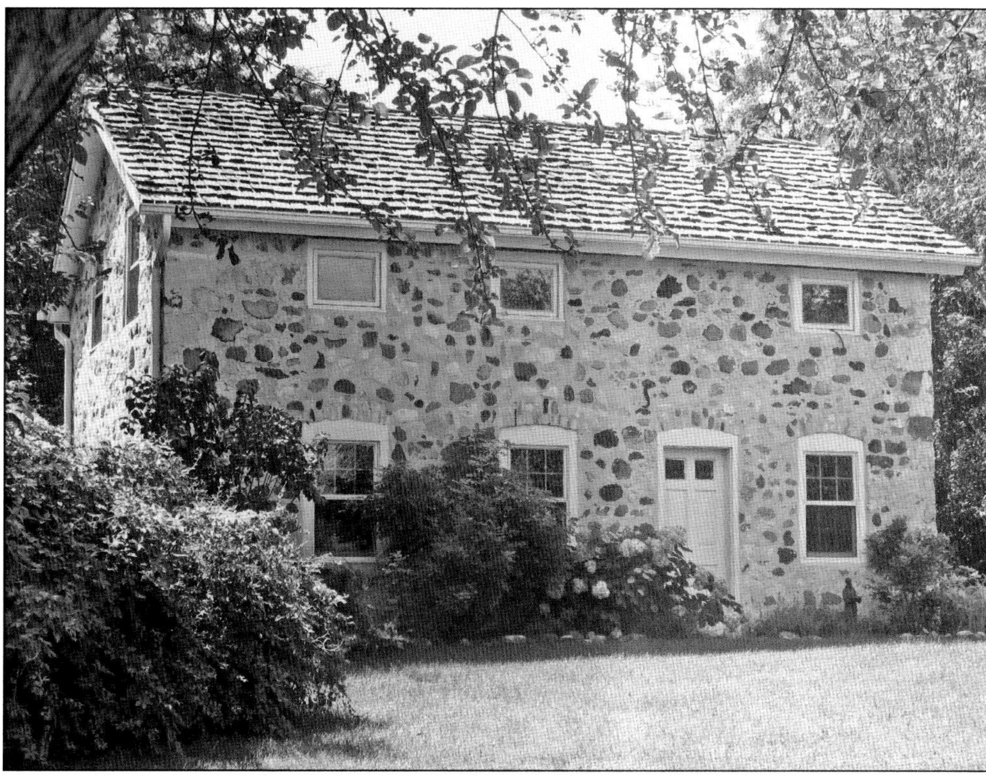

In 1860, Fr. Casper Rehrl completed the building in this photograph, his rectory, near the St. Agnes convent. Father Rehrl was a missionary priest, often traveling to far areas of his assigned parish in the Fox Valley area. His passion was education, and during his life he founded more than 30 churches, most with associated schools. The rectory is part of the St. Agnes site operated by the Washington County Historical Society.

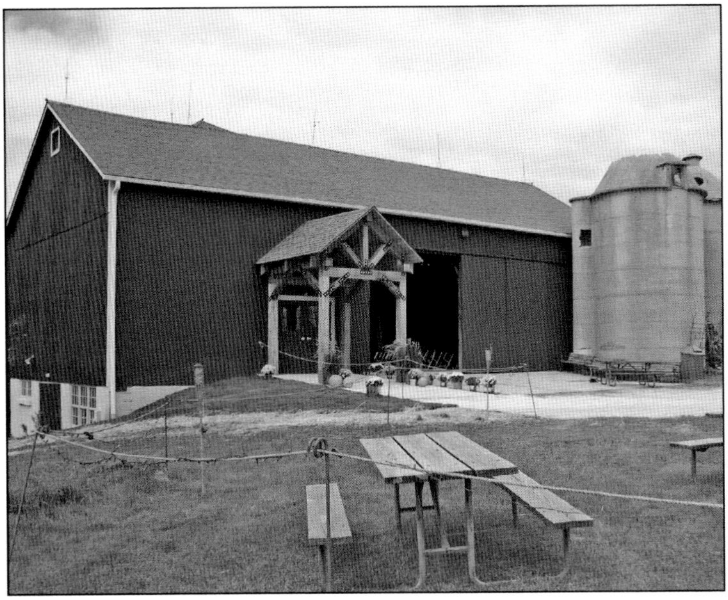

The land that would become Lac Lawrann Conservancy was originally part of the Schmidt Farm. One of the renovated barns on the property can be seen here. Lac Lawrann began in 1950 when Lawrence and Ann Maurin purchased 18 acres of the area and devoted it to nature conservancy. The area had long been home to squatters and was an unofficial junkyard for locals before the Maurins began cleanup efforts.

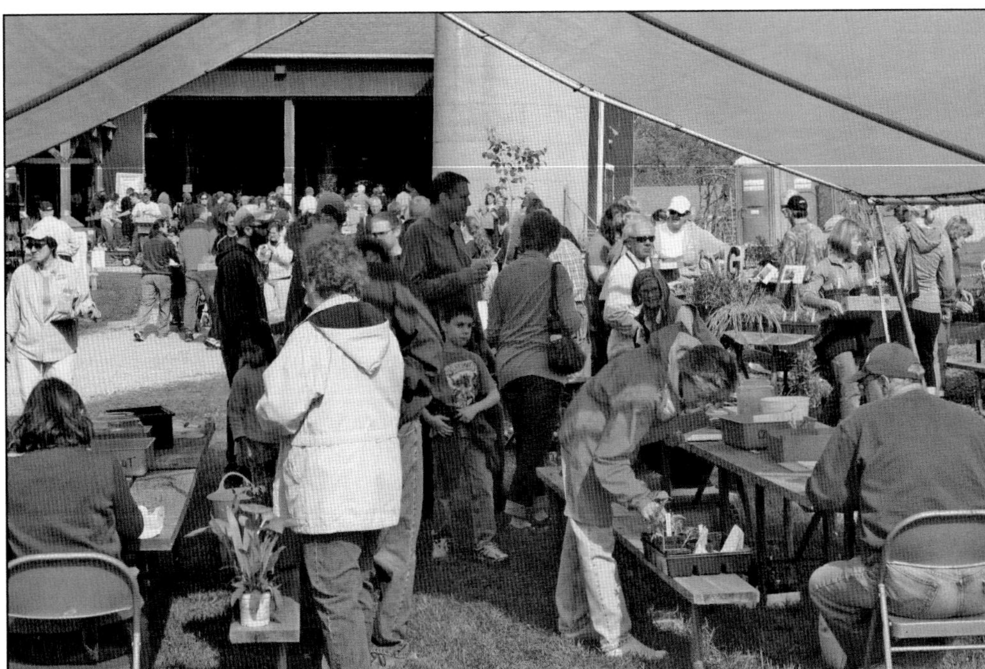

The annual Lac Lawrann Conservancy Plant Sale, seen here, is one of the ways the conservancy raises money to support its mission and nature and conservation programs. Public hikes through some of the 136 acres of the conservancy, youth camps, school trips, and the Nature in the Classroom program are only a few examples of Lac Lawrann's offerings each year.

Volunteers with Ozaukee-Washington Land Trust prepare a trail in Hepburn Woods. The land trust was founded in 1992 by a group concerned with the rapid population expansion and the loss of natural spaces. Its mission is to protect and enhance the natural environments of the area. The trust manages 15 properties throughout the two counties and partners with many others.

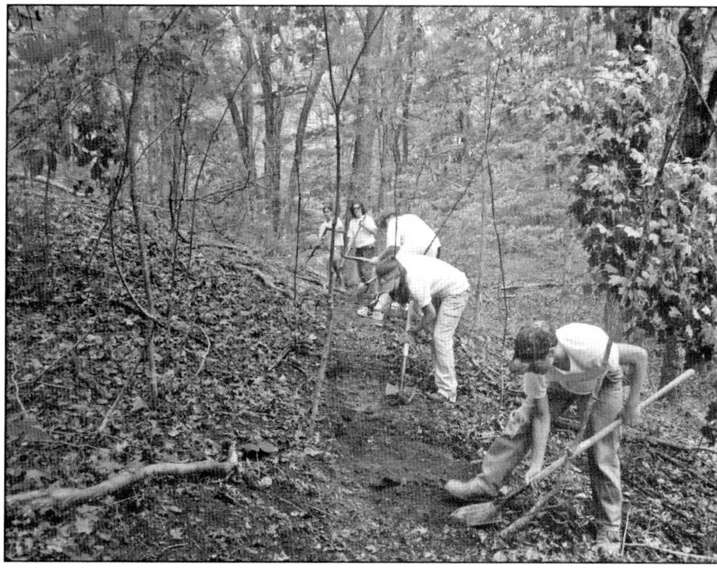

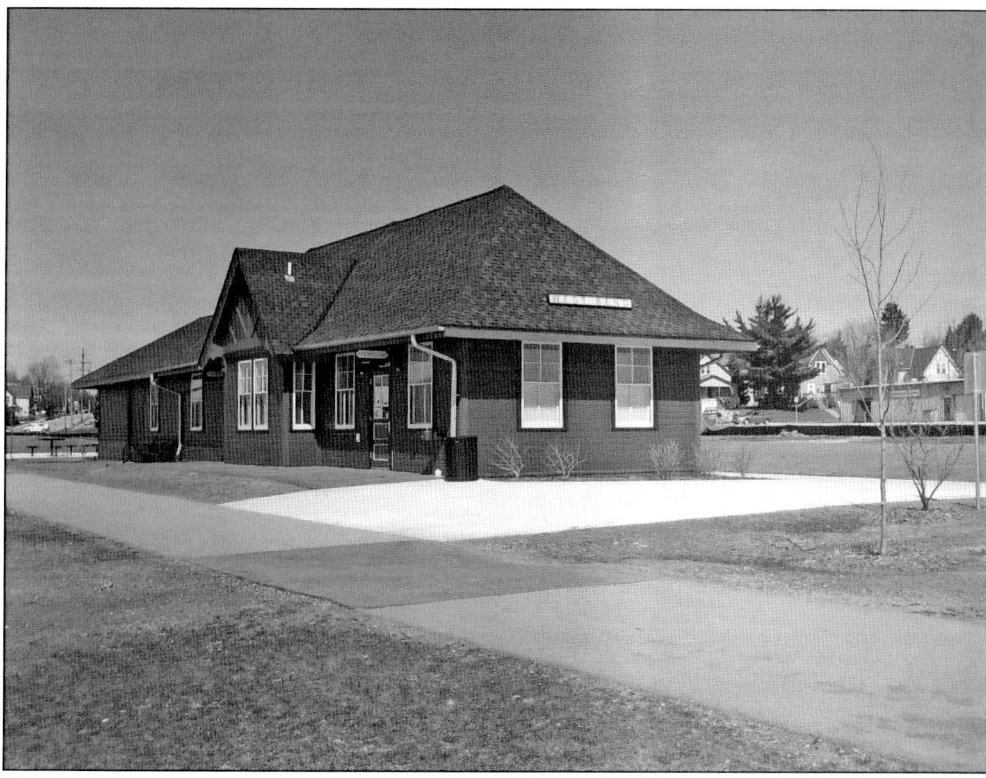

The Ozaukee-Washington Land Trust offices are located in the renovated Chicago & North Western Railway depot on Veterans Avenue in West Bend. Located along the Eisenbahn Trail, the former railroad bed has been paved; the building was abandoned in 2000. With state grant money, the depot was restored in 2006. It also serves as a tourist information center and restroom stop on the trail.

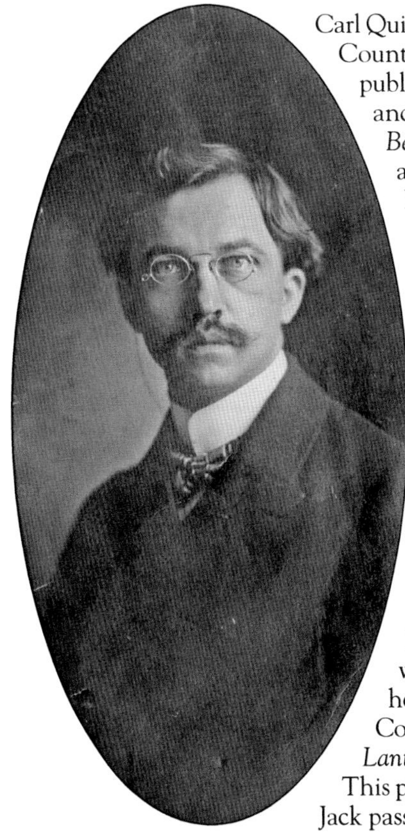

Carl Quickert is known for his books on the history of Washington County. He also wrote columns for the *West Bend News* and published a book of poems. Quickert was born in Germany and came to West Bend in 1889. He worked for the *West Bend Democrat*, *Beobachter* (a German-language newspaper), and the *West Bend News*. His work contained a wealth of historical knowledge and includes a personal touch with descriptions that make history come alive.

Jack Anderson was an investigative journalist and history writer who worked for the *West Bend News*. During his career, he won several awards and recorded much of Washington County's history though newspaper articles and the book *Dark Lanterns*, chronicling the lynching of George DeBar in 1855. This photograph was taken during his travels in Mexico in 1989. Jack passed away in 1993.

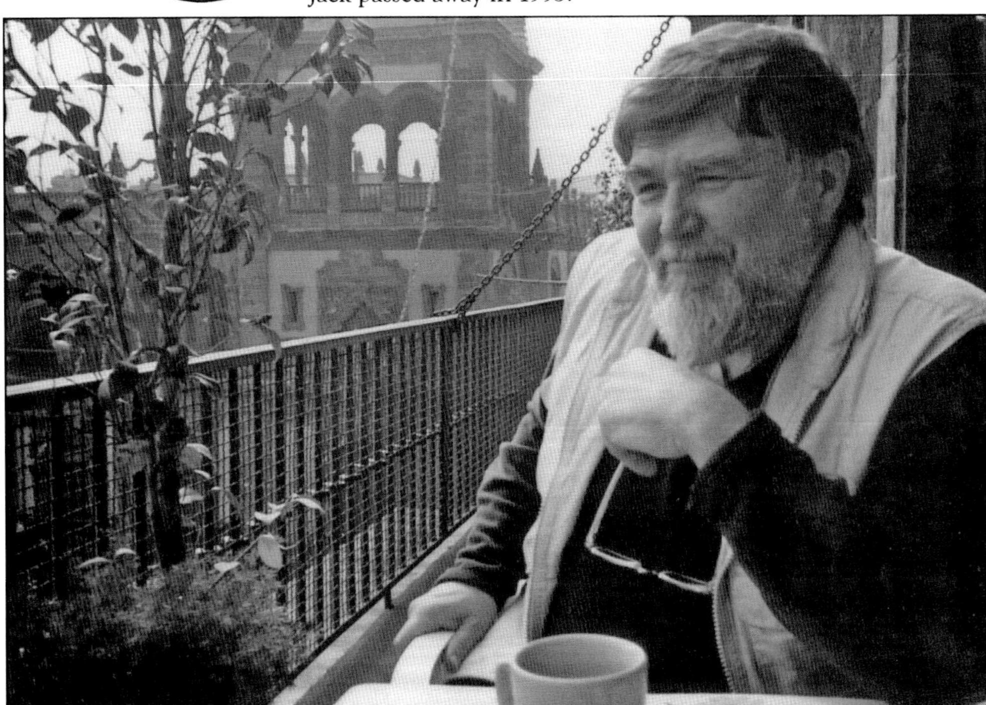

About the Organization

Since 1873, the Washington County Historical Society has been the steward of the rich history of Washington County. The society has preserved and interpreted the past through the operation of three unique museums and historic sites: the Old Courthouse Museum, the Old Sheriff's Residence and Jail, and the St. Agnes Historic Convent and School Historic Site. For over 130 years, the Washington County Historical Society has "captured the past" for future generations.

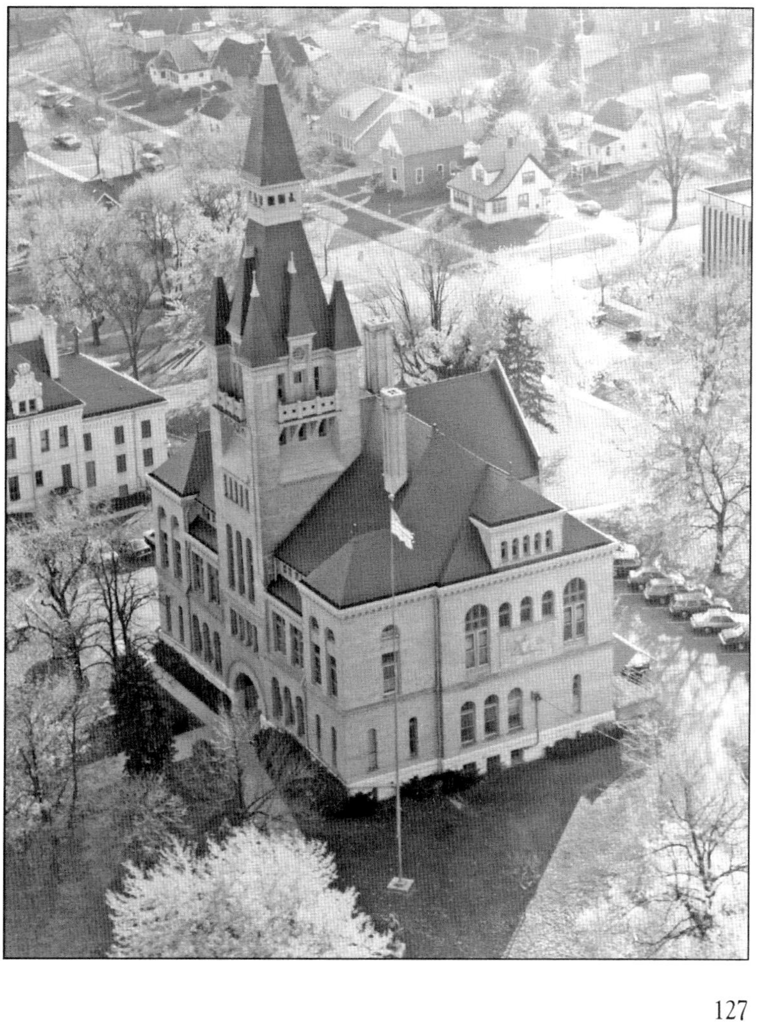